Internet Discourse and Health Debates

Also by Kay Richardson

NUCLEAR REACTIONS: a Study in Public Issue Television
(*with John Corner and Natalie Fenton*)

RESEARCHING LANGUAGE: Issues of Power and Method
(*with Deborah Cameron, Elizabeth Frazer, Penelope Harvey and Ben Rampton*)

TEXT, DISCOURSE AND CONTEXT: Representations of Poverty in Britain
(*edited with Ulrike H. Meinhof*)

WORLDS IN COMMON? Television Discourses in a Changing Europe
(*with Ulrike H. Meinhof*)

Internet Discourse and Health Debates

Kay Richardson
School of Politics and Communication Studies,
University of Liverpool

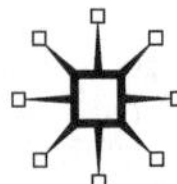

First published 2005 by
PALGRAVE MACMILLAN
Houndmills, Basingstoke, Hampshire RG21 6XS and
178 Fifth Avenue, New York, N. Y. 10010
Companies and representatives throughout the world

PALGRAVE MACMILLAN is the global academic imprint of the Palgrave Macmillan division of St. Martin's Press, LLC and of Palgrave Macmillan Ltd. Macmillan® is a registered trademark in the United States, United Kingdom and other countries. Palgrave is a registered trademark in the European Union and other countries.

ISBN 1–4039–1483–4 hardback

This book is printed on paper suitable for recycling and made from fully managed and sustained forest sources.

A catalogue record for this book is available from the British Library.

Library of Congress Cataloging-in-Publication Data

Richardson, Kay, 1955–
Internet discourse and health debates / Kay Richardson.
p. cm.
Includes bibliographical references and index.
ISBN 1–4039–1483–4 (cloth)
1. Internet in medicine. 2. Health risk communication – Data processing. 3. Public health – Computer network resources. 4. Internet – Social aspects. I. Title.

R859.7.I58.R536 2004
362.1′0285 – dc22 2004054898

10 9 8 7 6 5 4 3 2 1
14 13 12 11 10 09 08 07 06 05

Printed and bound in Great Britain by
Antony Rowe Ltd, Chippenham and Eastbourne

Contents

List of Tables

List of Figures

Acknowledgements

My major debt in preparing this work is to my research assistant, Marlene Miglbauer, who spent a full year collecting and examining newsgroup materials, to identify their most interesting features. I am very grateful for all the work she put into the project. I am grateful also to the Economic and Social Research Council who, via their E-society programme supervised by Professor Len Waverman at the London Business School, provided the money for the newsgroup part of this project (ESRC grant no RES-335-25-0024).

For permission to use screenshots from their websites I am grateful to John Moulder, Tim Bishop, Wang Jian Shuo, the World Health Organization and Stewart Fist.

I am also grateful to my academic colleagues in the Communication Studies section of the School of Politics and Communication Studies at Liverpool University – John Corner, Peter Goddard, Julia Hallam, Adrian Quinn, Piers Robinson. By taking on extra responsibilities in the early months of 2004, they made it possible for me to take a semester's research leave to prepare this book for publication. John Corner also read the whole manuscript in draft form and offered many useful comments. I am grateful for this support. I am also grateful to Jill Lake at Palgrave Macmillan.

1 Introduction

The research presented in this book looks at the internet and asks how people and organizations use it to communicate with one another about health risks. It is particularly concerned with forms of online communication that are public (that is, not formally restricted in any way to particular groups of people). Public communication does not begin and end with the internet. Where the internet goes now, the mass media have gone before, and continue to go. But public communication in the age of the internet is not what it used to be and it is important to set up some lines of enquiry to find out how it has changed and is still changing. The present book offers one such line of enquiry.

Public communication about health risks offers a useful point of entry into this territory because health risks are such a universally relevant topic, and the internet, in its public communication mode, is such a universal medium, in principle if not in practice.[1] Although health risks in general are universally relevant, particular health risks of course are not. Not everyone is at equal risk from HIV/AIDS, or lung cancer, or of contracting v-CJD from contaminated beef products. The risks examined in the present volume (cellphones and cancer, SARS, MMR vaccine and autism) were not chosen according to any particular principle, although all of them had at different times attracted mass media attention and all involved uncertainty as to whether there *was* a risk of the proposed kind, and/or what kind of behaviour would entail running that risk.[2]

Once Americans have internet access, it turns out that finding health information is one of the most common ways in which they use it (Pew 2003a). This is not so surprising in a medicalized world (Lupton 1994; Gwyn 2002).[3] Maintaining good health is a universal human priority. The medicalization of health turns over a lot of the responsibility for this to professional structures, dependent upon types and sources of information which are beyond the reach of the non-professional social networks of individuals. Using the net for health information and communication is potentially of value to the individual in four ways:

- Overcoming the problem of access to professional structures – no medical insurance; can't get an appointment until a week on Tuesday.
- Allowing access to non-mainstream information of which the medical establishment disapproves – such as how to avoid the controversial MMR vaccine whilst still immunizing children against measles as well as mumps and rubella.
- Expanding face-to-face social networks into cyberspace social networks, perhaps 'de-medicalizing' health knowledge, or mediating it via trusted personal contacts rather than 'authorities'.
- Buying drugs and other health related items – legitimately or otherwise.

The public sharing of information about health *risks* via the net introduces other considerations. From a 'top down', social policy perspective, public communication in relation to health risk is all about locating some health responsibilities with the individual, on the basis of knowledge about certain kinds of risky behaviour – unprotected sex, bad dietary habits, smoking; and public information campaigns are the usual approach.[4] These are unlikely to migrate in full from the traditional mass media to the net because they are less sure of finding their audience in this medium. From the perspective of the individual, traditional information sources may have been issuing confusing and contradictory 'risk' messages, so that the net is embraced as a way of trying to eliminate or reduce the confusion. Or the traditional sources may have compromised their public trust, making the net an option for seeking out different kinds of voices.

The above represents an account of the area which this research is designed to explore. What follows will place the research in the context of 'new media' studies and describe how the theoretical and substantive chapters which follow contribute to the general project.

New media research

Research on the new media is no longer novel. The internet itself no longer seems extraordinary: it is becoming integrated into the economic, social, political and cultural affairs of individuals, organizations and societies (Wellman and Haythornthwaite 2002; Liewvrouw 2004).[5] It is however not easy to establish an overall picture of just what the 'new media' are at this point in time, nor of where and how they are being used, and by whom. There is much discussion of the 'digital divide' (Ngini, Furnell et al. 2002; Rainie and Bell 2004) and the fear that in information-rich societies those on the wrong side of the divide will find themselves seriously disempowered. The digital divide operates both locally and globally; it divides different groups within a society from one another and also establishes a hierarchy of societies, with some being much better off for wired resources than others – an issue meriting the attention of the United Nations at a meeting in December 2003. In the present research a particular segment of the international 'general public' comes into focus. These people represent an English-speaking elite which not only has internet access, and has become accustomed to using it for international communication with known and unknown others, but which is also sharing with these others such concerns as the safety of international travel (in relation to SARS) and of the latest hi-tech consumer goods (cellphones).

The new media are also associated with various kinds of risks for the future. The most publicly prominent risk themes concern the online 'grooming' of children to ready them for offline sexual abuse and the circulation of child pornography in cyberspace. Governments worry about the ease with which crime can be organized with the help of new media technologies; individuals and companies worry about the security of financial transactions conducted online. There has been much practical rethinking of traditional concerns with privacy and intellectual property rights, to ensure an appropriate fit between these concerns and the new information and communication technologies.

Accordingly, research on new media has become multifaceted and multidisciplinary, with many points of entry. This fragmentation of research is reflected in a collection of papers for a special issue of the journal *New Media and Society*, entering its sixth year of publication, February 2004. These articles variously examine the new media in relation to politics and political activism; art, culture and design; communication and language; social theory; economic policy and others – all under the unifying theme 'what's changed about new media'? The collection shows a sustained focus upon the integration of new media with existing social, political and economic realities, and thus upon the reciprocal effects of 'society' and 'media'. Only one contribution to this issue is specifically concerned with changes in the nature (and study) of computer-mediated communication, often shortened to CMC (Herring 2004). This field, and this term, used to have a more prominent place in new media studies, and it certainly has a long history compared with some other areas – it can be traced back to Hiltz and Turoff (1978), when it came under the designation 'computer conferencing', pre-dating the internet.

The displacement of the 'communication' aspects of new media from a prominent place in the field of study is neither surprising nor regrettable. The displacement is not surprising because, firstly, as Herring observes, the basic forms of CMC are now well-established and have been well-examined in the literature. Newer forms of CMC, belonging to the first decade of the twenty-first century (for example, 'blogs'; see Chapter 5 below)[6] are variations upon more established ones. Secondly, it seems to be in relation to the *uses* of new media that the growth of research has taken place in recent years (Dahlberg 2004) and upon their impact in specific areas of social life, as well as the spread of net access from restricted groups of users to the mainstream. To study these kinds of developments it is not really necessary to understand in depth the particular communicative characteristics of the medium. Such understanding as is required is readily available from classic works and from secondary sources.

Another reason that the displacement is not surprising is that it took a while to learn the lesson that focusing upon 'new media' as some kind of free-standing enterprise, in relative isolation from the wider social context, offered too narrow a perspective on why these media took the forms that they did. Criticism of this tendency has now begun to take hold. Slevin, for example, believes that the study of the internet should be subordinated to the study of the kinds of social change which made the internet possible in the first place:

> I shall start out from three important developments that have transformed modern societies. These are described by Giddens as the intensification of globalization, the detraditionalizing of society and the expansion and intensification of social reflexivity. Taken together, these developments have resulted in the acceleration of manufactured uncertainty in our late modern world. It was not by accident that the internet originated under such conditions. Its emergence can only be understood if all these developments are seen to interlock. (Slevin 2000: 5)

Slevin's approach starts from a big picture of late modern society, indebted to the work of Ulrich Beck and Anthony Giddens – see, for example, Beck (1992) and Giddens (1990, 1999). There is, of course, room for disagreement about the characteristics of the 'big picture' and a danger that time spent debating the merits of the reflexive modernity/risk society thesis risks a long deferral of more specific questions about the internet and other new media forms, whilst the alternative, taking that analysis on trust in order to pursue particular enquiries, seems unduly deferential to the theorists.[7] Most research, in practice, will have either a theoretical or an empirical bias. In the present research the bias is empirical.

Internet research, health risk and the wider social context

It is of course possible to examine computer-mediated communication in its wider social context without a priori commitment to any particular theory of the contemporary social order. The present research does this in two ways. Firstly, this study makes use of what is *already* known about online communication in its various forms, including such characteristics as multimodality, interactivity and absence of social presence;[8] secondly, it approaches the internet as a context for public communication.

Rather than trying to develop fresh insights into the nature of computer-mediated communication in its particular forms, the research presented below takes existing ideas about communication over the internet, develops and extends these where appropriate, and uses them in an exploration of specific health risk concerns which have arisen over the last decade or so. The 'social context' enters the picture via the health risks, which are tied to their particular historical moment. Each of them can, for instance, be characterized as examples of 'manufactured' risk – side effects of social and technological progress. Progress in communications technology has given us the cellular phone – but maybe we need to be careful about how we use these machines? Long-distance travel is easier than it has ever been, but when we move between countries we now worry about SARS, as well as deep-vein thrombosis and international terrorism. Progress in disease control has produced vaccines which could in principle eliminate death and illness from measles, mumps and rubella (three of nature's risks) yet mass vaccination may also have its 'downside'. The manufactured risks discussed in this book – that excessive cellphone use will cause brain cancer, that international travellers will contract SARS, that the MMR vaccination will induce autism in susceptible children – are also characteristically modern risks because, thanks in part to internet websites and newsgroups, they are risks which are now discussed worldwide.

The other characteristic of the present research which locates it in a wider social context comes from the fact that it makes every effort to understand communication in terms of an epistemologically more important differentiation between *public* communication and *restricted* communication. Instead of setting 'the internet' *against* 'the mass media', the 'new' *against* the 'old', this differentiation recognizes the similarities between some kinds of internet communication and the traditional mass media. Public CMC comprises those forms which, in principle if not in practice (since governments such as that of the People's Republic of China can impose restrictions) are on open access, requiring no passwords or account numbers and involving no vetting procedures. The net of course is not just a forum for public communication in this sense. It can also carry more restricted forms of communication such as email. The most significant forms of public CMC are World Wide Websites and Usenet newsgroups. If you can get online, you can use these forms of CMC, as a reader and, with a bit more trouble, as a writer.

The chapters

The chapters below are arranged as follows. Chapters 2 and 3 together serve to frame the research. Chapter 2 reviews the CMC literature to identify the most important characteristics of public CMC, in relation both to the web and to newsgroups. Chapter 3 frames the research in relation to work on the social construction/representation of health and health risk, with particular reference to discourses of health and risk in the mass media.

The following three chapters each take one case study – mobile phones and cancer, SARS, MMR and autism – and conduct an in-depth study of particular online materials relevant to the topic. Each case study comprises one section which discusses resources on the World Wide Web and one section which examines discussions in Usenet newsgroups. Chapter 7 looks at all three of the case studies together, drawing out some similarities as well as differences. The book finishes with a final short chapter which offers some conclusions based on the preceding research.

The two forms of net-based communication which the research examines are World Wide Websites and Usenet newsgroups. Different considerations apply in respect of each of these, since websites are predominantly monologic in character where Usenet newsgroup threads (collections of messages linked to one another like the utterances in a conversation) are dialogic or 'polylogic' (Marcoccia 2004). Websites go much further than newsgroup threads in the direction of multimodality, that is, using more than one semiotic mode of communication simultaneously, principally combining the visual mode of communication with the verbal. The difference between websites and newsgroups can also be expressed in this way: that whereas websites are '*for* the public', in the same way as a TV news broadcast or documentary would be, newsgroups are '*by* the public'.

A note on terminology

The present research is heavily influenced by the linguistic study of discourse, but with a light touch. From a linguistic point of view the important thing is to employ the term '*discourse*' in such a way as to keep it distinct from other terms used in the literature, including *medium, register, style, dialect, channel, genre, speech event, text* and *literacy practice.* 'Texts' for the purposes of the present research are spoken or written material objects, though their meanings are non-material, since meaning calls for interpretation and is thus located in the subjective domain. Textual meaning can be discussed by analysts on the basis of assumptions about intersubjective convergence between groups of people sharing the same linguistic repertoires and communicative competence. Crystal (2001), in the most linguistic of all the recent treatments of CMC, uses 'medium' to distinguish writing from speech, and introduces 'Netspeak' as a new, third, medium alongside these two. This is the broadest possible use of the term, but the present research requires a narrower one. In this book, 'medium' is used with the sense that it has in the expression 'mass media', in which print is one medium, audiovisual broadcasting (television) is another and sound broadcasting (radio) is a third. For the internet, this means that newsgroups are one medium (any particular group is a forum) and the web is another. I have also referred to use of the web and use of newsgroups as distinct literacy practices, in recognition of the type of work which is required in the construction of texts for these media. The notion of *genre* captures the difference between a web page in the form of a blog (see Chapter 5) and one in the form of an FAQ or Frequently Asked Questions document – a question-and-answer format (see Chapter 4). I have used the term 'discourse' where Crystal prefers the term 'style'. *Style,* for Crystal, includes 'discourse features' alongside *graphic* features, *orthographic* features, *grammatical* features and *lexical* features. 'Discourse features' are defined thus:

> The structural organization of a text, defined in terms of such factors as coherence, relevance, paragraph structure and the logical progression of ideas; for example, a journal paper within scientific English typically consists of a fixed sequence of sections including the abstract, introduction, methodology, results, discussion and conclusion. (Crystal 2001: 9)

In multimodal texts such as web pages, where the structural organization is as much visual as it is verbal, it does not seem helpful to assign structure to discourse without elevating the status of 'discourse' to a higher level. The theoretical ramifications of these terminological distinctions are beyond the scope of the present work. There is also a degree of tension between the linguistic concept – after Sinclair and Coulthard (1975) – and a broader sociocultural concept of discourse – after Foucault (1972, 1977) – but the waters have been muddied because of the amount of research which strives to keep a foot in both camps (Fairclough 1992). Although both senses of the word are employed in the present research, the context will determine which meaning is most relevant. In speaking about discourse in relation to the 'social construction of risk', for example (see Chapter 3 and Chapter 8), it is the sociocultural perspective which prevails, since this perspective is as much concerned with *content* as it is with form: with what can (legitimately, authoritatively, sensibly) be said about a given topic. It is also concerned with the institutional arrangements underpinning speech and writing – discourses and institutions are mutually defining (Kress, 1989).

2
Computer-Mediated Communication and Language

This chapter provides a context for the subsequent case study chapters by discussing the study of computer-mediated communication. Pioneers in this field include Howard Rheingold (1993), Susan Herring (1994) and Sherry Turkle (1995). The more linguistic/semiotic aspects of this research have covered such topics as:

- 'Turntaking' and coherence in online interaction (Herring 1999; Beacco, Claudel et al. 2002; Marcoccia 2004).
- Topic development in newsgroup threads (Osborne 1998).
- Generic characteristics of online interaction, especially its relations with writing and with speech (Ferrara 1991; Hawisher 1993; Collot and Belmore 1996; Lee 1996; Yates 1996; Herring 1996a; Davis and Brewer 1997; Baron 1998, 2003; Osborne 1998; Gruber 2000; Harrison 2000; Crystal 2001).
- Gender relations in online textual environments (Dibbell 1993; Herring 1994, 1996/1999, 1996b, 2000, 2001; Turkle 1995; Bruckman 1996; Cherny and Weise 1996).
- Normative constraints on online interaction (McLaughlin, Osborne et al. 1995; MacKinnnon 1997; Burnett and Bonnici 2003).
- Web page genres (Crowston and Williams 1996; Kress 1997; Chandler 1998; Benoit and Benoit 2000; Cheung 2000; Lewis 2003).
- Cyberplay (Bechar-Israeli 1995; Danet 2001).
- Multilingualism online (Paolillo 2001; Danet and Herring 2003; Warschauer 2000; Warschauer and El Said 2002).
- Hypertextual discourse structure (Kaplan 1995; Mitra and Cohen 1999; Engebretsen 2000; Tosca 2000; Foot, Schneider et al. 2003; Schneider and Foot 2004).
- The semiotics of screen icons (Honeywill 1999).

However, the study of computer-mediated communication is not a field where disciplinary divisions run deep: experimental psychologists, information scientists, linguists and sociolinguists, as well as discourse analysts in sociology, linguistics and psychology, overlap with one another in the topics they examine and in the references they draw upon. The following discussion reflects that inter- and trans-disciplinarity and tries to do it justice, as well as emphasizing the themes which are most relevant for the present research.

The state of the art

February 2004 saw the publication of the first issue in volume 6 of *New Media and Society* (*NMS*), an international journal devoted specifically to the study of the new forms of media from the internet to the WAP mobile telephone. (WAP, Wireless Application Protocol, is a format to proride limited internet content to mobile devices.) This issue attempted to take stock of the field after the journal's first five years of publication. A common theme across many of the contributions was that of the 'mainstreaming' of new media, as the World Wide Web, email, wireless communication and so on ceased to be restricted to particular kinds of users and uses, and started to become ubiquitous in many developed countries in work, education, leisure, culture and politics (see Wellman and Haythornthwaite (2002) for more discussion along these lines; and Dahlberg (2004) for an overview of social science approaches to internet studies).

Among the writers in *NMS* volume 6 who developed this 'mainstreaming' theme, Herring (2004) talks about the development of newer forms of CMC (ICQ – 'I Seek You', IM – Instant Messaging, SMS – Short Message Service, blogs, streaming audio/video) alongside those which are now more established (the web, email, bulletin boards/newsgroups, chatrooms) while pointing out that 'the web' has a dominance now that it lacked previously, since so many CMC protocols, which used to be independent (including Usenet which is in essence a Unix-based protocol) can now be accessed by the user via a web browser interface. Herring also observes that the 'newness' of the recent innovations is a matter of modification: 'all involve text messages that are composed and read via a digital interface' (Herring 2004: 31). Electronic voice-based and image-based two-way communication have seen development too but they have yet to displace or even achieve parity with (written) text-based forms. Her prediction for the future is:

> Increasing technological integration, combined with the assimilation of day-to-day uses and the corresponding need to ensure the trustworthiness of one's interlocutors, will contrive to make the internet a simpler, safer and – for better or for worse – less fascinating communication environment. (Herring 2004: 34)

It is not remarkable to find that health risks are a subject of communication on the internet. Where online communication resources have become ordinary, even banal, the fact that they are used to communicate about any particular topic is not, in itself, interesting. Nor is it at all noteworthy that many different voices will want to have their online say – commercial voices, state voices, charity voices, individual voices, scientific voices, and so on – or that some will want to go public with their text/talk/image and others to target their discourse at more specific recipients. It may not be interesting *that* this happens, but it remains interesting to explore *how* it happens, and to reflect upon why it happens in the particular forms that it does. In relation to health risks and society, the big questions are why we (the public) worry about particular harms. Are we right to worry about such things? Are we indifferent to things that we should worry about more? Only some of these will ever be questions about the internet itself – for example, the issue of harm from internet pornography. In most cases the internet only comes into the picture as a provider of resources which contribute, for good or ill, to the social construction/representation of health risks. In this context the particular uses of CMC which are most worthy of attention are those which are publicly accessible on the widest scale. Subject to the reservations regarding economic, social, linguistic and political restrictions on internet access, the most public resources are those of the World Wide Web for one-way communication, newsgroups (Usenet) for asynchronous two-way communication, and chatrooms (IRC, Internet Relay Chat, the original and formerly best-known protocol for online 'chat', or synchronous computer-mediated communication) for synchronous two-way communication. Other online protocols and forums exist but they are deliberately restricted in particular ways. For example, websites involving commercial transactions have to be restricted to ensure security. Email is restricted (though less than many people would like to imagine) because the communication is intended to be 'private', between individuals. Listserv communication is restricted because it is conducted within self-defining communities of interest and some kind of subscription is required. Access to online textual resources in commodity form (for example, journals and their archives) is also restricted by subscription.

Communication about health risks occurs in these restricted contexts too, but they are beyond the scope and concern of the present research. By circumscribing the enquiry in this particular way, the point is to play *down* the connection between the web/Usenet and email, listservs and subscription products, and instead to play *up* the connection between the web and 'traditional' or 'old media' forms – specifically, broadcast and print mass media. There is a degree of convergence here between the old and the new. The traditional news media have used their news-gathering infrastructure as the basis of new web-based formats along-side their established outlets, some of them (the *New York Times*, the BBC) with considerable success. Before the coming of the internet it was these mass media which ruled the roost in respect of public discourse. They were the interface between other public forums (for example, parliament) and the wider audience. They still serve this function, but now it is easier for the 'wider audience' to access directly *some* of the source materials that the journalists themselves use as resources for their stories. In relation to health risk topics for example, it is the documents produced by such organizations as the WHO and the CDC which are offered via the web on 'direct access' not just to journalists (Trumbo 2001) but also to the browsing public, without national restrictions. This online presence is worthy of examination in its own right. It is also worthy of examination at second-hand, via an exploration of whether or not such resources are actually used by people with internet access.

It is an easy matter for organizations to monitor on an hourly, daily, weekly, monthly, annual basis, how many visitors their websites receive, what pages they access during their visits, what items they download, what domains they themselves are visiting from. The technical, 'behind the scenes' management of who goes where on the web, along with the politics and ethics of such management, is itself the subject of research activity (Rogers 2000). For organizations to know whether their visitors then go on to recommend the site to others and what they think of it, is not so easy. But other kinds of online materials can make a contribution here. Usenet is also a location for public discourse on all sorts of topics. Those parts of the wired population who participate in Usenet can and do employ it to tell one another which websites to visit and which ones to avoid.

Herring's observations about the changing contexts and forms of CMC are relevant to the present research in another way also. They have implications in respect of the question 'When was your research conducted?' This question is a more complicated one than may at first appear.

My dual focus upon websites on the one hand and Usenet discussion on the other is made more interesting by the fact that in the case of websites, I was only able to look at the most recent versions of those sites at the time of writing, whilst in the case of Usenet, I was able to take the study back in time to the earliest mentions of particular topics, using normal keyword search procedures. Notwithstanding extensive archiving on particular sites, the web is a notoriously unstable realm, textually speaking. Since editing is so easy, a webmaster might make an addition one day and remove it the next, leaving no traces.[1] Before the web era, such editing stopped at the point of publication. Thus, my discussions in the case study chapters below of particular websites are intended as 'synchronic' accounts, snapshots, circa February 2004, of what was available at that time. In contrast, my accounts of Usenet discussion are both synchronic and diachronic. The materials have been assessed as a synchronic body of texts principally because of the extensive *thematic* continuity in what people had to say about cellphones, and about MMR, across the 8–10 years that these topics have been available in public discourse. There is thematic continuity in the discussion of SARS also, though this is less surprising in a corpus which spans only three-and-a-half months. Diachronically speaking, the issue is how Usenet discussions responded to the developments in the narratives of cellphones, SARS and MMR, and this is discussed in Chapter 7 below.

The forms of public online discourse: websites and Usenet

The principal differences between the two forms of communicative practice examined in this book, from a CMC perspective, are firstly that websites are predominantly monologic in character where Usenet threads are interactive (Rafaeli and Sudweeks 1997), and secondly that websites are further along the continuum between monomodal and multimodal textual form. To put that another way, websites seem to be 'designed', Usenet messages, like emails, are simply 'written'.

Neither of these distinctions are absolute ones. Websites do not have to be monologic. They can refer to, summarize, quote from other texts in the usual 'intertextual' ways. But webmasters generally want to control the terms on which voices other than their own appear on the site. It is a rare website to which someone other than the webmaster can make changes directly. SARS Watch, discussed in Chapter 5 below, is such a site. People other than the webmaster can change the site. But they can only add material in certain defined places, where its authorship is also made clear, and they cannot edit the material of other contributors, including that of the webmaster.

Conversely, Usenet messages do not have absolutely to lack characteristics of 'design'. The language itself is designed for its purpose: that's what writing is, whatever the context (New London Group 1996). But 'design' in this context more usually refers to visual properties. Usenet contributions struggle against various obstacles to do anything 'visual'. They can try to employ alphanumeric characters for non-alphanumeric purposes (ASCII art – see Danet 2001; ASCII is the name of the original character set for keyboard/screen communication, limited to 128 characters and the English version of the Roman alphabet). They can also try to control layout. The latter is vulnerable to overlay by preference features and screen settings at the receiver's end of the communication, 'lost in translation'. Google, in archiving threads, overlays its own design forms for header section material upon those of any other software used to send and receive messages. Although email and newsgroup messages can now be constructed and delivered in HTML rather than text format styles (Hypertext Markup Language is the code used for presenting and interpreting web pages in a browser such as Internet Explorer or Netscape Navigator, with consistent instructions to display regular text, headings, images and so on), and a range of different character sets for other languages have become available, senders who employ character sets other than the basic ones risk having some forms converted 'back' into unintended keyboard characters on the screens of readers with more basic software.

Public online discourse part one: the World Wide Web

Is the World Wide Web all things to all people? No, not really. Most users will probably experience the web primarily in terms of the commercial voice in the first instance – selling, advertising, promoting, sponsoring. Information sources are plentiful despite this, although the problem of finding a needle in a haystack is real and search engines have become indispensable. Google is the most widely respected for the moment. The operators/owners of these engines well understand the commercial value of such widely-used resources.

Finding relevant sites and finding worthwhile sites are different kinds of work. The quantity of material on the web raises the problem of judgement. Search engine algorithms and protocols can only do so much to ensure that the sites they point to are good ones. Sites may benefit from having brand names that people think they can trust –

BBC, WHO, CDC. These particular brand names were acquired outwith the net – in contrast to Yahoo and Google, which are internet brands.

These considerations are all external ones – the internal questions have to do with what kind of texts websites are, and what they could be, what kind of genres and literacy practice(s) they represent. Although the range of possibilities is very large, two characteristics stand out as especially important. One is the multimodality of web design, variously mixing written linguistic form with spoken language, music and song as well as still and moving images, both figurative and non-figurative, some automatic and some activated by actions on the part of the receiver, all within a context where concern for overall graphic design has played a part, to a greater or lesser degree. The other key features of web materials concern their hypertextual capabilities: 'clickability' from place to place within a page, from one page to another within a site, from one site to another site.

History of the World Wide Web

The important moments in the pre-history of the web include the publication of an article in 1945 (Bush 1945) which described an imaginary new device to be called a 'memex', a kind of library of all sorts of materials, accessible on a screen through various techniques which anticipate those we have become accustomed to using in accessing resources on the web. The invention of the word 'hypertext' is credited to Ted Nelson in the 1960s, while the person who first attempted to develop the programming that would make these ideas a reality was Tim Berners-Lee in the 1980s, who also coined the name World Wide Web. Actual use of the web began in the early 1990s and its subsequent development was a crucial element in (re)constructing the internet as a domestic as well as a workplace technology. Its role in the commercialization of the internet, that is, its use by commercial organizations for advertising and promoting themselves, and selling their wares, whilst bearing much of the cost for the development of the system is likewise extremely important. Books about the history of the web include Berners-Lee (1999) and Gillies and Cailliau (2000), although there are also various useful sources online, including archived materials on the websites of ISOC (Internet Society) at www.isoc.org and of W3C (the World Wide Web consortium) at www.w3c.org.

Research on the World Wide Web

There are many practical books on how to design a website, for example, Lynch and Horton (1999); there is also plenty of advice online, for example, Pagetutor (no date) and criteria for judging sites good or bad

(Flanders and Willis 1998). On the more academic side, writers such as Benoit and Benoit (2000) assess US political campaign sites according to criteria of identification, navigation, readability, irritability, information accessibility, interest level, interactivity and adaptation to audience. Schneider and Foot (2004) criticize approaches such as this because what they attend to is web content, overlooking the equally important structuring elements of a web page or site. Further, these approaches are not, say Schneider and Foot, very good at making sense of hypertext intertextuality. Their own approach – 'web sphere analysis' – is useful for exploring the situatedness of particular sites within the larger web. Texts are no longer primary, in this perspective – connections are, reversing the traditional bias. Web sphere analysis runs the risk that other levels of meaning, including site structure as well as the interplay of visual, verbal and other modalities of communicative form, are lost from sight. To bring these other levels back into focus it is useful to take seriously Schneider and Foot's point that content and form must be analysed together, while ensuring that the 'form' which is considered is understood broadly, and goes beyond hypertextual linkage. Wakeford (2000) offers a useful overview of methods for analysing the web. The web page analyses in the case study chapters below draw from the literature on electronic/screen literacy (Snyder 1997, 2002; Hawisher and Selfe 2000) and from earlier studies of the semiotics of web page design (Crowston and Willliams 1996; Kress 1997; Chandler 1998; Cheung 2000; Lewis 2003) as well as studies of the history and forms of writing which take the story into the digital era (Baron, N.S. 2000; Baron, D. 2000) and those which discuss visual as well as narrowly glottic properties of writing (Harris, R. 1995, 2000). See also Goodman (1996), Kress and van Leeuwen (1996).

The question of hypertext and 'linkage' connects with another recurrent theme in discussions of electronic literacies: the radically unstable nature of the web and the implications of this for 'classic' concepts of text and author. These concepts were under attack in literary theory before the global spread of the World Wide Web (Fish 1980; Barthes 1977). Landow (1997) draws out some aspects of the connections between literary theory and new electronic textual practices, although he does not write directly about the World Wide Web. Bringing theory and practice together, an online electronic 'text' by Nancy Kaplan (1995), presents some of the arguments:

> **Hypertexts:** multiple structurations within a textual domain. Imagine a story, as Michael Joyce has, that changes each time one

> reads it. Such documents consist of chunks of textual material (words, video clips, sound segments or the like), and sets of connections leading from one chunk or node to other chunks. The resulting structures offer readers multiple trajectories through the textual domain (just as I have tried to do in this essay). Each choice of direction a reader makes in her encounter with the emerging text, in effect, produces that text. The existing examples of this form, especially the fictions, are so densely linked, offer so many permutations of the text, that the 'authors' cannot know in advance or control with any degree of certainty what 'version' of the story a reader will construct as she proceeds.

Add to this the instability which arises from the inclusion of external links, leading away from the original site, and the opportunities for textual construction by readers are without limit.

Time has passed since the original version of Kaplan's 'textual domain' in 1995, and any predictions that Kaplan's style of 'authorship' were poised to displace the older styles now seem forlorn. The tendency to confine external links to a 'page' separate from the 'internal', authored materials is one sign of this (Gauntlett 2000). Another is the preservation of very 'traditional' layout structures in pdf files (journal articles are an important species of this for academic web users) where the concept of authorship (and copyright) remains as important as it ever was. 'Conservative' practices can be preserved against the potentials of new technological forms where there are good social and economic reasons to expend money and effort in such preservation.

Public online discourse part two: Usenet

Usenet newsgroups are, for the purposes of this research, both an object of study and a resource. They are able to serve this function because, while they exist on the internet as a form of CMC, they also mention and discuss *other* aspects of the internet such as websites, so they can be used as a resource for establishing what people think about the web and the information it offers. As an object of study, newsgroups differ from websites firstly in the much reduced level of multimodality involved in the exchange of messages and secondly in the much enhanced level of interactivity that they demonstrate.[2]

'Newsgroup' here principally signifies publicly available asynchronous group-based online communication forums available via Usenet, although for some purposes, these forums can be discussed alongside other, less public, types of asynchronous group-based communication, such as bulletin boards, lists and conferences. Some of the published research which generalizes about asynchronous CMC as a whole is in fact based upon empirical research from only one of these contexts.

The description of newsgroups as asynchronous and as group-based is important in establishing how this form of discourse differs from chat and from email: all three are based upon the graphical representation of language (that is, writing) rather than upon its phonetic representation (speaking). 'Chat' is synchronous: the message exchange takes place in real-time (though not keystroke-by-keystroke: this is a more recent development and not as yet a widespread one). Newsgroups are asynchronous because, as with email, there is no expectation of an 'immediate' response to a message. Asynchronous electronic communication can be differentiated into the one-to-one form (email) and the one-to-many forms (newsgroups, bulletin boards, conferences and lists). Messages are sent to the whole group and/or to a central filestore depending upon the nature of the resource; in all cases, anyone accessing the resource may, but need not, respond to any given message there (or may indeed reply privately, via email, to the address of the person who sent the message). Responses by default retain the same subject line as the original. All collected messages which share the same subject line constitute a 'thread'.

The fact that Usenet newsgroups are in the public domain is important for the present research. Much asynchronous discourse on the internet is not fully public. The BBC website for example has, as of April 2004, over 400 'message boards'. The use of these requires registration, which involves acceptance of the BBC's terms and conditions. Registration in these cases may be a formality, in the sense that no one applying to join is ever rejected, but is useful to the BBC as part of the attempt to regulate online behaviour. For other groups, registration may be less of a formality: it may require the presentation of credentials or even payment, and the establishment of membership lists. Public newsgroups are indeterminate in 'membership', so that posting to a newsgroup is like broadcasting, except with a vastly smaller actual audience. The largest system of public groups is the Usenet hierarchy, with names like alt.culture.singapore, sci.physics.electromag and so on. An enormous archive of Usenet materials, going back to 1981, has been assembled and put on line by Google at google.groups.com. This archive includes, by arrangement, a few smaller collections from groups that were originally restricted rather than open. All of the materials consulted for the newsgroup sections of the following case study chapters are drawn from this archive.

History of newsgroups

Usenet newsgroups have existed since before the internet, that is, when communication between computers was managed via more localized computer networks and a range of different protocols. Usenet (in 1981) took over from the earlier 'bulletin boards'. Describing the history of Usenet up to the early 1990s, Howard Rheingold writes:

> The growth of Usenet was biological – slow at first, and then exponential. In 1979, there were 3 sites, passing around approximately 2 articles per day; in 1980, there were 15 sites and 10 articles per day; in 1981 there were 150 sites and 20 articles per day. By 1987 there were 5,000 sites, and the daily postings weighed in at 2.5 million bytes. By 1988, it grew to 11,000 sites and the daily mailbag was more than 4 million bytes. By 1992, Usenet was distributed to more than 2.5 million people and the daily News was up to 35 million bytes – thirty or forty times the number of words in this book. (Rheingold 1993, ch. 4: online at http://www.rheingold.com/vc/book/4.html)

There was further expansion throughout the 1990s but informed opinion (see Herring 2004) is that it is now on the decline, since, despite Google, it is less congenial to users who have become 'wired' during the era of the web browser as the principal interface with online resources.

Because electronic asynchronous group communication does go back to the earliest days of computer-mediated communication, it also predates the graphical user interface (GUI), that is, it pre-dates the innovations with mouse and screen of the Apple company, and Microsoft's Windows. The earliest forms of Usenet communication, like the earliest forms of email and of bulletin boards, were strictly text only, limited to ASCII keyboard characters, entered at a command-line prompt: c:>. This history is important because although the limitations of the medium have been overcome in many respects, there is a continuing 'drag' in this particular realm of CMC towards text format. Anything 'visual' is a compromise with the medium, not one of its affordances, and may become lost in translation, through transitions of platform, hardware and software.

Research on newsgroups

For research on asynchronous group-based computer-mediated communication, Hiltz and Turoff's (1978) *The Network Nation* is the landmark publication: it extolled many of the virtues of online communication which we now take for granted. In their introduction to the new edition (1993) they say that wired communication did not come about as quickly as they had envisaged, but of course there has been another huge wave of expansion in connectivity since 1993. The 1978 book talked not of 'newsgroups' but of 'computer conferencing'. At the time of publication there were not many 'users' who could be studied; the excitement was in the potential, not the actual use of technology for communication. The bias was towards restricted group formats, for example within particular companies. Unrestricted groups would not come into the picture until later. Gauntlett (2000) estimates that the expansion of the internet beyond the academic community followed ten years after the rolling out of the TCP/IP (Transmission Control Protocol/Internet Protocol – the standard protocol underlying communication between computers linked to the internet) nationwide in the USA in 1983. By this time of course, a graphical interface was nothing remarkable.

In the early years of research on group communication (not necessarily restricted to the asynchronous public kind), three themes emerged as being of particular interest, and these themes continue to be the subject of research: online community, online identity and interpersonal relations:

- The idea of CMC communication taking place within 'communities' has Rheingold (1993) as the pioneering text[3] (see also Jones 1995). More recent work on online 'togetherness' includes that of Bakardjieva (2003) whose ethnographic study offers a basis for distinguishing between different types of online involvement, serving different needs, with only a few living up to the value-laden name of 'community', and drawing upon different types of communicative resource both public and restricted, synchronous and asynchronous.
- The question of online *identity*, including its plasticity from forum to forum, and the visibility of the person behind the words, is where the work of Sherry Turkle (1995) gave early impetus to discussion. Ideas about the irrelevance of offline identities almost immediately came in for feminist critique, with particular reference not just to the different behaviours of males and females online (Herring 1994) but also to the effects of power on the interactional relations between the sexes (Camp 1996; Herring 1996/1999). Identity, like community, continues to attract the attention of researchers. Crawford (2002) offers a recent contribution in this area, challenging the idea of the 'unmarked' net speaker. Talking of a particular, hypothetical online participant, Crawford writes:

> Certainly her interlocutors will not be able to see her cultural background, markers of class carried in her clothing or the way she carries herself, her level of education, her gender, but does this mean that her speech will magically be freed of these extralinguistic facts of her everyday life when she goes online? On the contrary: Online speech is marked by a highly readable system of differences encoded in grammar and syntax, vocabulary, allusions, regionalisms, dialect and all the other ways in which we signify our cultural and class positions via language.
>
> (Crawford 2002: 98)

Though Crawford is right that we can hardly abandon all of the determinants upon our own linguistic stylings when we go online, there are some difficulties with this line of argument. One is this: that the codes which unlock the *meanings* of specific aspects of such stylings are not equally available to all who would participate in such discourse. If I use a particular word because I'm from Durham, who but someone else from Durham and its environs is going to know that, and allocate me to my correct place in sociolinguistic space? Another problem is the balance to be achieved by any particular online performer, between – in Goffman's (1979) terms – signs 'given' and signs 'given off', where the former are the ones under some sort of control for the purposes of impression management.

- The question of interpersonal relations online, with particular reference to the apparently greater incidence of 'flaming' – interchanges which take an abusive and insulting form – is discussed by Thompsen (1996), who reviews the history of online flaming as a topic of research and traces the earliest use of this word (albeit with a rather different meaning – some lexical drift having occurred in the meantime) back to Steele, Woods et al. (1983) (see also Kayany 1998; O'Sullivan and Flanagan 2003; Alonzo and Aiken 2004). This topic is closely connected with the previous one, since one of the popular explanations for the apparently greater extent of flaming in online communication has to do with the reduced social presence of interlocutors to one another, leading to misinterpretation of communicative intentions, to which the knowledge that 'so-and-so is not like that' cannot be a corrective (Kiesler, Siegel et al. 1984; Kiesler 1997). The question of gender difference in respect of flaming has also been addressed by researchers (Herring 1994).

Other disciplines which have contributed to research on newsgroups include information science (see Bar-Ilan 1997; Snyder 1996; Sallis 1998;

Savolainen 1999, 2001; Kot 2003), and psychology (see Granic 2000; Joinson 2001, 2002). There have also been some 'case study' enquiries into the power of newsgroup discourse to influence the 'offline' world (see Hearit 1999; Lewenstein 1995b). Research on CMC generally has also expanded since the early 1990s and is more conscious of the social/political/economic/cultural context of CMC (see Slevin 2000). But a discussion of research on newsgroups must begin from a consideration of their character as a form of discourse and speech event.

In previous research on newsgroups and health risks (Richardson 2001) I characterized newsgroup discourse in terms of the 'four I's': newsgroup conversations are Interactive, International, Intertextual and Interested. In a further article (Richardson 2003) I added a fifth – Interpersonal – in recognition of the fact that, overwhelmingly, messages sent to newsgroups are sent by, and on behalf of, individuals not institutions. Individuals write in their personal capacity, not as representatives of the organizations which they may work for, or the political parties to which they may belong. This is partly a legacy of the old 'electronic frontier' days in cyberspace when the corporate voice was treated with suspicion (Ludlow 1993). It is also one of the factors which can give rise to mistrust and even flaming in the threads. Other participants do not respond well to contributions which seem to promote the agenda of some group or organization. The corporate or party line 'voice' can be detected, even when a message is delivered by an individual, and such voices are still not welcome on Usenet. Many contributors use their sig (signature) files to make explicit that what they say in their messages represents their own opinions and not those of the company which employs them. This is particularly important for people using their workplace accounts to access groups:

Cellphone materials (2000) writer using a workplace email account

> xxx xxx, Nottingham, UK
> Speaking for myself, not my Employer

As for the original four 'I's', the Interactive characteristic does not need further elaboration; it is adequately covered by the previous discussion. The International aspect of newsgroup discourse recognizes that contributions can come from any part of the wired world. In the English-language materials I examined, to the extent that it was possible to judge, most contributors appeared to be based in North America

(USA and Canada), but the UK was also well represented, especially in relation to MMR, while anglophones in the Far East had a significant presence in relation to SARS. The extent to which participants explicitly reveal their country of origin varies. In some groups with a regional identity (for example, those beginning 'uk'; for instance 'uk.telecom. mobile') there may be a default assumption that all contributors are based in the UK, but regional newsgroups are also a way for diaspora populations to maintain a relationship with 'home' (Mitra 1997). Email addresses can be a guide to country of origin: my own email address ends with 'uk' for example. But this does not apply when people are using web-based accounts such as Hotmail.

The Intertextuality of newsgroup discourse in some ways is no different from intertextuality in other forms of discourse: all text draws from others (Meinhof and Smith 2000; Orr 2003). The distinctive forms of intertextuality in newsgroups include the reproduction of 'earlier' messages within 'later' ones, so that sometimes entire threads can be contained within a single message, marked to show how far 'back' particular elements go. Another is the extensive reproduction of full-text articles from other online sources, especially news sources. This kind of practice often results in single message threads. Such contributions, without any trace of the contributor's own voice, only that of the journal article being distributed in this way, seem to offer little for other participants to engage with. If such messages are cross-posted then they can constitute 'spam' and result in objections via the news.admin.net-abuse.usenet newsgroup. Yet the practice continues and does, often enough, result in further message exchange. The extensive referencing of other on- and offline sources and the varying attribution of trust to those sources is also of significance and has been explored in more detail in each of the case study chapters.

Messages on Usenet are Interested in that (in contrast to news discourse in the mass media), there is no attempt to construct an impartial speaking position. Participants are expected to write from their experience and their beliefs. The limits of this are tested by the general resistance to collective belief structures, the party or corporate line. For authenticity, the beliefs and experience should be genuinely personal, informed by experience (including experiences as a doctor, farmer, electrical engineer and so on). Speech of this kind shows little interest in the opportunity for online anonymity which has been proposed as an important characteristic of CMC – though less so in relation to asynchronous communication than to synchronous forms (Herring 2001).

The expansion of the agenda for research on newsgroups has involved some criticism of the early approaches and their findings. From the perspective of social theory, Slevin (2000: 107) argues that the classic accounts of 'virtual community' consistently cordon these off from the real world, while in his discussion of online identity, he brings to the fore other aspects of contemporary society which are having their effects upon the 'project of the self' (chapter 6), using arguments derived from Giddens (1991) and Bauman (1995). Taking a perspective from within CMC studies, Thompsen (1996) criticizes much of the research on flaming on the grounds that the early empirical studies were based upon unsatisfactory theoretical foundations, using variants of explanations based upon 'reduced social cues'. Thompsen also observes, as have others, that the early research (for example, Sproull and Kiesler 1986) relied too much upon experimental methods which are unsatisfactory for understanding this phenomenon as it occurs in actual online contexts; much of this research, furthermore, presumed that the interaction would take place within particular organizations rather than across cyberspace. As Thompsen observes, these explanations have ignored the influence of time, have displayed a bias towards face-to-face communication, have assumed that 'flames' can be objectively identified when the reality is that they are subject to interpretation, just as other aspects of communication are, online or offline, and have tended towards an unwarranted technological determinism. O'Sullivan and Flanagan (2003) share some of Thompsen's reservations, and they seek to rethink flaming to take account of the fact that senders, receivers and eavesdroppers may either converge or diverge in the normative perspectives they bring to bear in the interpretation of messages. Theirs is the first account to take this approach, and it is an improvement on previous work. However, their analysis is flawed because, in attempting to account for flaming in a way that is generalizable, that is, which will work for online as well as offline behaviour, they neglect the important public/private (or 'restricted') distinction. If newsgroups are a form of public discourse, like broadcasting, then there are no real eavesdroppers: messages are designed *for them* just as much as for their second-person direct addressees.

These criticisms of research on community, identity and interpersonal relations have been taken to heart in the present research, but it is nevertheless important to discuss how the present research relates to these themes. The idea of online 'communities' is still an important and interesting one. Much of the research on this subject, including that of Rheingold himself, relates not to public newsgroups but to more restricted forms of online interaction. This does make some sense, inasmuch as in a restricted forum there is more chance of the members becoming known to one another and more basis for the possibility of constructing boundaries between the in-group and the out-group – see Gaines (1997) and Harrison (2000). As for Usenet, there is evidence, especially from the work of Nancy Baym (Baym 1993, 1995a, 1995b, 1995c, 1996, 1997, 1998) that participants in some newsgroups do indeed construct relations with one another sufficiently strong as to merit the description 'community': see also Phillips (1996) on ingroup–outgroup tensions in a gay and lesbian newsgroup. Yet this is not the whole story. The primary basis of unity for any newsgroup is a shared interest in discussing a particular topic, hence the large number of groups with particular hobbies as a focus, or the 'fan' newsgroups. Others, such as many of the 'sci' newsgroups, have professional interests as their central focus. This is not a narrow or a utilitarian focus centring upon job opportunities in the field, conference announcements, calls for papers, announcements of new publications, and so on – restricted forums (lists) are better at serving this function than newsgroups are. It seems likely that some Usenet newsgroups are more tightly unified than others as regards their group cohesiveness. The kind of research presented here is not well designed to determine which of the groups are unified and which have much looser social bonds. The enquiry focuses upon particular *topics*, not particular groups and it was of significance here that, for example, SARS was a subject that golfers wanted to talk about in March 2003 just as much as jewellery makers. Communities based upon shared interests alone are unlikely to provide for very intense forms of solidarity, particularly on groups where the 'stick to the topic' rule is enforced. Wellman's (1997) 'social network' approach provides a more useful theoretical foundation for rethinking this issue. It may well be the case that, in some periods and/or for some groups it is the case that they are all acquainted with one another offline as well as online. But it is not possible to approach the interaction itself on the assumption that such acquaintance exists. It would not exist for a newcomer reading messages in a thread composed mainly by regulars. If the newcomer and the regulars interpret the same set of words differently, the interpretation of the regulars cannot be regarded as the 'true' interpretation with that of the newcomer somehow less valid. Such a position might be tenable in relation to communication in restricted groups but not in relation to unrestricted ones, which are indiscriminately open to regulars and newcomers. There are difficulties here which are compounded by reading threads in the context of an archive, many years after their original composition and without reference to concurrent threads on the same groups.

Similar considerations apply in respect of the construction of identity in newsgroups. In each of the three case study newsgroups there is a significant subgroup of participants who post under obvious pseudonyms, like 'elfchild', though most posting is done by people who offer a conventional name as their identity. What is important online for these topics is the extent to which someone can put aspects of their identity to work in the job of articulating, for their groups, reasons why their information should be trusted. Richardson (2003) addresses this in relation to newsgroup discourse about mobile phone health risks. In this context, the important factor is not that personal identities are unknown and therefore endlessly flexible online as between one area of cyberspace and another. It is more that, in these encounters, professional identities are masked: in principle, participants come naked into the discussion, except for whatever online reputation they have built up in the group itself – for flaming, for spamming, for pontificating, for being flippant, for going off-topic and so on. And even that reputation only holds for 'regulars' – while those involved in the thread as lurkers or as more active participants may include newcomers as well. To ensure that a professional background as a paediatrician counts for something on line, it is first necessary to inform the group that you have such a background. Then, like the rest of the discourse, this construct is up for negotiation as to its meaning, truth and value. One message in my collection passes on some 'information', and ends: 'You can trust me. I do work for the government.' There is enough indeterminacy in this speech act for a whole thesis. Expert *status* confers no privileges here because the task of discriminating the 'experts' from the rest is so uncertain.

'Flaming' can be considered as one of the distinctive characteristics of 'Netspeak' (Crystal 2001).[4] Flaming has been associated with chat as well as with newsgroups, but most of the empirical research has focused upon asynchronous forums. In the early research there is a strong sense that the amount of flaming encountered online comes as a surprise. It seemed wrong, shocking, certainly noteworthy, that there should be so much of it. By 1998 however, it is at least possible that the lesson has been learned. Newsgroups are for flaming. Could it be that in newsgroups characterized by much flaming there is a mutual *agreement*, in what has been, with exceptions, a male-dominated environment (Anderson 1996; Herring 1996b, 2001), to allow it here, to suspend any face-protection devices which might otherwise operate? Certainly there is some evidence of newsgroup participants who value the opportunity which newsgroups give them for expressing their feelings in a forceful way (see Phillips 1996).

The internet and health risks

The next chapter has more to say about communication and health risks, bringing in, among other things, insights and concerns from the literature on the public understanding of science. The purpose of the present chapter is more restricted: it outlines some current research which draws together the study of the internet and the study of health and risk. The internet/health interface can be approached in many ways, including from a managerial or a policy perspective. With the focus more specifically upon health *risk*, research is drawn towards the study of particular online resources – advice, information, support, treatment options – and how these might contribute to individuals' attempts to understand their own circumstances and arrive at personal decisions. According to Pew Internet (Pew 2003a), 80 per cent of adult internet users in the USA have searched for at least one of 16 health topics online. This includes immunization/vaccination, specific diseases and environmental health hazards, thus covering all of the areas relevant to the present research. What about Americans who do not search for health information on the internet? Is it because they do not trust this as a source of information? Only 12 per cent feel at all strongly that the net is untrustworthy in this respect (Pew 2003a: 33).

Current research at the University of Northumbria by Pamela Briggs and her colleagues (Briggs 2003) is especially interested in understanding the use that people make of online health resources. This research, funded, like the present research, by the ESRC's E-society programme, uses fieldwork methods involving diary protocols, interviews and observation in internet cafés with volunteers and questionnaires. The Northumbria research pays attention to the factors which influence trust for particular websites: such as source credibility and expertise; the degree to which the advice is personalized, the extent to which the process feels familiar or predictable and the consistency of advice across different sources.

There is, in this respect, some convergence between the Northumbria research and the research reported here. There are also important differences. Two in particular should be mentioned. In the first place, my research is more heavily influenced by the literature on computer-mediated communication and by particular areas of language and literacy research. This creates a different approach to the study of websites themselves. In the Northumbria research, analysis of key websites requires procedures of content analysis; in the present research, there is less content analysis and more analysis of textual form (visual, verbal and hypertextual) as this contributes to the construction of meaning.

The CMC approach adopted here also creates a difference in the way that 'the audience' for web resources is constructed. In the Northumbria research, participants are recruited for the purposes of the study from the (for want of a better word) 'real world'. In the present study, there is no attempt to go beyond the world of cyberspace itself. In my study of Usenet discourse about health risks, I have constructed this material both as an object of enquiry, just as the websites are, and also as a resource. It is a resource for exploring issues of trust on health topics, with particular reference in each of the case studies to trust of mass media sources and trust of websites. Despite the self-selected and small sample size the value of this approach lies in the possibility of exploring expressions of trust and mistrust as these are formulated spontaneously and interactively, in one particular communicative medium with its own distinctive characteristics. The medium/mode/genre of online expression is, to a degree, ignored in all forms of content analysis, and sometimes there is justification for this neglect. Some parts of my own analysis should be regarded as content-analytic, for example, the attempt to specify how many messages 'talk up' particular risks, as compared with the numbers who 'talk down' the same risk. As a result of these differences, there is in the present study less tightness of fit between the websites mentioned by the readers and those subjected to analysis in their own right than in the Northumbria research.

The research

In each of the case study chapters below I have chosen one or more websites as well as numerous newsgroup threads for detailed attention. In selecting websites, my purpose is somewhat different in each chapter. In the mobile phone chapter I sought to contrast two websites provided by two different individuals, one representing the mainstream view on mobile phone risk and one representing a minority view. In the SARS chapter the point is to examine how an 'official' website (actually that of the World Health Organization) compared with two contemporary blogs when dealing with the same topic. Finally, in the MMR chapter, the focus is upon a website which represents the extreme fringe view of modern medicine and its implementation. These accounts in each case present a textual analysis with particular reference to the structure of the site, to the graphic display of materials and to the types and forms of hyperlinks as they appear on the site in general, and especially upon the front page of the site or section.

In the case of the newsgroup materials, the object was to establish a corpus of 1000+ messages, organized by thread, for each topic, from the earliest mention of the topic in Usenet until the end of June 2003 which was the cut-off point. This produced a somewhat different number of threads in each case and a very different temporal distribution. The story of SARS only began in March 2003, while that of mobile phones and cancer began in 1993 and that of MMR began (slowly) in 1995 and intensified from 1998. The collections consist entirely of messages from English-language newsgroups which dominate the archive, although it is not an exclusively English-language resource. Each of the case study chapters (Chapters 4, 5 and 6) go into a little more detail about the procedures for the collection and the analysis of the textual materials, as well as the extent to which the analysed materials are representative of the full range of Usenet discussion on these topics during the relevant time periods.

Confidentiality

In this research I have quoted extensively from messages posted in Usenet from 1993 to 2003. Yet this is the tiniest fragment of Google's Usenet archive, and well within 'fair dealing' limits for copyright purposes. It is not the copyright issue which matters so far as this degree of citation is concerned, but the issue of confidentiality among Usenet contributors who may not appreciate that that their words are, thanks to Google, very much in the public domain. Google itself currently provides mechanisms for the deletion of particular messages from the archive.

It is important for this research to quote from actual messages rather than reporting, summarizing and quantifying them, because of the value of examining how health risk issues are debated in people's own words, within the limits and affordances of a particular medium. I have taken advantage of the public domain status of these materials. But I do have some concerns about confidentiality and I have taken some minor measures out of respect for the original participants.

In the first place it is important to note that some participants, on all three topics, took steps to protect their own online confidentiality by posting to Usenet under a pseudonym, like 'elfchild' (not an actual example). It is likely too that email addresses operative when some of the earliest messages were posted are so no longer, as people move their internet accounts between different ISPs (Internet Service Providers).

In the second place, I have not published the names of contributors, even when they are pseudonyms, alongside any of the citations, and I have substituted names within messages with placeholder characters.

In the third place I have refrained from advertising the name of the specific newsgroup where the original message was first posted. Instead I have identified messages according to the type of newsgroup on which it occurred. This level of identification is important to the research to the extent that different types of expression may be characteristic of different groups. The Appendix lists all the newsgroups which were consulted for this research.

Finally, to discourage easy recovery of particular messages from the archive, I have corrected obvious misspellings and typos and incorrect punctuation within messages. This does some damage to the authenticity of the data, but not much and not of a kind which compromises the analysis. 'Authenticity' is a difficult concept in relation to this data. In respect of formatting, for example, there is no single authentic form. The look of a text on a sender's computer screen is different from the look of that 'same' text on the screen of the receiver, and different receivers will also see different layouts from one another according to screen size, software, available fonts, display preferences and so on. The fact that Google has 'homogenized' all of these variations to its own formatting is a further complication. Typos and misspellings can distract from the textual features which are important for the analysis, and run the risk of creating inappropriate impressions of the writers. These corrections also make material harder to trace back to the originals in the archive. Overall, I have tried to ensure that this research is faithful to the spirit of the guidelines recommended by the Association of Internet Researchers (AoIR 2002) and those of the British Association for Applied Linguistics (BAAL 1994).[5]

3
Public Discourses of Risk, Health and Science

This chapter explores in more detail the importance of *discourse* (in the sociocultural sense) in the construction of contemporary risk. It continues the focus, introduced in the previous chapter, on the idea of *public* communication, which entails some attention to the role of the mass media in the representation of risk in general and to the particular health risks which have been examined in the present research.

Contemporary health risks are the subject of representations in talk and in writing.[1] Such discourse serves to 'construct' risks, by providing the concepts and language for making sense of them.

> [Risks] induce systematic and often irreversible harm, generally remain invisible, are based on causal interpretations, and thus initially only exist in terms of the (scientific or anti-scientific) knowledge about them. They can thus be changed, magnified, dramatized or minimized within knowledge, and to that extent they are particularly open to social definition and construction. Hence the mass media and the scientific and legal professions in charge of defining risks become key social and political positions. (Beck 1992: 22–3)

Of the many forms of communication which contribute to the construction of health risks – the scientific research, the policy documents, the newspaper reports, the gossip, and so on – it is the *public* forms which are of particular importance, because they provide the resources for popular understanding of what is at stake.

The chapter begins with a discussion of 'risk' as this has been written about in the social theory of the 1990s, drawing attention to three themes which are relevant to the present research: the idea of contemporary risks as manufactured risks; the considerable uncertainty which surrounds the possible outcomes of 'risky' behaviour; and the role of experts and expertise, foregrounding the problem of trust within this set of concerns.

The bulk of the chapter is concerned specifically with 'risk' in the context of communication and representation, so there is some discussion of the relevant channels of communication (including the internet) within the matrix of relationships which define public health issues: from channels of communication there is a shift to themes of communication in the discourse(s) of health risk and from these to the crucial 'meta-themes' of scientific expertise and of trust.

Risk and social theory

Beck (1992) and Giddens (1999), the theorists of reflexive modernization, say that the risks of today are *manufactured* risks, stemming from the created environment itself; that they have a potentially global sphere of impact, are interconnected across economic, political and social as well as geographic boundaries, are wrapped up within institutional frameworks, subject to widespread publicization and extend beyond what any particular knowledge system is capable of representing. They cannot be converted into certainties by any system of expertise such as religion. This is the 'downside' of risk, as opposed to 'risk' within an entrepreneurial frame, or a gambling frame, where 'he who dares, wins'.

For the purposes of argument, human health risks can be divided between the risks of accident on the one hand and the risks of disease/illness on the other; according to Gwyn (2002), 'disease' is the preferred term in expert discourse and 'illness' its lay equivalent. This distinction is an important one in the mobile phone debate where the risk of a car accident caused by people trying to use a phone and drive at the same time is constantly being traded off against the possible risk of cancer. 'Disease/illness' seems, symbolically speaking, to concern the body within, while 'accident' appears principally about the external body. Risks of either kind can produce health effects from the trivial to the fatal, but of the two it seems to be disease rather than accident which has the greater potency in our collective imaginings of risk and bodily harm.

All three of the case studies in this volume relate to the symbolic territory of human disease. The mobile phone study relates to cancer, which along with HIV/AIDS (although for a lot longer) is the most culturally salient of all diseases. The SARS case study relates to infectious diseases. These were, for a brief moment in the mid-twentieth century, thought to be under control or potentially so, thanks to the development of antibiotics and vaccines, but now seem to be extremely threatening once again, with the evolution of resistant strains of bacteria and new disease pathogens, while vaccination programmes prove hard to implement (Garrett 1994). The MMR study likewise relates to the area of infectious diseases, since the vaccine is designed to prevent three of them. But it also introduces an additional concern: the risk of autism (or an 'autistic spectrum disorder', which accommodates a range of conditions known under other names, including Attention Deficit Hyperactive Disorder or ADHD). Autism and brain cancer have in common the fact that they both implicate the brain. Threats to the brain have a special character inasmuch as the brain is the locus of the mental faculties as well as identity and personality.

In addition, the three risks fall within the sphere of public health, that is to say, where the public authorities at local, national and international levels share responsibility with individuals and other organizations. Public health authorities are involved here in various ways. They manage vaccination programmes, use standards legislation to regulate industries, invest public money in the science designed to explore causal theories, and respond to pressures from industry, the mass media, public opinion and so on, just as they do in other areas of public policy.

In the public health context, health risk issues such as the ones examined in this book are underpinned by connections between different participants in a public health matrix. One participant comprises individuals as actual or potential casualties of risk. Another comprises the industries and institutions distributing suspect product or managing suspect environments – airlines, mobile phone manufacturers, vaccine manufacturers, medical practices and so on. Then there are the authorities which regulate these industries and formulate policies in what they represent as the 'best interest'; and finally, research scientists conducting their varied enquiries so that policy and practice can be, or can claim to be, based on sound knowledge.

The problem with the 'risks' which are discussed in this research, particularly with the mobile phone and MMR debates, is that they do not allow us to use the word 'risk' with a stable meaning. If 'risk' in its negative guise is about doing something now, and possibly, but not certainly, suffering bad consequences afterwards, then the problem in these cases is about the extent of the uncertainty in respect of those bad outcomes. Variously, and on an ascending reality scale, the possibilities are:

- That there are no bad outcomes of the proposed kind
- That the potential risk under discussion is 'theoretical'
- That the bad outcomes depend on unknown factors deserving further research
- That the bad outcomes depend on knowable 'risk factors' concerning the individual prior to the risky behaviour
- That research and circumstantial evidence suggests a probability of bad outcomes
- That particular case histories demonstrate the reality of harm in the past, and thus confirm the possibility of harm for others in the future

and with a further possibility which goes beyond this scale:

- That *one* of the above is accurate but there is no present way of knowing which one.

To establish that this scale is not just a construct but represents the true range of opinion about these risks, I can offer illustrative quotations from the newsgroup materials:

No bad outcomes
Example no. 1 (1998) – cellphones

>Are there any health risks with cellular phones? If so, what are
>they?
xxxxxxxxxxxxxxxxxxxxxxxxxxxxxxxxxxxxxxxxxxxxxxxxxx
I know that the fanatics are going to love this!
There are no health risks.

Theoretical risk of bad outcomes
Example no. 2 (1998) – MMR

If no-one can give you a 100% guarantee that your child won't get the fatal brain-wasting disease Creutzfeldt-Jakob Disease (CJD) from the human albumin, a blood product, in the MMR vaccine how can you say it is a safe vaccine? Because the risk is described as theoretical and hypothetical doesn't mean it can't happen.

Further research needed
Example no. 3 (2002) – MMR

> I do believe that injections are a good thing but a lot more research needs to be done into the risks, but of course there's no time to carry out research without a big gap in the inoculations, it just seems a no win situation to me.

Susceptibility
Example no. 4 (2001) – MMR

> If your family has depressed folks, Alcoholics, ADD, ADHD or dyslexia of any kind, DON'T let the next generation get all the shots at once. Wouldn't it be better to err on the side of caution rather than create even more kids with autism???

Cumulative evidence
Example no. 5 (1998) – MMR

> There has been a sudden explosion of Autism in America. McKinney School district, 26 new students, Plano ISD, 60+ this year. Data backed by 5 more scientific studies soon to be published points to the MMR vaccine as the cause.

Case history evidence
Example no. 6 (1998) – MMR

> We do not have informed consent because regardless of what ever literature is given to you the attitude of the doctors is VACCINATE. It's a matter of risk vs. benefit – for the greater good of the majority a vaccine was given to all kids even though it was known a certain number of them would suffer dire consequences. Not a big deal unless your kid is one of the small percentage . . . I believe my daughter was. I am observing all of this with great interest.

Given this play of uncertainty, indeterminacy and ignorance, the use of the word 'risk' seems much too vague, though tending to point higher up the scale than 'theoretical'. The uncertainty of contemporary risk, and the consequences of this, is one of the themes in the risk society literature (compare Beck 1992: 71–2), although the explanations in this literature are at too 'macro' a level to account for the extent of the variations and the use to which they are put in actually occurring discourse about risks (Horlick-Jones 2003).

Risk communication in the public health matrix

The connections between these participants are relationships which depend upon the exchange of information, and information comes in the form of representations and constructions which are different for different parts of the matrix. The texts which realize these representations and constructions are 'public' to varying degrees. Intellectual property rights and commercial considerations keep some material out of the public domain, national security concerns may do the same for other material, but the matrix does require a public discourse, and by tradition this is where the mass media enter the picture. The mass media may enter from a number of different gateways, reporting variously upon public policy initiatives, new technological developments, unexpected scientific findings, public opinion surveys, changes in the economic fortunes of particular industries, or just unexpected 'health events' like the outbreak of SARS in March 2003.

The journalistic forms of mass media representations include not only news, current affairs, features and op-ed materials but also various kinds of fictional and dramatic representations, all contributing to the cultural framing of risk. With the coming of the internet there has been some expansion of public discourse beyond these familiar forms. Not only has the internet given the traditional mass media an additional channel of communication for their usual wares, it has also allowed for enhanced public access to hitherto more restricted materials such as parliamentary debates, standards legislation and other official documentation. Furthermore, the interactive capabilities of the internet have provided greater opportunities for public discussion of topics such as these.

In speaking of 'public discourse' there is an ambiguity which needs to be addressed. Does 'public discourse' refer to discourse which is addressed to the public, or does it refer to discourse in which the public actively contribute? In theory it could mean both of these, but in practice the participatory forms of public discourse are very restricted and lacking in power. Certainly people do form their own representations of health risk issues, and use these within their social networks, but the opportunities for these representations to mean something, to have consequences, depend upon people's involvements in activist and lobby groups, participation in opinion polls and direct communicative efforts, whether one-to-one (for example, the letter to the MP) or one-to-many (for example, the letter to the local newspaper). The internet, and especially the newsgroup arenas within the net, allow more scope for the views of ordinary people to enter the public domain, although in a way which still leaves this discourse isolated from the main arteries of public communication proper.

The widest definition of public discourse for the purposes of this study is 'discourse which is in the public domain'. This definition encompasses journalistic reporting, which is clearly 'for' the public, but it also takes in the kind of newsgroup threads analysed in this research – discourse by the public. The messages on these threads, are, like the journalism, 'on show' to unspecified, uncounted, uncountable others beyond the immediate participants who have composed the messages.

One of the important differences between the two forms of public discourse, for-the-public and by-the-public, is that although both kinds are multivocal, in the first kind, this multivocality is organized and patterned according to generic conventions. Different voices, for the most part, are clearly identified – the government spokesman, the opposition spokesman, the expert, the ordinary person, the industry representative, the trades unionist and so on. In the second, by-the-people kind, such external organization and patterning falls by the wayside, and identity, like everything else, becomes relevant only to the extent that the participants make it so. To make it relevant it has to be spoken: participants are free to say, or to conceal, what they do for a living, who employs them, how long they have been doing it, where they learned to do it, and other characteristics of this sort, and they have to have these credentials accepted as valid and relevant in this context. They may also reveal aspects of their identities in less deliberate ways through the forms of language they choose (Crawford 2002; Herring 2001). Not all participants will go to the trouble of articulating their identity explicitly. Plenty can be said and argued over, without reference to identity. Participants, including 'lurkers', are self-selecting and presumably do not 'join' newsgroups where they have no interest in the declared topic focus. This creates some unity and coherence within groups. But the coherence is managed internally by the participants themselves, not externally by professional organizations and individuals trained to produce texts in accordance with established and codified conventions.

Risk discourse for-the-people

Risk discourse by-the-people is amply covered elsewhere in this book, extensively in the case study chapters when they deal specifically with newsgroup materials. The present chapter offers an opportunity, by way of context, to expand a little more on risk discourse for-the-people, that is, on mass media and risk. Although the research in this book is not centrally about the mass media it is impossible to write about health risks intelligently without reference to the media. Mass media provide the archetypal for-the-public discourse about risks, with the internet now performing the function of an additional conduit for media materials. In by-the-public discourse there is constant reference to mass media sources: many newsgroup threads originate because some piece of reportage has introduced a new angle or new findings, and there is an important strand of media *criticism* within this material too. News values in the mass media, especially at the popular end, mean that health-related risk issues are certain to attract news coverage, since they have the potential to bring together some key ingredients of a good popular news story. Health risk stories offer the possibility of direct effects, as readers and viewers are invited to contemplate whether and how the problem might come to them and their families. They offer human interest, as audiences consider the fate of particular 'victims'. They offer opportunities for contemplation of responsibility – constructions of 'blame' in relation to particular public and private institutions and their duties towards citizens and consumers. Sometimes there are dramatic narrative values, for example the possibility of finding a particular hero-scientist, resisting the pressure to conform to majority opinions and becoming the champion for a challenge to orthodox views.

Discourses of health and risk in the mass media have been the subject of academic research in their own right. Two recent contributions are worth mentioning because both attend to a full range of media forms and genres, and discuss fictional as well as non-fictional formats. Allan (2002) writes about the ways in which science fiction from H.G. Wells to *Star Trek* and the *X-files* has provided pleasurable and worthwhile frameworks for engaging with scientific issues, and also reviews more factual treatments of science and scientists in the mass media. Gwyn (2002) devotes one chapter to media and health. He too examines fictional/dramatic representations of health issues, including an analysis of the 'plague' theme in the Hollywood film *Outbreak* as well as journalistic treatments of particular topics such as British newspaper coverage of an outbreak of a microbial infection called 'necrotizing fasciitis' in 1994.

Both Allan and Gwyn are interested in the power of mass media representations of science, health and risk within popular understandings of these topics, but for 'audience research' proper, the most relevant studies come from the stable of the Glasgow University Media Group. From this stable there are studies of audience reception in relation to the AIDS crisis (see Kitzinger 1993, 1998a, 1998b), as well as on food scares (Reilly 1999) and on mental illness (Philo 1999). Other relevant audience studies, without the Glasgow connection, include Corner, Richardson et al. (1990) on audience reception of TV and video representations of nuclear power, and Rogers (1999) on AIDS and on global warming. Audience research of this kind is necessary because the meanings of media texts are not 'given' and objectively available to an analyst, but have to be negotiated in the act of reading, viewing and listening: audiences bring to bear their own frameworks of value and of knowledge, and the interpretative result is never guaranteed.

The Allan and Gwyn studies of media and health offer accounts of media texts which owe much to the cultural studies tradition in media research, with their shared interest in fiction, myth and metaphor. There is another more social-scientific route into this territory, which connects with a 'public understanding of science' perspective. This perspective is drawn more towards the factual/journalistic forms of mass media coverage, and to concerns about the extent of the accuracy and fairness in media reports of health and science issues. Recent work out of Cardiff university (Hargreaves and Ferguson 2000; Hargreaves, Lewis et al. 2003; Lewis and Spears 2003) represents this trend, which also has an audience reception element. There is considerable overlap between the cultural studies and the social science branches of the enterprise of studying science and risk in the mass media.

In coming at questions of science/health/risk from a 'public understanding of science' perspective, recent work seeks to identify and to distance itself from a simplistic 'deficit model' of public understanding (see Hilgartner 1990). In a deficit model, popular views of science are simply wrong – ignorant, factually inaccurate and/or scientifically illiterate. The mass media, which could be contributing to a better understanding, are seen as part of the problem. The deficit model is unsatisfactory for many reasons. It eliminates all of the problems of understanding reality which originate within science itself – the disagreements, the uncertainties and indeterminacies, the ignorance, the amount of specialism insulating branches of science from one another. It ignores the ways that media representations and public understanding both seek a more contextualized view of science, placing it in relation to government and industrial interests. It ignores the importance of ethical frameworks in shaping science news – frameworks which the scientific community often tries to keep at arm's length. It does not give due attention to the nature and function of journalism which, without any particular hostility to science, necessarily privileges some aspects of science stories over others. It does not recognize that scientific authority has come into question: that knowledge presented in the voice of 'science' does not automatically command trust. 'The public' is viewed in an undifferentiated way, when the truth is that people are constituted differently by their experiences and their social backgrounds, so that the young parents of an autistic child may know all sorts of things that the elderly bachelor does not know when reading stories about MMR vaccine, just as the long-time amateur radio hobbyist knows things that the teenage mobile phone user does not know. There is no justification for the belief that the world would be a better place if science was reported always and everywhere on scientists' own terms, and if educational systems were more successful in training us to understand and accept the authority of those terms.

The range of problems with the deficit model point towards a need for a better model, and also for more empirical research on what people do understand and believe about science in general and about particular topics with a scientific component. The Lewenstein (1995a) model of science communication is one which is not restricted to the 'public' layers of communication, separated from other channels and forms of discourse (Figure 3.1).

The inclusiveness of this model is important to Lewenstein because, along with some others, he wants a model in which the for-the-public part of science communication is not a one-way street but can also lead back into the science itself. The 'messiness' of this model is precisely the point of it. Hargreaves and Ferguson (2000) describe it as 'a kaleidoscopic storm of competing and interacting lines of communication', predicting, correctly in their view, 'informational instability', at least in the early days of a new scientific project which is of public interest. Lewenstein's model is meant to account for science communication as it exists at this point in history, putting pressure upon more traditional relations between participants in communication processes. It is based not upon studies of the health/risk sciences, but on narrative accounts

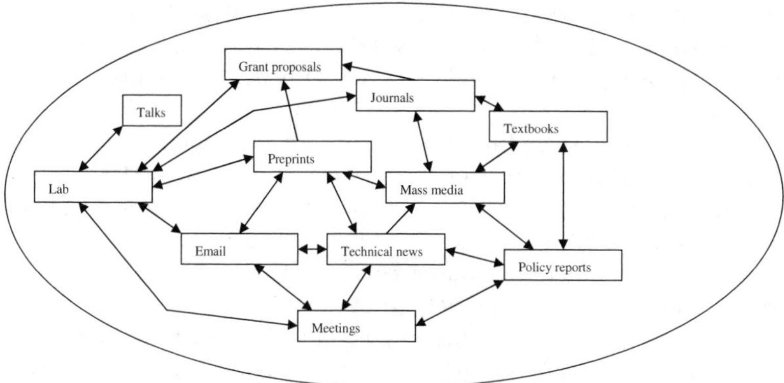

Source: Based on Lewenstein (1995a: 426).

Figure 3.1: Scientific communication

of 'cold fusion' experiments and discoveries in the late 1980s and early 1990s.

Some research into media coverage of health risks takes a more linguistic approach. A well-cited example of this is Fowler (1991). This is a critical linguistic analysis of press reports throughout the 'salmonella in eggs' affair in Britain, in the winter of 1988–89. This was an episode of public anxiety about the risk of food poisoning from eggs infected with the bacterium *salmonella enteritidis*. Fowler's interest is in the character of the episode as a kind of media event, and in the specifically linguistic characteristics of 'hysterical style', involving:

- Terms denoting negative emotional reactions, from the 'fear' semantic field
- An abundance of difficult technical and medical terms
- Agency imputed to the 'germs' and 'bugs' carrying the infection
- Metaphors of war against the bugs
- Intertextual allusions to horror and science fiction themes
- Heavy reliance on quantification, some of it involving very large numbers, as well as words like 'increase', 'rise', 'grow', 'spread', indicating growth in numbers

Whenever media/communication research turns its attention to health risk, the topic of HIV/AIDS provides one of the points of reference. Besides Allan, Gwyn and the Glasgow University Media Group, other researchers who have discussed media coverage of AIDS include Karpf (1988), Garrett (1997) and Wellings (1988). Susan Sontag's (1988) analysis of AIDS metaphors (war and invasion) is frequently discussed in these accounts.

A characteristic shared by the three health risk topics considered in the present research is that each of them involves, at the level of the individual, lifestyle choices. The luxury of these choices is denied to most of the world's population, but not to those adults who use the internet for information and/or communication. Internet users are people who can choose whether or not to buy a mobile phone, how to use it (with or without a hands-free set), and whether to pay attention to 'specific absorption rate' levels when they choose between models. They are people with opportunities for international travel, who have to decide whether to go ahead with planned visits to cities where substantial numbers of people have succumbed to SARS. If they are parents, they have to decide whether their fears about MMR are strong enough to induce them to resist official vaccination programmes. Only in the MMR case is the 'right' decision made by the authorities and not by the individual, and even then, it is negotiable.

Because it is individuals, members of the public, who get to make the final decisions as regards these lifestyle choices, the contribution of public discourse is central in the social construction of risk. It is the only layer of discourse within the public health matrix which ordinary people have access to, and/or the only layer constructed with their communicational needs in the foreground. Formal 'access' to other layers in the matrix, via the internet as described above, is not really relevant if the generic form and register of such texts makes them impossible to understand, although individuals with sufficient motivation can and do set out to 'master' the reading skills they need under certain circumstances. This possibility is dramatized to powerful effect in the Hollywood film *Lorenzo's Oil*, where the parents, played by Susan Sarandon and Nick Nolte, follow the research leads wherever they go, to the exasperation of most of the real 'experts' with whom they come into contact.

It is important that traditional public discourse in its journalistic forms is multivocal (Bell 1996): that it quotes and reports the voices of the interested parties in the world of science, in the relevant industries and in government. If the technicalities of risk issues go beyond what the ordinary citizen/consumer is capable of understanding (short of crash courses on the biomedical aspects of radiation exposure or the difficulties of mounting large-scale epidemiological research) then she will have to use more heuristic strategies in forming a judgement. Deciding which voice or voices to trust is one such strategy, and it will be from the mass media that she will learn which bits of information come from which sources.

Trust and expertise

Hargreaves and Ferguson, whose ESRC paper 'Who's Misunderstanding Whom?' was cited above, recognize that the old deficit model, while not exactly a straw man, is losing its hold in the arenas of debate concerned with public policy, where it is important not to oversimplify. For evidence of this they point to the Third Report of the Lords Select Committee on Science and Technology (Lords Select Committee on Science and Technology 2000), particularly its promotion of the idea of dialogue between the public and the scientific communities. Further evidence is available, for example, from the volume *Risk Communication and Public Health* (Bennett and Calman 1999). One of the editors of this book is Britain's former Chief Medical Officer (the British equivalent of the Surgeon-General), a post which he held throughout most of the BSE/CJD affair. His co-editor, in the preliminary chapter, writes about the importance of allowing 'expert' and 'lay' perspectives to inform each other as part of a two-way process:

> If scientific and lay perspectives are to inform each other, those responsible for communicating about risks have both to take public concerns seriously while still doing justice to available scientific evidence. This can be a difficult balancing act. As argued in subsequent chapters, very often answers have to be found in the *process* of communication and engagement with relevant stakeholders, rather than just the fine-tuning of words. (Bennett and Calman 1999: 4)

If it remains hard for Bennett and Calman to go very far beyond the traditional 'us' and 'them' view of scientists vs. the rest, any move in that direction is of interest, as too is their book's direct concern with the theme of trust:

> Put simply, the point is that messages are often judged first and foremost not by content but by source: who is telling me this and can I trust them? If the answer to the second question is 'no', *any* message from that source will often be disregarded, no matter how well-intentioned and well-delivered. Indeed, good delivery may even be counter-productive. There is some evidence that well-presented

> arguments from distrusted sources have a negative effect – as if people conclude that the sender is not only untrustworthy, but cunning as well. (Ibid.; see also Langford and Marris 1999)

It is interesting to observe from such quarters, acknowledgements of the importance of discourse, and interpretations of discourse (notwithstanding this gesture, however, their general perspective is realist rather than constructivist). On the main theme of trust, Bennett is certainly correct and there is considerable evidence from the newsgroup material in the present research to support his point about the importance of sources and their credibility. Trustworthiness is a constant theme of discussion in this material. It is used most powerfully in rhetorical moves against the authority of the voice of industry, powerfully against the authority of the government voice, and less powerfully against the scientific voice – except where science has been contaminated by its contact with less respected participants:

Example no. 7 (2000) – about mobile phones

> The industry and the government have too much at stake to be a reliable source of information. They will lie and deceive to protect their own interests. They put their interests above your health. Hence –
> RULE THREE: DO NOT TRUST INDUSTRY OR GOVERNMENT STATEMENTS ON SAFETY OF MOBILE PHONES
> That isn't to say everything they say is wrong, just that they are happy to lie and dissemble if it suits them.

Example no. 8 (2003) – about SARS

> Yeah xxx, you been listening to our two SARS 'experts' just happen to be company men. [. . .] Read up on xxx, a Wellcome man who is an HIV 'expert' and see how he arranged to have FMD under control by election time. [FMD = Foot and Mouth Disease, a cattle disease to which Britain succumbed in 2001–02.]
> I wouldn't trust him to tell me the time of day.

Example no. 9 (2001) – about MMR

> If you wish to place faith in the future good health of your children, in the hands of those propagating the destruction of the health service by means of PFI, then I guess its your decision. Personally I wouldn't trust these bastards with anything! [PFI = Private Finance Initiative, a Labour government policy for distributing the costs of national health care between the public and the private sector.]

There is nothing original in any of the above, the examples merely confirm what the public health experts have come to appreciate. It is important however, from time to time, to look at such unsolicited expression of mistrust, and the ways it is expressed, to understand that trust and mistrust are not just states of belief inside people's heads. They also exist in outward form as positions which people take up and defend in actual discursive situations.

Research focused on the discursive expression of trust can also complement more traditional survey-based methods for researching 'public attitudes to science', as represented, for example, by *Science and the Public* (Office of Science and Technology and the Wellcome Trust 2000). This report showed that among a sample of 1839 respondents, the sources trusted the most 'to provide accurate information about scientific facts' (p. 84) were university scientists and scientists working for charities. The least trusted sources for accurate information about scientific facts were people working for tabloid newspapers, followed by Government ministers/politicians (p. 86). This was a British survey: the patterns might have been different in the USA where tabloid journalism has a lower public profile. Like the House of Lords Select Committee, like Bennett and Calman, the bodies publishing this report want to dispense with the deficit model:

> The Wellcome Trust and the OST believe that an 'engagement model' of science communication – a two-way dialogue between specialists and non-specialists – is more appropriate than the 'deficit model' which just gives people more information about science. (Office of Science and Technology and the Wellcome Trust 2000: 10)

The trustworthiness of the mass media as information sources is complicated by the position of a media text as representing a voice in its own right while also mediating the voices of other participants. In putting it like this I am thinking in terms of the news media rather than the wider range of fictional and non-fictional media texts. This narrowing of focus is justified here because it is the news media which are in the front line when it comes to accusations of bias, distortion, sensationalism and hype. The OST/Wellcome Trust approach does not offer a useful methodology for exploring the complication of voice/authorship/footing as it affects trust. When someone picks 'Government minister' from a list of sources when asked to identify those they do not trust, we have to remind ourselves that their lack of trust is in their *versions* of what ministers are supposed to have said or done, though not necessarily any particular utterance or act. Questionnaire survey respondents have derived their versions of ministers and so on from exposure to mass media versions. Do we assume for the purposes of the OST/Wellcome Trust questionnaire that respondents have 'seen through' the mediating voice of the *Daily Mail* or BBC journalist and recovered/derived an accurate view of the minister's voice? (Granting here for the purposes of argument that accuracy is achievable in the first place.) It may be that they have not; that what they have derived from the *Daily Mail*/BBC account is only a distorted/simplified/biased/sensationalized/out-of-context version of the minister's words. One of the staple images of the British 'don't-trust-the-government' angle is an image we have learned to read as 'John Gummer (Conservative health minister) force-feeding beefburgers to his daughter to prove that they aren't going to kill anyone'. Gummer would see this as a very exaggerated account of what he was doing, and the exaggeration had a satirical purpose at the time, but it is hard now to recover any other version without some archive research.

There is another scenario in the literature which bears on the question of the media voice and its separability from the reported voices. Dearing (1995) and others have spoken of a situation in which the manner of reporting, by writers and editors trained in the protocols of 'balance', creates an impression of equality-in-argument between two opposed positions when within the scientific world no such equality exists, because one view is a majority/mainstream view and the other is a minority/fringe view. To trust the media in this case is to trust an implicit and probably unintended meta-claim: 'there is equal support for both of these views', while the scientific voices themselves have not made any meta-claims about the distribution of support, or have not been represented as making such claims. The individual voices are not distorted or misrepresented in any way in this scenario but the result nevertheless can be seen as unfair to the representative of the majority view. Furthermore, the OST/Wellcome Trust questions about trust are framed as questions about trusting someone 'to provide accurate information about scientific facts', and university scientists do well on this question. We have no way of knowing whether they would also do well on a question about meta-claims. Would questionnaire respondents be wont to believe the second part of this if a scientist said it: 'There is no evidence that MMR causes autism and no one else thinks that Andrew Wakefield's research has any merit.' Or are scientists only credible when they stick to 'the facts' or statements about their own beliefs? All of this is probably beyond the scope of survey research, but it is not beyond the scope of discourse analysis, carefully conceived.

Before leaving the subject of the mass media and trust, one other observation is worth making, based upon the research of Livingstone and Lunt (1994). Livingstone and Lunt are concerned with TV talk shows rather than with news media. This too is a context which involves the (re)presentation of different voices. Participants are recruited onto shows like Oprah Winfrey (in the USA) and Kilroy (in the UK[2]) on the basis of their relations to the topic of the show, which varies from week to week. An important differentiation of participants in this context is between the voice of experience and the voice of expertise. Some participants know about the topic because of what has happened to them or their families. Others know about it because it is part of their job to do so. These are the professionals, the experts, and they have the 'big picture'. Livingstone and Lunt's research, which includes an audience research element along with textual analysis, establishes that the voice of expertise has no particular privilege in this context, and if anything it is the voice of experience which is more highly valued:

> The programme [Kilroy] . . . invites the audience to ask whether the experts are credible, helpful to ordinary people, comprehensible, trustworthy, attractive, in tune with ordinary experience, and so forth. Broadly speaking, the viewers are thus invited to identify with the studio audience and to be critical of the experts.
> (Livingstone and Lunt 1994: 117)

This is further evidence, from a different vantage point, both of the problems which ordinary people have with experts and their forms of knowledge, and of the role of the mass media in managing the 'expert'/'lay' relationship in a particular way.

Trust discourse by-the-people

The audience research component of the work done by Livingstone and Lunt begins to move the discourse-analytic focus away from discourse for-the-people and towards discourse by-the-people. The most valuable study to date in this area is the work of Myers (2004 forthcoming) which looks at the discourse of focus groups convened to discuss environmental hazards. This is not 'public' discourse of the kind explored in the present volume but it does represent another methodology for exploring popular constructions of risk, expertise and trust. Myers raises objections to questionnaire methods which are similar to the ones presented above: 'these responses to set questions do not reflect the ways people talk about experts in interaction, and the ways they use such talk to display opinions and construct identities'.

Myers' work, like parts of the research in this book, is focused upon discourse 'by-the-people', albeit not for public consumption except via his mediation. There are differences other than the public/restricted status of the talk, between focus group interaction and newsgroup threads which are methodologically important to recognize. Focus group discussions generate interaction which is solicited for research purposes, whereas newsgroup threads are unsolicited. On the other hand, focus group methods can be selective about the participants they recruit, while newsgroup participants are self-selecting and exclude many kinds of voices, either because they do not spontaneously wish to enter into discussion of the topic, do not wish to do so online, or do not have internet/newsgroup access. In both cases the generic character of the interaction-type has to be factored into the analysis. Newsgroup threads for example are 'polylogic' (Marcoccia 2004) and in focus groups there is a possibility that one member will come to dominate the others. In focus groups, people talk their opinions and identities into being, in newsgroups they do something comparable through writing. Myers observes, in his material, a propensity to avoid disagreement. In many newsgroup threads there is no such propensity and flaming is common (see previous chapter as well as Chapter 7).

Bearing in mind these similarities and differences between Myers' material and the newsgroup material, some common themes about the evaluation of experts emerge. Myers argues that experts are represented as 'indefinite, interrelated, inconclusive and interested'. Indefiniteness comes across in the tendency to characterize experts with nothing more explicit than a third-person plural pronoun. Interrelatedness comes across in the tendency to compare different risk issues, not on the basis of the science itself but on the basis of similar patterns of advice between cases. In Myers' research, as here, the BSE/CJD affair (a 'media template' in Kitzinger's (2000) terms), while not itself the focus of discussion, was constantly being brought into the frame via comparisons. Inconclusiveness comes across in the focus groups through the tendency to present experts as divided and unable to come up with definitive answers. The newsgroup discussions manifest exactly the same tendency, and this is demonstrated extensively in the case study chapters below. Myers' fourth characteristic is interestedness. In the focus groups, as in the newsgroups, 'Participants . . . also trace the problem, nearly always, to money.' Here are some examples from the newsgroups which relate to these four characteristics:

Example no. 10 (2003) – Indefiniteness

They are calling it SARS

Example no. 11 (1996) (the caret character at the start of a line indicates text from a message to which the following one is a reply) – Interrelatedness

>there is, at present, no clear evidence to support a link between
>mobile phone use and risks to health.
xxxxxxxxxxxxxxxxxxxxxxxxxxxxxxxxxxxxxxxxxxxxxxxxxxx
Sounds frighteningly similar to the Government's BSE statement of some time ago. Just substitute 'Mobile Phone' for 'BSE' or whatever issue you are trying to ignore up at the time – never fails!

Example no. 12 (1999) – Inconclusiveness

The jury is out. Some studies even indicate they can even improve memory! There's definite evidence they heat the brain, whether or how dangerous this is is undetermined. I recommend if you have a mobile get some sort of handsfree kit. No point taking a risk if you don't need to!

Example no. 13 (2000) – Interestedness

> Comment by Swedish journalist:
> I have plenty on this Finnish study – the main thing being that the monitoring system in Finland is completely flawed – they too have a rise in autism incidence but are yet to find out why . . . They don't monitor long time effects . . . And besides – this study was financed by Merck – they admit it at the end of the study!

The strength of Myers' approach is that he does not only discuss what focus group participants say about experts and expert knowledge, drawing out the characteristics listed above. He takes it further to show how and when these characteristics are invoked within the discourse, the kind of rhetorical work which these 'commonplaces' as he terms them, are called upon to do. What emerges from the study is the provisionality and negotiability of the trust accorded to any particular voice, including their own and one another's. Among themselves, their own expertise/knowledge gives them entitlements to speak within the group, and Myers goes on to observe:

> Experts can come across as participants who do not allow their claims to be evaluated, who expect their opinions to finish the matter, regardless of their practical experience, the placement of their claim in the talk, their timing or their relation to the group. It may be this communicative demand, as much as any epistemological privilege, that is being resisted in the widespread scepticism about experts shown in surveys.

There is also the question of how the internet is involved in the mediation of relations between experts and non-experts. Leaving to one side the functions of the World Wide Web in this respect, and concentrating specifically upon the newsgroups, it is important to point out that in this kind of by-the-people public discourse it is hard to see the expert/lay distinction as an applicable one, for four reasons:

1. Newsgroup discourse cannot be regarded as exclusively 'lay'. Participants have various kinds of expert/professional competencies, by virtue of which they choose to participate in particular newsgroups and not others. When they 'talk shop' they are taken seriously at that level, within the limitations of the medium (that is, the fact that it

is not well-adapted for the presentation of scholarly argument and data).

2. Newsgroup discourse cannot be regarded as exclusively 'expert'. Newsgroups are open access, so anyone can join in; there is plenty of evidence from the material itself that non-experts do join in – they ask questions or make statements which are treated as naive or ignorant by other participants. Risk topics get discussed on a multitude of forums, not just those which are narrowly specialist in the appropriate way.
3. Newsgroup discourse makes identity problematic (see Chapter 2), including the production of expert identities. Someone might write 'like an expert' online, that is, by making statements in a register that sounds 'right', and even vouch for him/herself *as* an expert, but such credentials are vulnerable in this part of cyberspace.
4. When experts are talking to one another about *uncertain* science, as they are on some of these topics, their expertise is not necessarily going to get them very far in terms of persuasiveness.

Observations such as this are congruent with questioning of the 'expert'/'lay' divide, (see above), recognizing for example:

- that the microbiologist is no expert in astrophysics and vice versa
- that 'expertise' comes in different forms: scientific expertise is not the same thing as the professional expertise which comes from working in a particular industry
- that the 'layperson' might, in the right circumstances, seek to acquire some expertise in order to pursue a subject in which they have a particular interest
- that the language of science is not sealed up in such a way as to be beyond the reach of folk theories, images, metaphors and rhetorical devices

If news media accounts of health risks go beyond what other institutions regard as warranted, how do we separate the genuine public interest component here from less worthy motivations for playing up the controversial and the dramatic aspects of risk stories. Perhaps such accounts are justified, 'in the public interest', because of real limitations in the perspectives of those other institutions. The scientific frame may fail to consider fully the ethical implications of their proposed research; governments may seek to play down risks for fear of the effects on company profits. Alternatively, news organizations which have their own economic bottom line know what kinds of representations will boost their sales figures/ratings, and this calculation may weigh more heavily than cool, careful analysis.

Mass media discourse on topics such as these is important because of the potential influence over public opinion. Media discourse can, among other things, teach readers and viewers to be suspicious of science, industry and the government or other vested interests. Yet as the case studies below will show, people are also suspicious of the mass media per se, and this seems to be one of the reasons that they now value access to the internet. The net seems to promise something different. But this difference may reside in a number of different properties: it may reside in access to different kinds of text, to interaction with other concerned and/or knowledgeable individuals, or to the opportunity for an individual to present his or her own views on the subject.

4
Mobile Phones and Brain Cancer

The spread of the mobile telephone and of the internet into the general population have taken place over roughly the same period of time; the late 1990s and the early 2000s. From a health perspective, it is not the use of the phones themselves which has given the most cause for public concern during this period but the erection of masts or 'base stations' in particular locations to improve the network coverage. People living in the vicinity of phone masts, or facing the prospect of doing so, quarrel with the companies for choosing their neighbourhood, and with the local authorities for allowing them to do so. Once erected, the masts are permanent fixtures, constantly in use, and may, it is feared, inflict health damage as well as interfering with other domestic equipment and creating an unwanted visual presence. Whereas individuals can choose whether or not to buy themselves a mobile phone, how much to use it, and whether to employ a hands-free attachment, they have no such personal control over the operation of the base stations. This aspect of the masts issue gives it a political edge that is much more muted in relation to the phones themselves. Meanwhile, the personal choice element in relation to the actual cellphones introduces an important component of reflexivity. 'I must decide what is best for *me*, knowing what I know/believe not just about the technology, but also about *myself*.' Although this chapter is mainly about phones not masts, it is not always possible to separate these in practice when the issue comes up for discussion.

The internet has offered opportunities for people and institutions with an interest in this topic to 'have their say' online. Some have chosen to do so via websites; some have chosen to do so in more interactive ways, including via Usenet newsgroups; some have done both. Views 'for' and 'against' mobile phones have been put into circulation, for the benefit of the 'don't knows'; the 'don't knows' too have left traces of their online quest for information.

This chapter begins with a review of wireless telephony, with particular reference to the ways in which this technology has been constructed as a health risk issue over the last ten years or so. It is followed by a discussion of the forms that this debate has taken on the internet, or at least in those areas of the net which are primarily for public communication purposes – websites and Usenet newsgroups.

My discussion of websites compares two sites designed with public information in mind, one produced by an active research scientist and one by a journalist with a particular interest in this area. It shows that each of these has appropriated the medium in different ways, as well as taking a different position on the issue. In relation to newsgroups, I have tried to find pattern in the 'noise' of this material by concentrating upon a few specific aspects of the discourse: the balance between confidence and scepticism, recurrent themes of argument, recurrent motifs of expression, relevant comparisons and forms of intertextuality.

The story of mobile telephones

The technological principles which enabled the development of mobile phones are based upon the science of microwave radiation and the technology of the cellular principle, whereby the radio transmission can make use of short wave frequencies because the distance of transmission, to the nearest base station, is very low. Around 45 million Britons now own a mobile phone – Jeremy Clarkson, in a British TV documentary, *Inventions that Changed the World: the Telephone* in February 2004 said that this amounted to almost everyone in the country capable of using one.

Domestic uses of microwave radiation are many, and they are increasing thanks to the steady development of practical applications for wireless communication in the home, in connection with security devices such as burglar alarms, entertainment technologies such as television, and of course computers. The term 'microwave' itself is obviously associated with one domestic technology above all others, and that is the ubiquitous microwave oven. Microwave radiation affects living tissue by heating it. Microwave cookery makes deliberate use of this effect but in relation to communication devices, heating is just a side effect. Biomedical science is also interested in the possibility of other side effects, besides that of heating, as the basis of any possible health problems.

The idea that mobile telephone use might pose a health risk for humans seems to have begun in approximately 1992/3. At that time cellphones were not in general use to the extent that they are now. A court case in Florida, brought by the widower of a woman who had died of a brain tumour attracted some mass media attention, thanks to the Larry King show on television in the United States. The basis of the case against the manufacturer was that the woman had used her cellphone much more than was wise, and had died as a result, because she had not been warned by the company of the potential risks. The scientific evidence at that time did not support such a case. The position accepted by the court was that there was no principled reason, let alone any concrete evidence, to suspect a causal connection between microwave radiation at the levels concerned, and damage to cell structure observed in cases of brain tumour.

Throughout the 1990s the use of mobile telephones saw phenomenal growth. Public anxiety also grew, and so did the amount of independent as well as industry-funded research. There are three principal areas of concern. One centres upon the use of mobile phones in cars, yet another risk factor for road traffic accidents. Another strand has to do with the siting of base stations by the operating companies to improve network coverage across a given region. The third strand, which centres upon the risks (if any) from exposure to microwave radiation from cellphones themselves, is the one with which the present research is concerned. Mobile phones are 'transceivers' of microwaves: they both send and receive wireless signals. The base station issue and the transceiver issue are both concerned with exposure of living tissue to microwaves, but in the latter case, the concern has regard to something we do (or don't do) to ourselves with radio waves, rather than something done to us by profit-seeking corporations (although corporations will have a case to answer if they know there is risk involved and don't pass this information on). The fact that the tissue at risk is *brain* tissue, and that there might in consequence be effects on *mental* processes, is of significance here, and so too are questions about proximity (the transceiver is very close to the body); to length of exposure (phone calls can go on for a long time) and to the amount of exposure over time (people can become very regular and long-term users of their phones).

The 'precautionary principle'[1] is relevant here. This looked set, certainly in Britain, to become rather popular in the wake of the BSE crisis,[2] a very important reference event in the area of public health risk. The precautionary principle has been adopted in the UK to some degree in regard to mobile phones: it has led to a policy of advising against the use of these phones by children (IEGMP 2000 – the 'Stewart Report'), although there has been no legislation to prohibit such use. The Stewart Report influenced the European Union to require the labelling of all mobile phones with their radiation emission levels, so that concerned consumers could choose a lower-rated model if they wished. In relation to base stations, the Stewart Report invoked this principle to justify considerable tightening of the planning regulations. There was never a question of a moratorium on further development of networks.

Individuals can also exercise their own precautions of course. There are a range of options available. The extreme position is to refuse to use a mobile phone at all, or to refuse, as parents and guardians, to allow children to use them. Others might be cautious enough to ration their use and to use landline phones instead when these are easily available (most landline calls will also be cheaper). Another option is to use a hands-free kit so that the phone itself and thus its radiation is further away from the body; various companies have brought on to the market protection devices such as 'radiation shields' which attach to the phone. Both of the last two options have attracted controversy. In 2000 there was a dispute over hands-free kits, with some research suggesting that these devices served to channel the 'radiation' more effectively (and thus more hazardously) direct to its destination – the brain (Consumers Association 2000). As for radiation shields – the primary point of contention here is their effectiveness. To the extent that a shield is effective it is interfering with the very process which makes the communication possible. No radiowaves, no talk – so the argument goes. Perhaps because of the absence of any very obvious 'effects' of mobile phone (mis)use – there's no smoking gun, no 'thalidomide babies'[3] to point to – perhaps because users appreciate that, as with smoking and lung cancer, this risk is a personal choice, the issue is now a fairly quiet one, as these things go. In Britain the most recent official report on this issue (NRPB 2003) did make the national news, but neither in the press nor in the broadcast media was it thought deserving of headline/front page treatment. The report mainly confirmed the conclusions of the earlier and more newsworthy Stewart Report, and was published at a time when the British public was preoccupied with major political stories. Nevertheless, the low-key treatment of the mobile phone report is significant.

As for the current state of scientific opinion on the likelihood that the use of cellular phones represents a hazard to human health, there is a degree of consensus claiming 'no evidence' that mobile phone use constitutes a health hazard.

> In aggregate the research published since the IEGMP [Stewart] report does not give cause for concern. The weight of evidence now available does not suggest that there are adverse health effects from exposures to RF fields below guideline levels, but the published research on RF exposures and health has limitations, and mobile phones have only been in widespread use for a relatively short time. (NRPB 2003: 148)

But since 'no evidence' does not mean 'no risk', and since there is extensive if muted public concern, funding for research continues, along with moderate use of the precautionary principle as described above.

It is a matter of general knowledge that overexposure to radiation can cause many different forms of illness, some of them life-threatening. It is less well known that the worst effects relate specifically to 'ionizing' radiation, which is at much higher frequencies than those characterized as radio frequency radiation. X-ray technology is hazardous to health because it involves ionizing radiation. Radio frequency radiation includes, but is not restricted to, those frequencies used for wireless telephony. Non-ionizing radiation can heat tissue, as it does, by design, in the case of microwave ovens, but the balance of expert opinion is that the heat levels associated with mobile phones are not sufficient to produce adverse health effects on human tissue. Some research is exploring whether there could be 'non-thermal' effects on human tissue from non-ionizing radiation. Cell studies test this by applying radiation to cell cultures; animal studies test it by applying radiation to animals (principally mice); and epidemiological studies test for correlations between actual human beings who have undergone radiation exposure, for example, in the course of their work, with increased incidence of particular health conditions (not just brain tumours). Experimental studies use human volunteers under laboratory conditions to test for cognitive effects such as memory improvements.

It is in the area of non-thermal effects that we get closest to the limits of current research. 'Non-thermal' is a catch-all category. It says, in effect: 'We are exploring processes, including ones which may be as yet unknown to science, by which microwave radiation at cell phone frequencies under particular conditions of exposure might present a risk to humans.' This is much too speculative for some scientifically-minded temperaments, prone to ask, rhetorically, 'Why should we even suspect the existence of such processes?' But, in turn, this reaction is much too complacent for others. Whether this constitutes *scientific* controversy is debatable. It represents the point in the argument where suspicion towards the industry and the profit motive is likely to rear its head. When scientists funded by the industry say 'There is no evidence for non-thermal effects' their critics riposte 'They would say that, wouldn't they?'

Both of the key British reports on this subject (IEGMP 2000; NRPB 2003) have, in reviewing the available evidence, been sufficiently cautious to take the possibility of non-thermal processes seriously. The relevant research is what some sociologists of science have termed 'science-in-the-making', where considerable indeterminacy, dispute and negotiation surround particular findings (Durant 1993; Gregory and Miller 1998). For example, in discussing the evidence that mobile phone-type signals could affect brain function, the NRPB writes as follows:

> The IEGMP report noted that there was evidence from volunteer studies that exposure to mobile phone signals at intensities within existing ICNIRP guidelines had direct short-term effects on the electrical activity of the human brain and on cognitive function. These could have their origin in a variety of biological phenomena for which there is some evidence from experiments on isolated cells and animals. IEGMP concluded there was a need to establish whether these direct effects on the brain have consequences for health because, if so and if a threshold could be defined, then exposure guidelines would have to be reconsidered. It was also important to determine whether these effects were caused by local elevation of temperature or by some other 'non-thermal' mechanism. Studies on the effects of mobile phone signals on human brain activity and cognitive function published since completion of the IEGMP report are reviewed in chapter 5. (NRPB 2003: 8)

The degree of doubt here is indicative of the current state of the art: to begin with the report recognized that further studies were necessary, following the IEGMP report, to get more evidence of these supposed effects. Although it now provisionally accepts these effects, the NRPB group does not know if they matter, from a health point of view, or at what level they might matter, or whether the effects happen because the microwaves heat the brain cells or for some other reason. So they recommend further research in this area:

> Further research is needed to investigate what impact, if any, neural activity changes after RF field exposure have on cognitive performance

> – for example, by measuring EEG patterns during specific cognitive tasks that have previously shown sensitivity to RF field exposure. Any possible health outcomes that may be associated with the altered EEG patterns caused by RF fields from mobile phones should also be identified. Finally, the biological mechanism whereby RF field exposure could alter EEG patterns remains unclear. Future cellular and animal studies may provide useful information about possible mechanisms underlying any EEG effects. (NRPB 2003: 150)

On the internet

This chapter looks at some of the ways the internet contributes to the provision of publicly accessible information and opinion in relation to the cellphone debate, via World Wide Websites and via Usenet discussion.

The war of the websites

On the web there are extensive resources available for people interested in mobile phones and their safety. Some of these resources are official, sponsored by governments – for example the documents of the National Radiological Protection Board in Britain,[4] or those of the Federal Communications Commission in the United States;[5] or of non-governmental organizations – for example the World Health Organization.[6] Some are scientific, sponsored by universities (for example the FAQ on cellphone antennas and health, produced by John Moulder at the Medical College of Wisconsin, discussed below[7]); some are scientific with no apparent sponsorship. Some are commercial (for example the sites of Motorola,[8] a company which makes mobile phones, or Aegisguard,[9] a company which makes radiation shields). Some are none of the above. These sites do not all agree with one another in their assessment of the risk posed by the use of cellphones. This section examines two websites with contrasting views of this risk.

No scientific consensus is ever complete. The sociology of science is familiar with the figure of the 'maverick', the one who is bold enough to stand up against the consensus, to throw a spanner in the works of what seems to be an acceptable overall account and one which the public has been happy to take on trust (Dearing 1995; Gregory and Miller 1998). Dearing is particularly concerned with the way that news coverage can, inappropriately and misleadingly, put the maverick voice and the mainstream voice into an apparently equal relationship. This has also been documented, as we shall see in Chapter 6, in relation to the debate over the adverse health effects of the MMR vaccine, compounded by the fact that the claims of the maverick in this case are also widely misreported in the journalism (Lewis and Spears 2003).

It is difficult enough for the public when the science is genuinely contested – for example in the early phase of the 'cold fusion' debate (see Lewenstein 1995a, 1995b, 1999) – to know which 'side' to believe. If the mass media, by reporting unconventional science 'in balance' with conventional views, creates this same indeterminacy where it is less appropriate, a possible result is that the public will form the view that nothing in science is decidable. 'Precautionary' behaviour looks entirely reasonable in these circumstances – it simply 'brackets out' the controversy to exercise a different order of rational thought. But this scenario also makes it reasonable to stop reasoning – 'I might as well do what I want' – or to rely on values which go beyond those of the scientific enterprise, such as trust in certain kinds of voices rather than others, or even religious faith ('If God had meant us to fly . . .').

The principal public 'maverick' in mobile phone research is George Carlo (Carlo and Schram 2002). Carlo does not have his own website, though he was the driving force behind the Mobile Telephone Concerns Health Website, which provided a facility for collecting anecdotal evidence of health problems from individuals (Mobile Phone Health Registry 2002). The most prominent *online* critic of the industry is not a scientist but a 'journalist, columnist, and film-maker' – albeit one with general scientific credentials (Fist 2000a). His website goes by the name 'Electric Words'. Fist is a sceptic rather than a maverick: he believes the dominant view is that there are no safety concerns not covered by existing exposure guidelines; this view for Fist is complacent rather than wrong; the complacent view is the dominant one because the voice of the industry is too strong an influence over the scientific research. On one page of his site he says:

> I've still not concluded that cellphones are necessarily dangerous – and, in fact, I promote the use of radio in the Australian country. I think the evidence shows however, that radio frequencies at the power output by handsets can have some substantial (and possibly dangerous) biological effects – and there is good reason to suspect that this may be cumulative over time. (Fist 2000b)

The Electric Words website is usefully compared with an online site representing the mainstream view. The mainstream website for these purposes is an FAQ document (FAQ stands for 'Frequently Asked Questions') and goes by the title 'Cellular Phone Antennas (Mobile Base Stations) and Human Health' (Moulder 1996–2004).

There are some problems with such a comparison. The two sites are not equivalent. Moulder is a professor of radiation oncology, Fist is principally a journalist. The cellphone antenna FAQ is primarily concerned with the health risk from base stations: Electric Words deals with cellphones and with base stations. The FAQ focuses exclusively on scientific issues: Electric Words has a broader agenda in which politics and economics are also brought into the debate. Furthermore, Electric Words does not deal only with mobile phone technology but also provides access to some of Fist's other work and interests. The FAQ is regularly updated: Electric Words carries a copyright date of 2000. Word for word, there is more on Electric Words about cellphone safety than there is on the FAQ. The FAQ is written from a position of scientific detachment – 'let the results speak for themselves' – where Electric Words represents the journalism of personal conviction, using knowledge of science to support an argument.

Nevertheless, the comparison is worthwhile because, in their different ways, both are offering a kind of 'one-stop shop' for exploration of the wireless radiation issue, with extensive references out to other sources, online and/or print, resulting in considerable overlap. Furthermore, both are well-signposted from other places on the internet and use just the right kinds of keywords to ensure that they turn up in a search engine hit list.[10]

Literacy practices: print culture versus screen culture

From a sociolinguistic perspective, the differences between the two sites is striking. Each points towards different forms of literacy practice (Street 1984; Barton 1994) despite the fact that both have been produced for the same medium of communication – the World Wide Web. One (the FAQ) is oriented towards academic print literacy, with adjustments appropriate for the new medium. The other (Electric Words) is characteristic of the new screen literacy (Snyder 1997, 2002; Hawisher and Selfe 2000), and for a readership comfortable with these types of expression. Table 4.1 shows the principal differences between the two sites in respect of their textual form.

Textual structure. Figure 4.1 below gives a screenshot of the opening material in the cellphone antenna FAQ. Although FAQ documents are very much associated with the World Wide Web, 'catechism' style

Table 4.1: Literacy practices in two websites

	Cellphone antenna FAQ	**Electric Words**
Textual structure	Linear	Non-linear
Use of hyperlinks	Narrow	Broad
Multimodality	Minimal	Moderate

question-and-answer texts are not new in print culture and the FAQ genre has become popular now with banks and other institutions for particular types of documents intended for customers. This particular example is highly structured, offering (following the extensive preliminary material) 15 sections, many with subsections. There is an initial Table of Contents, where the entries are 'bookmark' hyperlinks to take the reader direct to the corresponding section, overriding any necessity to read from beginning to end in linear fashion. This is, in effect, the faster and easier equivalent of turning to the right chapter from an entry in a printed Table of Contents. All sections are on the same page/ document within the website – if printed, it runs to more than 60 pages of continuous A4 paper. Scholarly conventions are a strong influence on the presentation of this work, especially the requirement that all information be thoroughly referenced. Numbered references fulfil this requirement: there are 250 such references and they too are 'electronic': each number in the text hyperlinks to the corresponding entry later in the document.

The chosen form of presentation is thus one which in several ways carries with it the prestige and authority of scientific registers, while exploiting the affordances (Kress and van Leeuwen 2001) of the new medium in ways which make it easier for academically trained readers to use their customary literacy practices such as following up the sources of particular pieces of information.

By contrast, Electric Words is structured in a form that has taken a further step in the direction of screen literacy. The site is not assembled as a single page but as a collection of related pages (or nodes) with an initial gateway or 'home' page. Figure 4.2 illustrates how that home page looked in March 2004.

The subsections of the site are accessed via the button links in the centre of the page, and the layout indicates that these belong in a hier-

Cellular Phone Antennas (Mobile Phone Base Stations) and Human Health

---

Version: 6.0.2
Last-modified: 1-January-2004
Author: John Moulder, Professor of Radiation Oncology, Medical College of Wisconsin, Milwaukee, Wisc, U.S.A.
Address: jmoulder at mcw dot edu

GO TO: Home

- **This FAQ addresses the issue of whether base station transmitter/antennas for cellular phones, PCS phones, mobile phones, and other types of portable transceivers are a risk to human health.**
- Issues surrounding the phones (transceivers) themselves, including the regulation of radiation-frequency radiation from the phones, are discussed only indirectly. For detailed discussions of the evidence that RF radiation from mobile phones is associated with cancer or other health risks see:
  - JE Moulder et al: Cell Phones and Cancer: What Is the Evidence for a Connection? Radiation Research 151(5):513-531, May 1999. (http://www.radres.org/rare_151_05_0513.pdf)
  - KR Foster and JE Moulder: Are mobile phones safe? IEEE Spectrum, August 2000, pp 23-28. (http://www.spectrum.ieee.org/publicfeature/aug00/prad.html)
  - Human Exposure to Radio Frequency and Microwave Radiation from Portable and Mobile Telephones and Other Wireless Communication Devices. IEEE Eng Med Biol, Jan/Feb 2001, pp 128-131. (http://ewh.ieee.org/soc/embs/comar/phone.htm)
  - H Frumkin, A Jacobson et al: Cellular phones and risk of brain tumors. CA Cancer J Clin 51:137-141, 2001. (http://www.cancer.org/eprise/main/docroot/PUB/content/PUB_3_8X_Environmental_C-Cellular_Phones_and_Risk_of_Brain_Tumors)
  - Research and regulatory efforts on mobile phone health issues (GAO-01-545). US General Accounting Office, Washington, D.C., 2001. (http://www.gao.gov/new.items/d01545.pdf).
  - Mobile telephones: an evaluation of health effects. Health Council of the Netherlands, The Hague, 2002. (http://www.gr.nl/pdf.php?ID=377)
  - Cell Phone Facts: Consumer Information on Wireless Phones, Food and Drug Administration and the Federal Communications Commission.. (http://www.fda.gov/cellphones/)
  - JD Boice and JK McLaughlin: Epidemiological studies of cellular telephones and cancer risk -- A review. Stockholm, Swedish Radiation Protection Authority, 2002.

http://www.mcw.edu/gcrc/cop/cell-phone-health-FAQ/toc.html 08/03/2004

Figure 4.1: Cellular phone antenna FAQ (Moulder 1996–2004)

archical structure. But this hierarchy is not overlaid across a linear flow as it was on the FAQ. There is no strong sense in which 'Other arts/columns' comes either 'before' or 'after' 'Telecom and internet', even if there is a preferred reading path (Kress and van Leeuwen 1996)

ELECTRIC WORDS

Telecommunications–Cellphones–Health–History–Politics–Economics

The site of Stewart Fist, journalist, columnist, and film-maker.

Current CrossRoads: this week's column in *The Australian* newspaper.
Selected Column Archives held at the Australian Broadcasting Corporation's on-line site. General archive material, see below.

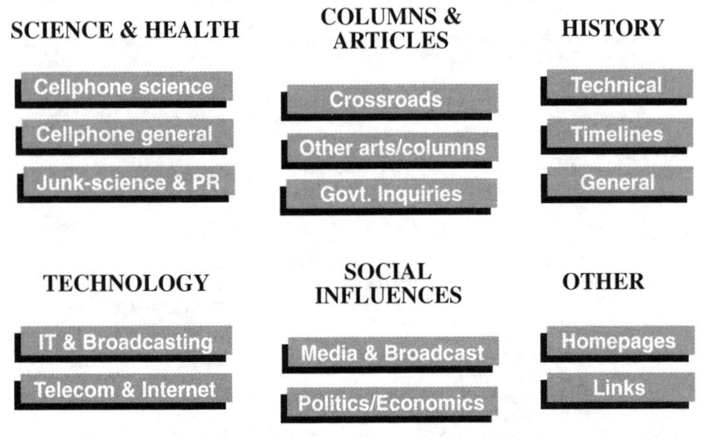

The material at this site is all copyright. However it can used freely for non-commercial purposes. If you have any doubts, check the copyright statement in the homepages and/or contact me at the address below.

© Stewart Fist, Sydney, 2000
Contact Stewart Fist

Figure 4.2: Electric Words (Fist 2000a)

for the buttons which access those sections. The most likely reading path for these buttons would be top to bottom, by column, three times.

Within specific sections, a side menu (a 'frame' in HTML terms) preserves this potential to move between subsections without authorial direction as to the suitability of doing so in any particular order. Readers may choose their own paths through the site and are not necessarily expected to read all of it, so each section is more or less 'free-standing' textually, that is, it does not assume that any other section has already been read (though there is the same cross-referencing, via hyperlinks, between sections). The significance of a menu in a side frame is that it remains on screen even when the reader changes the main frame by clicking a hyperlink.

Hyperlinks. In Table 4.1 the use of hyperlinks in the FAQ is described as narrow and that of Electric Words as broad. As befits scholarly discourse, the FAQ external hyperlinks are mainly to online academic papers, including one of the webmaster's own publications (Moulder, Erdreich et al. 1999). Of course, not all research literature is on public access online, thus the majority of the bibliography is to traditional print references without hyperlinks. The external hyperlinks on Electric Words are more varied. They include more journalistic literature and more references to commercial sites. The webmaster's interest in the politics and economics of the issue come through strongly in his range of references: furthermore, in commenting upon the various sources, he gives readers indications as to where any particular site or person fits in to the contours of the debate and what their biases are likely to be.

Multimodality. As Figures 4.1 and 4.2 clearly show, the relations between visual and verbal semiotics are very different in the two sites. This is largely tied in with the differences of textual form discussed above, for example, the FAQ site, a single document, is much more like a printed page in its visual appearance than Electric Words. This is especially true on those pages of Electric Words which are divided into a side frame and a main frame, which has become a very common navigation aid on web pages with no corresponding element in a traditional printed document.

Science text is necessarily visual whenever it needs to use diagrams, graphs and tables, and there are some of these in both sites. But there is no photograph of the author on the FAQ, and the graphic box which appears at the top of the page, incorporating the logo of the webmaster's institution, is the only concession to the kind of visuality which has to do with branding, house style and 'design' generally. In contrast Electric Words has its own visual house style – not especially elaborate, but consistent, expressed for example via the choice of a colour other than white as the background to the screen image, in the styling of the hyperlink buttons, in the variations of font colours used and the different purposes served by these – not just the 'regular text' black and hyperlink blue preferred on the FAQ site. There is also a much more considered use of white space on Electric Words – between the two frames, between the edge of text and the edge of screen, between headings and text, between paragraphs and so on. It is not surprising that someone with a journalism/film background is more conscious of visual design than someone from a more academic background. In academic culture the tradition is that the values of visual display are potentially a distraction from the serious business of purveying information and conducting rational discussion.

Theorists of screen literacy have frequently observed that writing on the net is significantly less stable than printed writing, and have discussed the end of the 'fixity' of print culture and the possible consequences of this (Yates 1996). Both resources examined here are testimony to this characteristic. When the FAQ is updated, which happens several times each year, previous versions then become inaccessible. Meanwhile, an older version of the FAQ is preserved on Electric Words where the webmaster has reproduced it in full, but in order to 'intercut' his own critical commentary, section by section, in a contrasting red font. Both of these are ways of 'unsettling' earlier text – and both do so in ways that leave traces.

Content and rhetoric. What we need to consider now is the relationship between visual/textual design and the substance of the communication. These two webmasters have different idioms for addressing the same issue. It is not a simple case of one interpretation of the science in confrontation with another, although this is part of it. It is also that each writer takes a different view of how the issue is to be framed.

The controversy in the cellphone debate pivots upon the claim that there is as yet no compelling evidence that the use of mobile phones can hurt you. Literature reviews such as that of the NRPB (2003) come to this conclusion even after reviewing research which suggests that cellphone radiation can affect living organisms. In the NRPB report (which neither of these two sites mentioned at the time of writing, since it was too recent) there were two predominant moves made in response to findings of this kind. Move no. 1 was to accept the findings provisionally and call for further research, as in the work on electrical activity in the brain (see above). Move no. 2 was to find fault with the research, or to quote from other published work which found fault with it. For example, the *Which?* Report (Consumers Association 2000) suggesting that hands-free kits did not protect the brain from radiation exposure but instead channelled that radiation more directly to the brain, is disparaged by referring to another article which objected to the research design of the *Which?* study (Bit-Babik, Chou et al. 2003). The difference between the NRPB and Electric Words is essentially the difference between 'talking down' and 'talking up' an accepted set of findings.

Electric Words, espousing the sceptical position, eschews both move no. 1 and move no. 2 and comes up with move no. 3 – a *less provisional* acceptance of results which indicate that mobile phone radiation has biological effects.

For example:

> The Adelaide Hospital study
> This was a major report from Adelaide Hospital in Australia, which established a clear link between GSM phone handset radiation levels, and tumor promotion in genetically-engineered mice. The importance of this study is that it kills, once and for all, the old 'Thermal Only' claims. (Fist 2000a).

Writing about the same study, a key reference point in this literature, three years later, NRPB said (partially repeating IEGMP 2000):

> The authors reported that the incidence of all lymphomas (lymphoblastic and non-lymphoblastic) in the exposed mice was almost double that in the sham exposed. However, lymphoma incidence was increasing rapidly in both exposed and sham exposed groups at the time when the study was terminated; in addition, only moribund animals were examined histopathologically.
>
> More recently, an attempt to replicate the above study, using larger numbers of animals with improved dosimetry, a longer follow-up period (24 months) and complete histopathology on all animals did not confirm these results . . . However, the study size (120 transgenic mice per group) was too small to detect a low or moderately raised risk. (NRPB 2003: 72)

This is an example both of move no. 1 (provisional acceptance subject to further research) and move no 2 (objections to the research design): furthermore, there *has* been further research, with results at odds with the earlier study. It too has problems of research design (low sample size).

Another element in the sceptical response to the 'no evidence' conclusions of mainstream positions stresses the *amount* of research supporting the case that this kind of radiation can affect the body.

> Scientific papers and lectures
> These are some of the many scientific papers and reports which support the case that radiofrequency signals at cellphone levels can, and probably do, have biological effects. This is not an attempt to provide a complete picture of the state of the research, but rather to provide some balance to the constant lies that 'there are no studies which show cellphones have a health problem'. (Fist 2000a)

This brings us on to the third key element in the quarrel that Electric Words has with dominant opinion: suspicion of the vested interest.

> In the last eight years, the major funding for health research into cellphones safety has been in the hands of the Wireless Technology Research (WTR) group, funded (supposedly) at arm's-length by the US Cellular Telephone Industry Association to the tune of $27 million. This money was spread over six years, and is now all spent – with almost nothing to show for the delay or the funds. (Fist 2000a)

Electric Words is by no means alone in taking the line that the industry can buy scientists who will deliver congenial findings. This by itself is not a strong line of attack. Scientific evidence which is simply 'bought' in this way ought not to stand up to critical scrutiny if it is, actually, wrong. So long as the institutions of peer review exist, and the 'bought' scientists have to submit to peer review judgement alongside more independent researchers, this should offer some guarantee against abuse. If Fist and others who share his views about corruption in the profession cannot fault the science, it will be hard for them to make the ad hominem argument stick. Significantly, Electric Words combines its ad hominem arguments with scientifically grounded forms of criticism, and takes this combination into the opponent's territory to the point of direct, point-by-point, confrontation with the FAQ material. The FAQ site does not show a reciprocal interest in Electric Words.

Newsgroups

The principal difference between newsgroup discourse on mobile phone health risks and the web page accounts discussed above, is that newsgroup contributions, for the most part, are extremely brief. Writers, some of them, do take up positions for or against the likelihood of harm, but they do not have to elaborate or sustain a position or try to ensure its internal consistency. Although newsgroup discourse is interactive, individuals can drop out of the conversation at any time, so they do not necessarily even have to respond when the position they have taken is criticized (although of course they often do). The kinds of groups where messages have been circulating since 1993 include some very specialist ones close to aspects of science involved in the debate, such as sci.med.diseases.cancer, as well as others which are unlikely to include technically knowledgeable people amongst their regular contributors or 'members', or at least only by chance – aus.tv, for example. Thus, expertise has no privileged place in this discourse, although it is clear that some people do expect to find in the group others who have information which they do not have.

The material

Searching the Google Usenet archive for discussions about mobile phones and health is not quite like looking for a needle in a haystack, thanks to the power of the Google Groups search engine, but quantifying the amount of such discussion does present problems. One is the variety of names by which wireless transceivers are known: cell phone, cellular phone, mobile phone, cellphone, wireless phone, wireless telephone, wireless transceiver, wireless handset, flip phone, mobile, cell . . . Another is the extent to which messages are cross-posted to a number of newsgroups: responses are sometimes posted on all of these groups but sometimes not. Thread names (a 'thread' is a sequence of messages on the same topic) are not always a good guide to content: a thread might be called something useful like 'Cancer from mobile phones' but it might also be just 'Dangers', much less helpful.

Nevertheless, by concentrating on threads rather than individual messages (so that it is not necessary to examine whether every single message in a thread is on-topic), it is possible to offer an impression of the amount of Usenet discourse on cell phone health risk from 1993 to 2002 – ten years in all. According to these estimates, Table 4.2 shows the numbers of threads which were wholly or primarily about mobile phone risks during each of these years, and the following numbers of individual messages on those threads, in aggregate.

There are some exclusions from Table 4.2 which must be mentioned. It excludes all threads which are primarily about the risks from base stations rather than transceivers. It also excludes all threads which comprised only a single message or just two messages. Such threads are not interactive, and it is the interaction between different voices which is the focus of enquiry here.

Table 4.2: Usenet messages about mobile phones and health, 1993–2002

Year	Threads	Messages
1993	2	22
1994	4	59
1995	7	104
1996	24	303
1997	11	135
1998	28	489
1999	52	722
2000	61	1246
2001	19	504
2002	13	230
Total	**221**	**3814**

Of the threads which were included in the count, the length varied between 3 and 118 messages in length. Average thread length was 17/18 messages. It should be remembered that while interest in the possible risk of mobile phones certainly did increase during this period, so too did access to the internet and the total number of Usenet newsgroups, so the large increase in threads on this subject from 1997 to 2000 is likely to reflect greater opportunity as well as greater concern in those years. Usenet activity may well be static or even declining now, with many more ISPs and websites providing other forums for online discussion of topical issues.

These 221 threads were distributed over 84 different newsgroups, as shown in Table 4.3. The newsgroup 'uk.telecom.mobile' had the most threads (23); 12 of the 34 threads in science-related groups also had a health focus. The non-scientific health related groups include, for instance, groups for those suffering from particular health problems (cancer, tinnitus, multiple sclerosis, asthma and migraine).

This material was sampled for the purposes of more detailed analysis of online conversation about cellphone risk. The sample comprised about 1400 messages on 82 threads, distributed across newsgroups and across years roughly in proportion to the numbers shown above. Within this sample, 681 participants contributed messages: the most messages contributed by any one person was 55 and there were 445 people who only contributed a single message.

Table 4.3: Distribution of threads by type of newsgroup

Newsgroups	**Numbers of threads and percentage**		**Example**
Science	34	15%	Sci.med.diseases.cancer
Cellphones	92	42%	Alt.cellular-phone-tech
Telecommunications	20	9%	Uk.telecom
Radio hobbyist	16	7%	rec.radio.amateur.antenna
Non-science health	20	9%	misc.health.alternative
General regional	18	8%	Soc.culture.singapore
Miscellaneous	21	10%	Alt.folklore.urban
Total	**221**		

Confidence and scepticism

There is considerable evidence within this material of doubts about the safety of mobile phones, as in this example:

Cellphone messages example no. 1 (1994) on one cellphone newsgroup

> The danger is real, but don't start to panic. The best way you can protect yourself is with moderation. If you're on the phone continuously, for huge periods of time, your chances will increase. A normal 3 watt carphone antenna has the waves travel through your rear window, rather than drilling through. Now, if it can easily go through your glass window, how easily can it go through your skull? The good thing about that is that handhelds are only .6 watts. Also, switch ears often. With these careful hints, you shouldn't have anything to worry about.

This many not be a very striking finding on the face of it, but it is worth spelling out because of the bias of the research. 'Technophobes' might well be fearful of mobile phone technology, but they must be under-represented in this material. Conversely, however, techno*philes* could be over-represented. This would account for the assertiveness of the tone when mobile phone safety is being defended:

Cellphone messages example no. 2 (1996) on two science newsgroups

> There is no known physically plausible mechanism whereby non-ionizing electromagnetic radiation such as the radio waves from cell-phones could cause cancer. Such radio waves do =NOT= have sufficient energy to =directly= damage anything in a cell, nor do they resonantly interact with anything that we know of existing within a cell. There is simply =NO= physically reasonable mechanism that could possibly justify the claim that cell-phones can cause cancer.
>
> About the only plausible effect the radio-waves from a cell-phone can have on you, is to warm up the skin on your scalp next to your ear by a minute fraction of a degree . . .

Notice the use of the = symbol as a bracketing device to indicate emphasis. This medium does not allow underlining, which requires the combination of two characters in the same character space. But capital letters alone do not give this writer enough emphasis for his purposes.

Confident contributors such as the author of the one above will concede the point that 'no evidence' does not mean 'no risk', but their answer to that is a variation on the theme that 'you can never prove a negative' – the implication being that 'no evidence' has to be enough, and not just for this issue. One writer contributes an anecdote about fears of electric blankets which he treats as analogous:

Cellphone messages example no. 3 (1993) on a science newsgroup

> A friend just returned an electric blanket after she heard about ELF. I tried to convince her it wasn't worth worrying about, but was unable; its not my field (pun intended) and I don't have the info at hand. Also, my friend brought up some European standards in rebuttal. She also used the 'well, we don't know everything' ploy; a scientist can't argue that one, though a good skeptic/statistician can say that we do know that some effects are almost certainly not larger than X.

Not everyone online takes a position with respect to the issue. Some use the medium because they want other, more informed, participants to tell them if there is anything to worry about. Indeed, this is the way most threads begin – with a question, as in example 4.

Cellphone messages example no. 4 (2001) on one cellphone newsgroup

> Subject: 3310s and 6210s radiation
> Kindly confirm if said phones cause radiation and there are already people died due to the use of these phones.

It is in responding to such questions that the more committed attitudes emerge – attitudes which may then be subject to online negotiation:

Cellphone messages example no. 5 (1993) on one science newsgroup

> I appreciate the comments about non-ionizing exposures and cancer induction. It is quite a public-relations time out there for radiation-related folks. My concern hasn't been about thermal effects. It is the non-thermal effects, which would occur at possibly very low exposures. For microwaves and RF these would include general malaise, anxiety, headache, but, cancer induction is not one of them. Or could it be? And I think that is the question. SARs [SAR = Specific Absorption Rate, a technical measurement of the body's absorption of radiation] are of importance if you are getting diathermy or hyperthermia treatments, but it is of little concern to the exposed public. My question about non-thermal effects comes because I poorly understand the biochemical changes which go along with EMF exposures. As usual, its not the high exposures that are the problem, its the low level stuff! But I do agree, that telephone pointed at head causing brain cancer is not a valid conclusion! The other types of claims are from policemen with radar guns (sarcoma of thigh). I'm gonna have to pull out last year's Health Physics Newsletter that was dedicated to non-ionizing. Again, from the SARs, there is no risk of thermal effect. Its the non-thermal effects I wonder about.

This message follows a sequence in which mobile phones have been defended. Sociolinguistically, what stands out here is the 'face-work' or politeness which has gone into the writing. The writer goes to some trouble to express the limits of his knowledge (last sentence but two); to compliment the research efforts of others whose view is different from his (first sentence); to sympathize with their communication problems (second sentence); and even to agree with them, as far as he is able

'I do agree, that telephone pointed at head causing brain cancer is not a valid conclusion.'

As the above discussion shows, the positions which writers take involve delicate matters of expression and are realized in different ways according to the context, and negotiated interactively within the thread. Faced with a question related to the safety of mobile phones, writers may choose to confirm that there is a risk, or deny it; they may equivocate, they may change the subject; they may make a joke or flippant remark. They may displace the issue from disease to the risk of accident; they may point the writer elsewhere, give safety advice, criticize protective devices or amplify the question by asking another. Consequently any attempt to quantify the proportions of messages in each category must necessarily be crude and potentially misleading. For example, is the writer of example 5 talking up the risk or taking a 'don't know' position, given that his predecessors have talked down the risk and he is politely disputing that stance?

Only by ignoring details of this kind, and making judgement calls on hard cases, is it possible to classify messages according to their stance on the issue. For what it is worth, Table 4.4 shows the results of this exercise.

Taking the 18 'ambivalent' and 124 'neither' messages along with the 'talking up' messages gives a proportion of 29 per cent not sharing the confidence of the 24 per cent where the risk is actively talked down. This seems surprising, in view of the sheer numbers of mobile phone users, the fact that this not an issue with a very high public profile, and the bias of the sample towards technophiles.

Table 4.4: Evaluating mobile phone risks in newsgroups

Orientation to risk	**Number of messages**	**(%)**
Talking up of risk	261	19
Not applicable (for example, off-topic)	631	45
Talking down of risk	334	24
Putting both sides, i.e., ambivalent	18	1
Putting neither side, for example, asking a question without presupposition	124	9
Unclear, i.e., difficult to classify	26	2
Total	**1394**	

Themes of argument

People argue about a lot of things in this material. Sometimes they argue about points of scientific knowledge, for example, whether radio frequency radiation has non-thermal biological effects. Sometimes (as in the 'electric blanket' example above) they argue about the general rationality of scientific enquiry, for example, 'nothing can ever be proved "safe"', and sometimes they argue about the personal choices people have to make, for example, whether it is good idea to play safe and avoid using mobile phones until the evidence is more conclusive. I have taken one example of the first type, the issue of 'non-thermal effects' and one of the third type, the issue of 'taking precautions' for in-depth analysis.

The understanding that microwave radiation has 'thermal effects', leads to a debate about whether it also has *non-thermal* effects. This is an issue which arises in just eighteen threads of the sample using the word 'thermal' and in a further six using 'heat/heating'. Basic knowledge permits some writers a fairly brisk dismissal of other people's concerns:

Cellphone messages example no. 6 (1997) on two cellular groups and one miscellaneous

> The only clearly known biological effects from non-ionizing radiation are thermal, and very bluntly, the power levels from handsets are clearly insufficient for that. Maximum average power for a GSM-900 handset is .25 watts. I believe GSM1800/1900 uses even lower levels.

Greater knowledge opens the door to the possibility of non-thermal effects:

Cellphone messages example no. 7 (1993) on a science group

> My concern hasn't been about thermal effects. It is the non-thermal effects, which would occur at possibly very low exposures. For microwaves and RF these would include general malaise, anxiety, headache, but, cancer induction is not one of them. Or could it be? And I think that is the question.

More knowledge still allows people to talk about what the non-thermal effects might be and to evaluate the evidence for them. In reply to the writer of the above, the response comes:

Cellphone messages example no. 8 (1993) on a science newsgroup

As for non-thermal effects of RF/MW; there is evidence that such effects exist. I don't find the laboratory evidence for non-thermal effects very convincing, but in any case most of the evidence for non-thermal effects does not point to a human health risk. Some recent articles relevant to non-thermal effects:

If people can't specify what they mean by 'non-thermal effects' they are liable to be challenged:

Cellphone messages example no. 9 (2000) on a cellphone newsgroup

>>there is a non-thermal effect that is poorly researched
xxxxxxxxxxxxxxxxxxxxxxxxxxxxxxxxxxxxxxxxxxxxxxxxx
>What is this 'non-thermal effect' and what evidence do you have
>of its existence?
xxxxxxxxxxxxxxxxxxxxxxxxxxxxxxxxxxxxxxxxxxxxxxxxx
Don't ask me what they are, I'm not a godamn scientist, but there has been much reference to them in the more serious media reports on mobile safety.

Debates like this generally go unresolved: neither side can accept that the other knows what they are talking about.

The extent of someone's grasp of the key difference is not simply a matter of whether they use the terms 'thermal' and 'non-thermal'. The scientific community, here as ever, prefers this classical term to its demotic equivalent, 'heating'. But the fact that these terms are broadly equivalent is useful when more knowledgeable people on these threads are explaining the science to less knowledgeable ones. When they are confident about cellphone safety, they are apt to say that heating is the only way that cellphone radiation can affect the body:

Cellphone messages example no. 10 (2000) on a cellphone newsgroup

> The frequencies being used are what is known as 'non-ionizing' radiation which means that individual photons do not have enough energy to disrupt chemical bonds. That means that the only possible form of effect they could have on you is by heating. Enough heat is capable of disrupting chemical bonds (that's why cooking works) but it takes a lot of heat.

In the following case, a writer challenges a previous sceptic on the thread to provide evidence of a harmful mechanism, ruling out both ionizing and heat effects first. The implication is that there is no such mechanism:

Cellphone messages example no. 11 (1996) on a cellphone newsgroup

> There are rumors that RF fields are somehow damaging to the nervous system or to other human cells, but I will consider it when somebody gives me a reference to a peer-reviewed article! It cannot be the ionizing effect, since there is none. Nor can it be the heat effect at 600 mW. It would have to be something else. Pray show me!

It is not just the confident contributors who use the 'layspeak' idiom rather than the technical one: sceptics do so too:

Cellphone messages example no. 12 (2000) on a cellphone newsgroup

> As far as I know the safety regulations relate only to the 'heating' effect. There may well be other effects of RF exposure that are less well understood, and certainly not incorporated into safety regs. The heating effect anyway may have dangers, particularly to the eyes.

The precautionary principle and personal choice. People also argue about their own personal choices, which may seem a strange thing to do in a discourse environment based around minimal personal involvement between participants. Why should any writer care what another may choose to do, or not to do? The problem is that assertion of a behavioural choice based on the precautionary principle (as a guide to individual conduct not to national policy) strikes some contributors as so perverse that they cannot help but say so, and to get annoyed when their ideas on this are rejected.

The precautionary principle is an idea which many Usenet contributors are capable of working out for themselves:

Cellphone messages example no. 13 (2002) on one telecommunications newsgroup

> Whether we decide to take the risk is ultimately a personal choice we may decide that the convenience of using a mobile outweighs any risk or potential risk. However in making this decision it may be well to look back at history; 50 years ago Thalidomide was the wonder drug, with initial concerns after a few years of use, and conflicting reports of its dangers it was 15–20 years before its dangers were recognized and the consequential litigation; DDT the great insecticide; asbestos not to mention tobacco, the list is endless All of these characterized by an initial reluctance to accept that they was any risk involved, rebutting of concerns by manufacturers and others with a vested interest, large scale propaganda campaigns of miss-information, and eventually ending in the courts where the truth finally emerges. Is it 'scare of the week' or a genuine concern you be the judge but I prefer to maintain a healthy scepticism especially when my health may be at risk!

In other cases, precautionary advice is offered as a way of putting an end to further discussion, by those who do not themselves think it is necessary:

Cellphone messages example no. 14 (1997) on a science newsgroup

> There is no clinical, epidemiological or laboratory data to support a connection between use of cell phones and brain cancer. But if you are worried about it, don't get a cell phone. Or get the type of phone where the antenna is not right next to your head.

The logic of precaution gets argumentative, when confident contributors try to reason them out of their doubts. In one remarkable, and very long, thread, a precaution-minded individual repeatedly resists all arguments to the effect that his behaviour is irrational, accuses his critics of being the unscientific ones, points out that he is only exercising personal choice, not trying to persuade anyone else to follow his example – yet there is something about his line (especially its reliance on sources which his critics find untrustworthy) which provokes ridicule and animosity along with the criticism:

Cellphone messages example no. 15 (2001) on one cellular phone newsgroup

>This is my last response to [*xxx xxx*]. He obviously uses a mobile
>phone so probably won't be fit to understand the results in 10
>to 20 years time. To the others reading this hoping for guidance.
xxxxxxxxxxxxxxxxxxxxxxxxxxxxxxxxxxxxxxxxxxxxxxxxxxx
The best they can do is totally ignore you and your ilk.
xxxxxxxxxxxxxxxxxxxxxxxxxxxxxxxxxxxxxxxxxxxxxxxxxxx
>you can do what the phone companies want and take the risk,
>or you can play it safe and refuse to use them. I choose the latter.
>After all there are so many ways to communicate these days that
>I don't need a phone in my pocket where ever I go, and it does
>mean I will be OK whether [*xxx xxx*] turns out to be right or
>wrong!
xxxxxxxxxxxxxxxxxxxxxxxxxxxxxxxxxxxxxxxxxxxxxxxx
Next he'll be telling us that the only way to salvation is through
his particular brand of religion.
Keep on babbling, [*xxx*]. I spent a lot of my youth poking fun at
your brethren on street corners. You're amusing.

Relevant comparisons

Argument by analogy is common in this material, and it comes in different forms. Some comparisons, from sceptical participants, look back at recent history, suggesting that we should learn from past experience not to be too quick to call something 'safe'. More confident participants prefer to invoke other 'lifestyle hazards', to argue that they are as bad as, or worse than, the risk from cellphones.

'Learning from experience' is brought into play with reference to three significant historical parallels. For United States' contributors the key historical parallel is the history of smoking and lung cancer; for British contributors it is as likely to be the BSE/CJD affair, and in one case, it is the history of the drug thalidomide (see message no. 13. above).

The smoking analogy is raised thirteen times in the sample, across 22 newsgroups. Here is an example:

Cellphone messages no. 16 (1999) on one cellular phone group and one radio hobbyist group

> I just read about a 50 page article prepared by an Oncologist (medical doctor) which states that there is absolutely no evidence to suggest that Cell Base Station Antennas can cause cancer. This is the same sort of nonsense we have heard from the tobacco industry for years.

The BSE/CJD affair is referred to in five different threads, across seven newsgroups and over a period of eight years. Here is one example:

Cellphone messages example no. 17 (1996) on a cellphone newsgroup

> Sounds frighteningly similar to the Government's BSE statement of some time ago. Just substitute 'Mobile Phone' for 'BSE' or whatever issue you are trying to ignore up at the time – never fails! Just wait for the public reaction to the Mobile phone 'Cull' in a few year's time:-)
> Not funny really is it?

Comparisons with other lifestyle hazards such as driving a car feature strongly in the rhetoric of those disposed to talk down the cellphone risk.

Cellphone messages example no. 18 (1999) on one cellular phone group

> >SUBJECT: S.O.S. Can anyone help to provide the bad effect to
> >body by cellular phone?
> xxxxxxxxxxxxxxxxxxxxxxxxxxxxxxxxxxxxxxxxxxxxxxxxxxxx
> NONE. You get more radiation from your microwave oven, your TV or your computer monitor you are looking at to read this!

Another response displaces the health concern from the issue of *disease* to that of *accident*: cell phones may indeed kill you but by involving you in a car smash not by giving you a brain tumour:

Cellphone messages example no. 19 (1999) on four cellular phone groups

>Are Cellular phone are hazardous to health?
xxxxxxxxxxxxxxxxxxxxxxxxxxxxxxxxxxxxxxxxxxxxxxxxxx
Yes, if you try to operate them while driving, or while walking in a hazardous area. The distraction of the phone could cause you to have an accident.

A further variant invokes the twentieth and twenty-first-century condition: life's too short to worry about everything that might be doing you harm:

Cellphone messages example no. 20 (2002) on one cellphone newsgroup

The logical answer is to say we have a considerable body of evidence to say they are not harmful, but it cannot be said with absolute certainty. Exactly the same statement can be made about Coca Cola, Beer, Chicken Nuggets and almost everything else in life. Do you worry about all those as well?

Sensational language

The scientific community and the industry are concerned that popular attitudes to mobile phones are based upon ignorance, misinformation, misunderstanding and fear. This is the old and much-debated argument that if only people *understood* the science better they would share the scientific view, and is often accompanied by criticism of the mass media for serving the public so badly (see Hargreaves, Lewis et al. 2001 for a critical discussion of this in relation to the mass media). Markedly figurative language stands out because it contributes to the discourse an element which scientific and rational approaches strive to avoid in their own use of language. In a journalistic context such language would be called 'sensationalist'. The particular expression which emblematizes the 'sensationalist' element in this discourse involves the collocation of the verb 'fry' with the noun 'brain', and related usages.

Certainly the newsgroup material reveals a fair degree of naivety about the technology, as example 29 above shows. Generally such lack of information is corrected by the better informed – often with scorn and ridicule:

Cellphone messages example no. 21 (2001) on a cellphone newsgroup (LOL stands for 'laughing out loud')

>>Kindly confirm if said phones cause radiation and there are
>>already people died due to the used of these phones.
xxxxxxxxxxxxxxxxxxxxxxxxxxxxxxxxxxxxxxxxxxxxxxxxx
>Of course it radiates – its a radio transmitter. They don't work
>otherwise.
xxxxxxxxxxxxxxxxxxxxxxxxxxxxxxxxxxxxxxxxxxxxxxxxx
LOL

The idea of mobile phones 'frying the brain' stood out as a motif which encapsulated the kind of 'wrong-headedness' that the industry is concerned about. The element of truth that it expresses relates to the thermal/heating effects of non-ionizing radiation discussed above. This takes the transformation of the scientific register one stage further: if 'heating' is the more or less literal alternative in layspeak of 'thermal', then 'frying' is a metaphorical alternative. It is a metaphor derived from the domestic realm, but also an elevated or poetic use of language, which injects positive emotional excitement into the repertoire. It is a bad kind of excitement because the process is 'not natural'. Frying your own brains makes the activity sound like extreme self-abuse.

The image occurs on eight threads out of the 82 in the sample, and in two of these it is part of the subject line. This may not sound a lot, but it is the only image to recur at all in this way, and there were many more examples in threads which did not form part of the sample. It has passed the stage of being a creative metaphor, and has started to enter the language:

Cellphone messages example no. 22 (2000) on a cellphone newsgroup

All cellular phone generate electromagnetic radiation . . .
yes . . . use a headset if you're worried . . . that's what I do . . .
no point frying my brain and risk getting a brain tumor and cancer . . .

Furthermore, this is a generative metaphor which gives rise to implicatures (Lakoff and Johnson 1980). Frying is a type of cooking. Using a mobile phone is frying the brain, therefore using a mobile phone is cooking the brain. This usage occurs in an additional ten threads of the sample.

Cellphone messages example no. 23 (1999) on four cellphone groups

> Incidentally, my phone really heats up after an hour of usage . . . which intensifies the psychological factor of feeling like my brain is being cooked.

Although 'brain frying' and 'brain cooking' can both be understood as metaphorical uses of language in this domain, the linguistic relationships here are not straightforward. The verb 'cook' in this context also bridges the gap between the effects of two different technological devices, both based on the use of radiation. With microwave ovens, we are asked to understand that the radiation is *literally* cooking the food objects exposed to it – it heats those objects and changes them so that they are ready to be eaten. With cellphones, if our ears get warmer after 20 minutes use, this can be called 'cooking' too, but we are meant to construe this as a metaphorical use of language (there is scope for dispute on whether it is the radiation or the pressure or the electric power which is the cause of the heating in these cases). The metaphor effect is stronger with the verb 'fry' than with the word 'cook' because the latter is a specific *type* of cooking and conjures up certain prototypical elements such as cooking-fat and a frying pan. These elements do not easily map on to the elements in the activity of using a cellphone. 'Cooking' by contrast is susceptible to a more abstract interpretation and does not call for such cognitive mapping.

Sources

This part of the chapter focuses upon explicit references in newsgroup messages to sources in print and on the internet, as well as to the evaluation of those sources in positive and negative ways. The majority of writers do not give references: they speak their knowledge 'straight' if they have it, and if they are asking questions they do that without references too. Some may refer to their background by way of warrant for their information: their academic knowledge ('I'm studying physics . . .'); their occupational training ('I'm an electrical engineer . . .') their

Table 4.5: Types of reference in mobile phone threads

Type of reference	Number of threads
Science references, including to the cellphone antenna FAQ	42
Popular/mass media references	44
Commercial references	
Mobile phone manufacturers and phone networks	11
Manufacturers of protective devices	11
Governmental references, including regulatory bodies	11
Miscellaneous references	21
No references	8

experience ('I've never had headaches . . .'); their hobbies ('I've been around this radio stuff all my life. . . .'), and some may refer to members of their social network (friends, family, workmates, customers and so on) and possibly *their* backgrounds: 'my father/boss/brother's girlfriend told me . . . and he/she works for Motorola/British Telecom/the company that makes those radiation shields' (see Richardson 2003 for more discussion of 'warranting' in this material). Reference to sources is another very common form of warranting. The two most common sources acknowledged in this material are (i) the mass media, and (ii) the cellphone antenna FAQ website, analysed earlier in this chapter.

Table 4.5 gives a general indication of how, within the 82 threads examined here, references to different information source types were distributed.

The total in Table 4.5 is greater than 82 because many threads involve more than one kind of reference. It should also be noted that many of the references to governmental and commercial sites are made for the sake of the scientific/technical information to be found there, so the above categorization is somewhat artificial. As for 'miscellaneous' references, this is a broad collection of infrequent types of reference, including the following:

- Books, for example, the Carlo and Schram (2002) book on mobile phone radiation
- Documentation produced by campaigning groups
- Literature of the specialist press for example, trade journals
- Databases, for example, Medline
- Internet search engines, for example, Altavista

- PR organization documents
- Personal web pages
- Newsgroup discussions

As with other tables in this chapter, Table 4.5 is a crude approximation to fact, because of the wide range of forms which a 'reference' can take. I have construed the idea of reference very broadly because this gives a better indication of how particular kinds of voices are regarded in this material.

In relation to mass media references, for example, there are references of the following types;

1. Generic: 'all that media rubbish'
2. Vague: 'I read an article somewhere last week'
3. Series based (or the print equivalent): 'I don't trust anything on *Watchdog*' (*Watchdog* is a consumer affairs programme on BBC in the UK)
4. Episode based (or the print equivalent): 'Last night's *20/20* had all the facts wrong' (*20/20* is a news magazine programme on ABC in the USA)

References can be critical of media reports, can praise them or simply reproduce their information, without explicit judgement, for further online discussion. Reproduction of information from a media text may treat the media source as the author of all the information contained therein or may respect the idea of the media text as a vehicle for other voices: the difference between 'that programme was so biased' and 'that speaker was so biased'. Media references may paraphrase the content of a print article or TV show, or may cut-and-paste full or partial text from a website. Similar variety is possible in relation to the other categories in the table above. In the 'Comparisons' chapter of this book I will have more to say about relations of trust in different source-types across all three of the case studies. For now, and bearing in mind the foregoing reservations about oversimplification, I want to examine in more depth the range of mass media references and the attitudes towards mass media which this reveals.

Using and evaluating the mass media. At the generic level, there is some degree of hostility towards the mass media in the newsgroup material, mainly coming from those who hold the media responsible for creating an improper level of fear:

Cellphone messages example no. 24 (1993) on one science newsgroup

> we've got to fight this junk by convincing people to look at the actual data, not the media interpretation or special interest group interpretation of that data.

Most media criticism is expressed in these general terms, but some people have an antipathy to particular programmes:

Cellphone messages example no. 25 (1996) on one telecommunications group

> I don't believe anything coming from 'watchdog' or 'news at 10'.

Occasionally it is particular episodes of programmes which are specifically criticized:

Cellphone messages example no. 26 (1999) on one science group

> The 20/20 show was high on hype and low on science, so don't expect to learn much real science from a transcript.

In the sample there were just 19 threads where mass media reporting is dismissed in these ways, as against 25 where the uptake could be regarded as uncritical, including press reports 'recycled' on the newsgroups to see what others make of them. There are a large number of messages which simply report information from a media text as fact, or at least as worthy of consideration:

Cellphone messages example no. 27 (2001) on one cellular phone group

> I did however saw on the newspaper saying that a researcher at the medical school of Hong Kong University has invented a sticker that could dramatically reduce the radiation emitted by your cell phone once it attached to your cell phone.

Such favourable and neutral uses of mass media as a source of information are present on 25 threads in the sample. This does not mean that such newsgroup contributors uncritically 'trust the media', but it does mean that the mass media is where they get their information from, many of them, and they need more informed people to tell them whether there are reasons to disbelieve what they have heard or read:

Cellphone messages example no. 28 (1996) on one miscellaneous group

I do not wish to do any scaremongering but I read a brief article in the British press yesterday (Mon 15th April) about Mobile phones causing cancer. How the heck can a mobile phone do any damage? I have a phone myself, but I am not familiar with the science of it . . . is it from the radio waves? In fact what do mobile phone use – radio or microwaves?)

The World Wide Web. Most of the specific, as opposed to generic or vague, textual references in the list above are actually references to websites in the first instance. The references are to websites which belong to news media organizations, commercial companies, and so on. There are thus web references on 56 of the 82 threads in the sample. But there is very little duplication of reference to particular websites – with one exception. In 22 threads out of 82 there are references to the cellphone antenna FAQ.

Cellphone messages example no. 29 (1998) on one science newsgroup

>To all the EM experts,
>I don't trust the businessmen when they say mobile phones are
>safe. I just started a course in EM theory and I don't feel safe
>about the phones. Can the experts assure me about its safety?
xxxxxxxxxxxxxxxxxxxxxxxxxxxxxxxxxxxxxxxxxxxxxxxxx
No, they cannot. But they will readily sell you a mobile phone. The other way round is, that no expert can prove how dangerous the cellular phones really are. For more information you might read the FAQ by John Moulder and do a search in WWW with AltaVista for 'emf and health'.

The webmaster responsible for the FAQ contributes messages himself on 10 of the 82 threads, but only mentions the FAQ on four of these. Elsewhere on Usenet he routinely draws attention to the FAQ after he has updated it, sending a message to his preferred newsgroups saying how it has been updated, reproducing all of the main headings, and providing the URL so that readers of the message can access the site.

There is a downside to reputation on the newsgroups – it is also a place to criticize and condemn as well as praise. The FAQ is valued by most of the newsgroup contributors who are familiar with it or with its author. Less commonly, the site or its webmaster are attacked – one writer, on a science newsgroup in the year 2000 (this example is not from the sample) refers to a comment on the FAQ as 'displaying characteristic Moulder propensity to peddle disinformation'. However, the positive and neutral references outnumber the negative and questioning ones by a considerable margin. In the sample there were in the region of 25 positive references, about six questioning ones (can this man/site be trusted?) and no negative ones.

Discussion

It was my intention in this chapter to use 'naturally occurring' materials to explore the range of public opinion with respect to the issue of mobile phones and human health, across the first ten years that such phones have been available; to develop this as an account of how the internet can be used as a forum for establishing and negotiating positions in regard to the issue, and to do so in ways which respected the distinctive communicative characteristics of the two most important channels of communication in this context: the World Wide Web and Usenet.

Of these two channels, the web gives rise to more 'monologic' text types, where writers construct and sustain their own voice/position, and where reference to other voices and views are subordinated to that position, as for example in the intertextual use of the cellular phone antenna FAQ on the Electric Words site. Usenet is, by design, overtly dialogic with no master voice. Individual writers have to contend with views they do not agree with, or, sometimes, even sympathize with. Behind the rough balance between sceptical/uncertain and more confident online voices there lie a range of ways for engaging with the issue. Some of these follow the contours of the scientific debate itself; specifically the line which divides those for whom the concept of 'non-thermal effects' points to an area of serious concern, and those for whom there is little or no concern in this area. Some participants seek to bypass debate by appealing to the principle of personal choice. Unable to agree with interlocutors on the risk itself, they announce their decision to behave 'as if' the risk is real, by avoiding mobile phones altogether, rationing their use or using hands-free sets. Often, however, this move does *not* put an end to debate, because others in the newsgroup regard this exercise of a personal 'precautionary principle' to be positively scientifically *ir*rational and as such, objectionable.

The line between the confident and the sceptical/cautious is drawn in other ways too. It is drawn, for example, in the divergence of preference for relevant analogies, with the sceptical preferring analogies of the 'learn from experience' type and the more confident asking others to think about other, more accepted, lifestyle hazards and stop worrying about phones. Confident writers are also more likely to affiliate to the idea that the mass media are responsible for misleading and inaccurate representations of what this risk might amount to. Both confident and sceptical writers can use their texts to draw attention to websites supportive of their own views. Sceptics refer to a wide range of different sites: confident participants do so too, but they also converge in drawing support from the FAQ page which is analysed in the internet section of this chapter. For the most part this particular 'public' has not been in the grip of 'sensationalist' ideas about mobile phone risks. There is a ready-to-hand idiom for the sensationally-minded: 'brain frying'. It occurs sufficiently often, along with the implicated 'brain cooking' to be considered as a generally available usage, but it is not the preferred lexical frame for serious discussion: it remains poetic.

5
SARS

SARS stands for Severe Acute Respiratory Syndrome, the new infectious disease which began in China in the second half of 2002 and was introduced to the world in March 2003. SARS as an 'issue' is different from mobile phones and cancer. Where the mobile phone debate begins with the 'cause' and reasons or speculates about effects, the discussion of SARS begins at the other end, with illness and death, and tries to work backwards to the probable causes of infection in particular cases. But there is similarity too. In both cases public interest in the topic has for many people a personal character. People are anxious to know if their normal behaviour – which might include travelling on a plane as well as using a cellphone – is going to put them on a danger list. In one case the risk is open – the danger might be cancer, or something else, or nothing at all – in the other case, it has a name – SARS – and a list of bodily symptoms.

This chapter begins with a brief account of how the world learned about SARS in 2003. It is followed by a discussion of the role of the internet – websites and Usenet groups – in disseminating information and opinion with respect to this new disease on a global scale.

My discussion of websites compares the online voice of global authority – that of the World Health Organization – with two other web contributions to the story of SARS. These are two very different 'blogs' – 'SARS Watch', a news digest, and 'Wangjianshuo's blog', a diary-style account of one man's life and thoughts within a Chinese city affected by SARS.

In relation to newsgroups, the chapter focuses upon the three-and-a-half months following the crisis announcement. This is in contrast to the ten years of Usenet activity which were reviewed in the mobile telephone chapter. If the mobile phone issue is chronic, then the SARS issue was acute. Yet many of the headings which were significant in relation to the cellphone material are also relevant here, and the chapter examines the balance between confidence and doubt, lexical expression, associations and sources.

The story of SARS

The story of SARS broke in March 2003, when the World Health Organization issued a global alert as the unidentified disease, which it had been monitoring as an 'atypical pneumonia' for about a month (although cases had occurred in China as early as the preceding November), began to spread in Vietnam, Hong Kong, Singapore and Canada. Its second public communication on this topic, on 15 March 2003, took the form of a 'travel advisory' whose purpose was to attract the attention of governments, airlines and other interested parties, with advice about the treatment of possible sufferers. This document introduced the name 'SARS', and prompted the global news media to devote airtime and column inches to the topic. Over the next few months the disease spread to yet more countries and claimed more lives: precautionary measures were instituted and by July 2003 the disease was considered to be contained, although there have been additional reported cases into 2004, for example, on 8 January 2004. A WHO paper of 20 May 2003 describes SARS as 'a puzzling and difficult new disease' (World Health Organization 2003a). Throughout March, April and May it remained an extremely hot topic, competing with the Iraq war for the global headlines.

As with other health risk topics, there are issues here about the relationship between expert or otherwise 'authoritative' discourse and the terms upon which this makes its way into public frameworks of knowledge, understanding and belief. SARS was presented to the world, by the WHO, from within the domain of medical science; but in the wider public domain, medical science becomes just one element in a much wider play of ideas. As yet, there has been no published work on the public discourse of SARS with the exception of Eagleton (2004). Eagleton focuses upon the local response to a global issue in the *South China Morning Post* (*SCMP*), the major English-language newspaper in Hong Kong, analysing several aspects including the move from neutral to more emotive reportage, as well as the spread of SARS-related material beyond the news pages into features, editorials, letters, medical advice columns and an email discussion list. There are many similarities between the discourse of the *SCMP* and the more internationalized patterns found in the Usenet newsgroups discussed below, including shifts and ambivalence about the naming of the disease as well as the attempt in some articles to link the SARS outbreak and the Iraq war. There are also distinctively local aspects. For example, personal hygiene is one of the themes in the Usenet materials, as well as in the *SCMP* as in this piece of advice to children:

> So, did you have a good 'holiday'? Have you been wearing your mask properly and washing your hands regularly? Did you take your body temperature this morning before you headed out for school? I hope all your answers are yes!
>
> (*SCMP*, 28 April 2003, quoted in Eagleton 2004: 43)

Eagleton, however, argues that in the context of Hong Kong this theme is actually an issue about 'loss of face' and that the *SCMP* is in fact attempting to handle the implication that Chinese culture has something to be ashamed of in respect of personal hygiene.

On the internet

This section explores some of the ways in which the World Wide Web and Usenet are being used for public communication about SARS.

The official voice and the blog

The variety of web resources for public communication about SARS is less extensive than those for communication about mobile phones and risk. Search engine enquiries inevitably pull up the World Health Organization website and that of the CDC (Centres for Disease Control and Prevention, a US government agency). Other national government health departments also maintain resources for enquiries on this subject and there are various research centres based at universities which have their own websites. Journals with websites, such as the *New England Journal of Medicine* offer resources, and so do non-governmental organizations like the Red Cross. Sites like this are essentially official because they are produced within organizations: they contrast with sites produced by individuals without such institutional backing, mainly in the form of blogs.

One kind of complaint about finding information on the WWW is the uncertainty about the 'status' of particular sites and the views expressed therein. In a world where there is no 'peer reviewing' of content and anyone can say anything within any legal limits which are enforceable, this gives rise to a sense of the WWW as a chaotic multivocality. 'Branding' of output becomes very important in such a context, some brands carrying more weight and authority than others. The rise of the 'blog' and the styling of some sites as blogs, allows the 'unofficial voice' to express opinion and purvey 'information' from a personal perspective.

This section compares official online discourse about SARS with two unofficial contributions. The official voice is represented by the materials on the World Health Organization website;[1] the unofficial voices are represented by two blogs. One of these, called SARS Watch,[2] is maintained by Tim Bishop, who describes himself as 'a sometime entrepreneur, engineering manager, product manager, project manager and writer who has been working in high tech start-ups for over a decade'. This blog was most active between late March and mid-June 2003, although there have been occasional contributions to the site since that date. The third contribution is Wangjianshuo's blog.[3] The author, Jian Shuo Wang, simply says of himself that he lives in Shanghai and works in IT software. The significance of these three sites will become apparent below.

The three sites

The WHO website is an essential resource for finding out about SARS. Much of its material is either biomedical, or else bureaucratic, to do with control measures and their implementation. By contrast, SARS Watch mainly draws its material from public domain sources – journalism, printed and online, as well as material from the aforementioned official sites, including the WHO (which it praises). It can be regarded as a kind of 'news digest' on this one subject, though its materials go beyond mere news reports, as will appear in the analysis below. Wangjianshuo's blog is rather different, and more typical of blogs in general – an online web diary and 'commonplace book' for public consumption. This website, like that of the WHO, does not have SARS as its single focus of concern, but it does carry a large range of entries about SARS during the key months of the outbreak, because the author was resident in a city affected by the disease.

Textual structure. The WHO's work on SARS fits within its own organizational structure, belonging to the branch of the organization dealing with communicable diseases. This has its own English acronym, 'CSR', but the full title is 'Communicable Disease Surveillance and Response'. The structure of the website is mapped on to the structure of the organization, so the SARS section of the site is embedded at the third level of structure: the site possesses the usual search engine and alphabetic browsing facilities which have become familiar on very complex sites such as this. As the screenshot shows (Figure 5.1), the multi-section

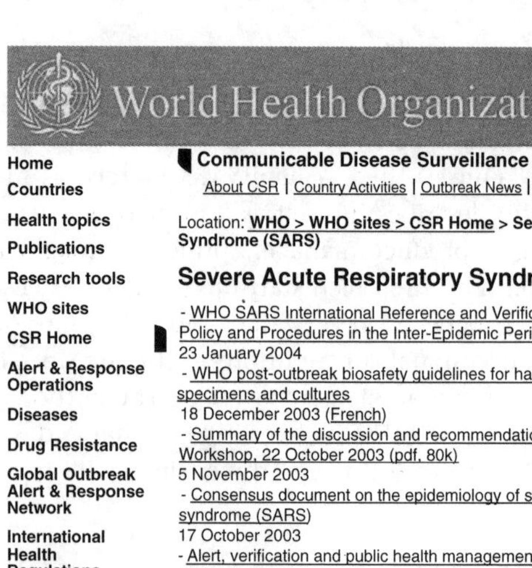

Figure 5.1: WHO SARS section

format, created through the use of cascading style sheets, is one which is familiar from other organizational websites, such as that of the BBC, and the division of the 'page' is reminiscent of modern newspaper layout, minus the photographs. This is a page of headings and links. The prominence and top-down order of the three headings again reflects the internal arrangements of the WHO as an organization, with 'World Health Organization' at the top, elaborated by a logo, followed by 'Communicable Disease Surveillance and Response' and then by the actual page title: 'Severe Acute Respiratory Syndrome (SARS)'. The text following this title offers up a bulleted list of five hyperlinked texts, each identified by the name of the corresponding document. So much for description. The textual structure here suggests that this is a site designed for the needs of those users who already know what they are looking for. The more casual citizen/consumer, without a specific focus for their enquiry, would not find it easy to know what links to follow and perhaps would be unsure even of what to enter in the search engine.

By contrast, SARS Watch (Figure 5.2), typically for a blog, is organized primarily in diary form. Blogs provide for the needs of writers who want to alter their site a little every day by adding new information. The newest material goes at the 'front' or 'top' or 'beginning' of the document. Earlier material is not deleted or changed, it just gets demoted to a place further down the screen, or away from the main front page. The basic organizing principle is that of date sequence; the headings under which new text is added are date headings.

SARS Watch offers (on another page) a table of contents comprising just the headings of each entry; alternatively, readers can choose, from a different menu, to look at one of the 10 most accessed entries, or one of the 10 most commented-upon entries. There is also a search engine for those who are looking for something in particular, for example, how many cases of SARS were recorded in Toronto during the outbreak. But, essentially, the assumption is that the reader will be interested in whatever the author has found out, or has thought about, most recently.

Wangjianshuo's blog follows the same basic design principles as SARS Watch (Figure 5.3), with differences related to the design of the software which are not relevant to this analysis. An alternative menu allows readers to access items not by date (the default approach) but instead by category.

As the screenshot (Figure 5.3) shows, on this blog SARS is not necessarily mentioned on the gateway to the site: this will depend upon how recently Wang has written about SARS. He wrote about it a few times in March 2003, but by April it had taken over and most of the daily

SARS Watch™ Org

following **Severe Acute Respiratory Syndrome** around the globe

Home Table of Contents SARS Links Books SARS Weblog News Feeds SARS Media News Feeds Discuss Join Archives

January 06, 2004

It's official: SARS is back

WHO has **confirmed** that the 32-year-old television producer in Guangdong province suspected of having SARS actually has the disease.

> Results from laboratory tests over the weekend have led the Ministry of Health of China and the World Health Organization (WHO) to upgrade the suspected SARS case in southern China to a laboratory-confirmed case.
>
> The latest results were obtained from virus neutralization antibody tests carried out by two laboratories in Hong Kong SAR, China, that are part of the WHO international laboratory reference network, as well as by a laboratory under the Chinese Centre for Disease Control and Prevention in Beijing.
>
> The virus neutralization tests from all three laboratories indicate that the male patient, a 32-year-old television producer in Guangzhou, Guangdong Province, has recently been exposed to a SARS coronavirus (CoV).
>
> The tests compared the level of SARS neutralizing antibodies in the patient's blood over recent days with levels found early in the course of his disease. The results showed that the level of these antibodies had risen significantly, fitting the laboratory definition of SARS.

This is the first case of SARS (other than the two laboratory scientist who contaminated themselves) since China and WHO declared SARS eradicated last July. So the inevitable question arises, how did the man contract SARS?

I've seen a number of theories advanced over the last week, everything from **suggestions that the victim had a mild case of SARS last year and that this is a resurfacing of the virus to suggestions that he contracted SARS from rats**. Clearly, nobody knows. WHO is reminding people that even though the SARS virus has been identified in civet cats, it isn't known if the cats are the reservoir for the disease, or if they contracted it from another animal in the Guangdong wild animal markets. The Chinese government isn't taking any chances – **they have decreed** the closure of all wildlife markets and the killing of the estimated 10,000 civet cats in the markets, by **"boiling and drowning, electrocution and incineration."**

The man himself has recovered from SARS, and the Chinese authorities are planning to release him on Thursday, according to **a**

Figure 5.2: SARS Watch.org

Wangjianshuo's blog

Events (in Shanghai) that affect my life (and others')

Home | Life | News | Shanghai | Tech | Travel | WWW | Random | About me

BENZ TAXI IN SHANGHAI

Friday, February 20, 2004

Hey. Take a look. I finally saw and took a shot of the hot Benz taxi in Shanghai. It is reported that 50 Benz taxi were put into operation but I never seen one. This morning, when I arrived at Metro Tower, a shining car passed by. It was a Benz. At a second look, I realized it was a...

FULL STORY 4 comment(s)

PREVIOUS HEADLINES

- Foggy Shanghai | 2 comment(s) | Thursday, February 19, 2004
- Professional English | 6 comment(s) | Thursday, February 19, 2004
- Receiver Pay SMS? | 3 comment(s) | Thursday, February 19, 2004
- About Jian Shuo Wang | 7 comment(s) | Wednesday, February 18, 2004
- Wifi Hotspot Competion Becomes Hot | 2 comment(s) | Tuesday, February 17, 2004
- Always-Red Pedestrian Signs | 2 comment(s) | Thursday, February 17, 2004
- China Internet Market Analysis | 2 comment(s) | Tuesday, February 17, 2004
- Beijing Impression | 10 comment(s) | Monday, February 16, 2004
- Read: **Other entires** (complete list)

SEARCH THIS SITE

Search

DIRECTORY

Life
Entertainments
Friends
Fun
Holidays
Learn
Me
Wendy

Tech
Backstage
Movable Type
Review
Spam
Usability
Webcam
Wireless

News
Blogging
Muzimei
SARS
Space

Travel
Airlines
Cities
Cycling
Daocheng
Dreaming

我在这一站 | cn
Wendy's | Map

COMMENTS

- oshee
- Michael Darragh
- James
- Sekhar
- FRANCIS
- bugs
- pablo
- Apple
- Lee
- Jen
- Jian Shuo Wang
- Jian Shuo Wang
- Last 20 comments

Figure 5.3: Wangjianshuo's blog

entries are about the outbreak in his city, or about SARS in China generally. The following entry was written before the first officially confirmed cases of SARS in Shanghai were reported.

> April 6th 2003
> The sunny weather continues. The rumor of SARS discontinued. With the recent official news on SARS from the Ministry of Health, the ban for news on the topic of SARS is lifted. Newspapers, TVs, radios and websites rush to report SARS in one night, just as the speed of spreading <u>Bill Gate's</u> news.
>
> I haven't tried metro since the first day I heard about SARS. Yesterday, I had a try. I didn't see any one with a mask then. It is said that about 5–20 people wearing facial masks in metro during the rush hours.
>
> In the bus, I didn't find **any** one wearing masks too. People insists to open the window eve in the air-conditioned bus. The only <u>two masks</u> I have ever seen is in the bund areas. The official news reports again and again that there is NO SARS in Shanghai. Shanghai is clean and safe. Don't need to wear masks . . .

Hyperlinks. There are various ways of managing the insertion of hyperlinks. Since any screen element can function as a hyperlink, images will do as well as words, nor do the words which function as hyperlinks have to be the same as the title of the page to which the link leads. Another difference is that hyperlinks can stand apart from running text or they can be part of it. The WHO site is conservative here. Its hyperlinks are verbal, not visual and most of them are free-standing. SARS Watch is a little more ambitious. The right-hand frame (not shown in Figure 5.2), used mainly for links and supplementary information, includes some visual links to other sites, and in the main frame it makes extensive use of hyperlinks which are part of the running text – recognizable as such through the use of the familiar convention that hyperlinks are in a blue font and underlined.

> January 6th 2004
> I've seen a number of theories advanced over the last week, everything from <u>suggestions that the victim had a mild case of SARS last year and that this is a resurfacing of the virus</u> to <u>suggestions that he contracted SARS from rats</u>. Clearly, nobody knows. WHO is reminding people that even though the SARS virus has been identified in civet cats, it isn't known if the cats are the reservoir for the disease, or if they contracted it from another animal in the Guangdong wild

> animal markets. The Chinese government isn't taking any chances – they have decreed the closure of all wildlife markets and the killing of the estimated 10,000 civet cats in the markets, by 'boiling and drowning, electrocution and incineration.'

All of the underlined phrases in this passage are hyperlinks to online articles in the *New York Times, Washington Post* and *Straits Times*. Wangjianshuo's blog adopts this style as well. The underlined words in the 6 April story are both hyperlinks to other entries in the blog.

Interactivity. Discussions of the value of the internet as a revolution in communication always mention the greater potential for interaction between reader and writer as compared, for example, with mass media where the communication is principally one way. Organizations routinely provide for 'feedback' from their readers on their websites, and individuals too invite their readers to enter into correspondence with them via email. It is instructive to compare the different forms in which the WHO site and SARS Watch provide for interaction with readers: in both cases this provision is highly structured, but with very different effects.

The WHO has a 'Suggestions' page. The wording on this page does not invite suggestions regarding the regulation of health policy, only suggestions in regard to the design of the website, and it seeks to know something about the person who is making the suggestion:

> Thank you for taking the time to comment and help us improve our web site. We have included a few questions about you and your interests, to help us better identify who is accessing our information. If you would like a response to your message, there is the possibility of including your email address, which will not be used for any other purposes. The questions marked with an asterisk (*) are required. With your suggestion, please try to give as much information as possible so that we may clearly understand your comment.

There are not very many personal questions, and they are optional: WHO is interested to know your organization, your area of work, the type of information you are looking for and the focus of your suggestion (design, search, language/translation, content, other).

The communication between the WHO and the reader thus starts in the public domain, from this page, but immediately goes 'private' – the readers' messages themselves are not for public consumption, and may or may not have any practical consequences in relation to the organization, content and appearance of the WHO site.

SARS Watch does things differently. First, it is organized so that readers can if they wish also become members, and provide some minimal information about themselves in the form of a 'profile', including name, email address, location, website URL, occupation, birthday and interests. Apart from name and email address these fields are optional, and SARS Watch, unlike the WHO, does not want to know what kind of organization you work for. Second, it provides, after every new entry, a hyperlink called 'comments'. By following this link the reader comes to a new page with the following elements: the item itself is repeated at the top; if the webmaster has any more information, that goes in the next section; a third section shows what other readers have written on this aspect of SARS (if anything); and a fourth section has fields for the current reader to complete with their own comments. This section offers the option of having the comments added to the SARS Watch site.

So long as readers are interested enough to want to join or at least to say something from their own perspective and with their own information about the topic, the site itself must constantly change, and not because the author has changed it. A final section allows the reader to 'Send this story to a friend'. The arrangements in place for structured multivocality are working: despite its relatively short lifespan the site does (did?) have members, and attracted a considerable number of responses which were added to the site in the manner described. Wangjianshuo's blog also invites and incorporates comments from readers on the site and the webmaster offers, as a less public form of communication, between himself and his readers, an email newsletter to update interested readers on new additions to the site.

Content. Just as there are differences between the WHO, SARS Watch and Wangjianshuo's blog in their use of the medium, so there are differences in content and linguistic style. As indicated above and in the screenshot (Figure 5.1), the WHO is in the business of producing and distributing official papers, many of which have a regulatory function, including documents of record for the use of national governments who may need to implement their own policy measures in order to control the spread of SARS. SARS Watch in contrast is a news digest. It is interested in WHO documentation and provides many links to these as well as to more informal statements originating with WHO personnel. But it is interested in other things besides, especially those with a 'breaking news' character which would be of much less interest to the WHO. If a typical item on the WHO website is: 'Summary of the discussion and recommendations of the SARS Laboratory Workshop, 22 October 2003', then a typical SARS Watch entry (29 April 2003) is 'The Lancet publishes study of SARS in children'. There is a 'human interest' dimension to some of the SARS Watch entries, for example, a story about a 'special doctor' in Toronto. Some of the themes which arise are also concerns of the newsgroup participants whose discourse is discussed below, for example, on the cultural acceptability of spitting in public. Wangjian-shuo's blog also carries news: one of his entries discusses the report by the WHO following their visit to Shanghai to assess the situation there. But since the purpose of the blog is broadly the author's life, experience and opinions, and since he surely knows that the wider world is interested in the Chinese experience of these things, many entries are about the impact of the outbreak upon daily life in the city:

> 29th April 2003
> Taxi drivers are among the most sensitive people for any changes in the city. I initialized a chat with the third taxi driver after SARS hit the city. If you still remember, the first taxi driver told me on April 17 that his car was disinfected once every month. The second taxi driver told me on April 23 that his car was disinfected every morning from April 21. Let's see what the third taxi have to tell us after one week.
>
>> You see the green label at my front glass? We are required to return to taxi company once from 10:00 PM to 8:00 AM the next morning everyday. The taxi company will organize disinfection for each car carefully. It is done very careful now. The cover of the seats are changed everyday.
>>
>> Meanwhile, every taxi is equiped with a bottle of disinfectant. We are required to spay the disinfectant every noon when I leave my car for lunch. I will close all doors so the spray will work better. Then open all the windows after I return. If I meet any passenger who goes to hospital or I suspect he/she is ill, I will also spray the disinfectant after he/she leave.

Whereas the WHO, in publishing its documents, is stamping them with its authority, the standard practice on SARS Watch is to link to, quote from, or reproduce, with attribution, other people's documents. It clearly attributes any authority to the original sources and not to itself – it is just a route to the words of others – while it still maintains the right to add commentary and interpretation to those words. There is no place in WHO documents for first-person address, but there is on SARS Watch:

> April 30th 2003
> I have linked to a lot of stories criticizing the actions of China's leadership, but the media need to spend more time looking at what the U.S. is doing to prepare for SARS, this summer's expected West Nile virus epidemic, and other public health threats.

As befits its 'personal experience and opinions' brief, the move to the personal mode is even more marked on Wangjianshuo's blog. The 'non-native-speaker English' is a feature of the language but not one which impedes communication, though Wang sometimes apologizes for it.

Newsgroups and SARS

The material

In the previous chapter, the newsgroup material examined covered ten years of Usenet traffic. In this chapter, the data covers a mere three-and-a-half months – from mid-March to the end of June 2003 – as does the sample of about 1000 messages which I have used for the purposes of focused analysis. During this period there were between one and two thousand threads of four messages or more which are wholly or mainly about SARS. Because of the very large numbers involved it is impossible to do an accurate calculation of the total amount of Usenet 'traffic' on this subject. As the months unfold, it becomes more likely that when contributors mention SARS in Usenet messages (which they often do) this will be an 'incidental' mention in the context of a message with different primary concerns. It is impossible to determine when a mention is 'incidental' except by reading all the candidate threads – the subject line alone does not give enough information. Table 5.1 does give some indication of the scale of response to SARS on Usenet, by quantifying the number of threads (4+ messages long) which were wholly or mainly about this subject during the last two weeks of March 2003.

Thread length varies between 373 messages and 4 messages (threads of fewer than four messages were not counted): average thread length is 24 messages. In March the newsgroup with the most interest in this topic was soc.culture.singapore (36 threads). One of the reasons that there is so much discussion of SARS on groups devoted to hobbies and

Table 5.1: Usenet threads about SARS, last two weeks of March 2003

Newsgroups	Number of threads and percentage from 15 March to 31 March		Example
Health	11	7%	misc.health.alternative
Hobbies and fanclubs	20	12%	rec.arts.movies.current-films
Lifestyle	12	7%	misc.survivalism
Politics	12	7%	alt.politics.liberalism
Regional	77	47%	soc.culture.singapore
Religion	5	3%	alt.bible.prophecy
Science	4	2%	sci.med.nutrition
Travel	11	7%	rec.travel.asia
Miscellaneous	14	8%	alt.prophecies.nostradamus
Total	**166**		

fan clubs is because of world conventions and other meetings due to take place later in the year in cities affected by SARS. Hobbyists take advantage of their global network to discuss whether their meetings will be cancelled, whether they will take a risk in travelling there, and so on.

As with the material in the cellphone chapter, more detailed analysis is based upon a sample of threads. The sample examined in this case is drawn not only from the threads exchanged in March, but also covers April, May and June 2003. Fifty-five threads were selected, so as to ensure a 'spread' across the following parameters: (a) the growth and then the decline of the issue as a 'hot topic' through these three-and-a-half months; (b) the length of message, between 4 messages and 140 messages, to reflect the variation in length of the threads exchanged in the late March list above; (c) the type of newsgroup, covering all of the categories in the list above. Five hundred and twenty-four different people contributed relevant messages within this sample. The greatest number of relevant messages contributed by any one participant was 34; 308 people contributed only one on-topic message.

Confidence and doubt

Table 5.2 gives a general picture of the balance between confidence and doubt among the newsgroup participants. As in the previous chapter,

Table 5.2: Talking up and talking down of SARS

Orientation to risk	Number of messages	(%)
Talking up of risk	224	17
Not applicable (for example, off-topic)	484	36
Talking down of risk	193	15
Putting both sides, i.e., ambivalent	27	29
Putting neither side, for example, asking a question without presupposition	392	2
Unclear, i.e., difficult to classify	9	1
Total	**1329**	

this analysis is the result of a process of interpretation which does not do justice to the range of expression. As a crude indicator therefore, and ignoring everything except the 'talking up', 'talking down' and 'ambivalent' categories, it is clear that there is no consensus regarding the hazardousness of SARS.

Online conversations about the SARS outbreak begin when someone either provides information, seeks information or expresses an opinion about some aspect of the SARS story:

Providing information
SARS messages no. 1 (May) on three health newsgroups

> As a registered user of www.thelancet.com, you might be interested to know that research by UK epidemiologists and scientists from Hong Kong, fast-tracked for publication on THE LANCET'S website, reports results of the first major epidemiological study about severe acute respiratory syndrome (SARS). [This introduction is then followed by a summary of the Lancet report.]

Seeking information
SARS messages no. 2 (April) on one lifestyle newsgroup

> The cause for SARS has still apparently not been absolutely tracked down. I understand that the cold-like coronavirus that was thought to be at the root of the disease is absent in something like 60% of the cases. Anybody have any later info?

Commenting
SARS messages no. 3 (April) on one lifestyle newsgroup

> I am surprised to hear that the USA, Britain and Australia have apparently issued travel warnings about coming to Canada due to the SARS in Toronto. I find it odd, since there are cases in ALL of those countries (in fact, more in the USA than in Canada, according to WHO), and the Canadian outbreak is primarily limited to hospitals in Toronto, leaving rather a vast expanse of country disease free.

All such initiations, whatever the content, can be seen as responses to the news story as it broke and developed across the globe, following the WHO alert of 15 March. Such responses testify to the concern which the outbreak provoked, even if some respond by attempting to minimize suggestions of serious risk to health and life on a global scale. For every writer who initiates a thread in a voice of concern, there is another expressing doubts about the outbreak's seriousness.

Fearful
SARS messages no. 4 (June) on one travel newsgroup

> SARS is a real worldwide epidemic. People are dying, there is no cure, thus I have the right to be worried for my family. Wouldn't you be worried?

Sceptical
SARS messages no. 5 (March) on one regional newsgroup

> 'SARS survival rate higher than pneumonia'. Surprise, surprise. If its not killer dogs/sharks/men, it's killer household appliances or killer bugs. The list goes on. All to sell a few more papers and fool the stupid hippy masses.

However it is only with the development of online interaction, beyond the first message, that we can study in more depth the patterns of response to the news of this new virus and of the people and places which it affected. As with many issues of risk and health, it is useful to explore these patterns in terms of the writer's propensity either to accept the reality of the risk and 'talk it up', or else to remain sceptical and 'talk it down'. These choices are best seen as dialogic engagements in the sense of Bakhtin (1981). They involve either taking issue with a previous contributor on the thread (or on an earlier thread), or with a different contributor on an earlier thread; or with what someone else has said or is reported to have said, such as the prime minister, or with some unspecified source. Dialogic engagements in this sense are most apparent when they involve *contestation* with earlier/other views: *agreement* with another, also dialogic, is somehow less visible.

Here is a sequence of messages from one particular thread in which the various contributors accept the threat and amplify it, in various ways (the number of '>' characters at the start of the line indicate how far back this message is from the most recent one, which is at the end of the sequence). Text in square brackets summarizes material from the original message rather than quoting it:

Talking up
SARS messages no. 6 (April) on one regional politics newsgroup (separate messages numbered a–e)

SARS virus killing 5% & 20% need mechanical respiration
a) >>>>SARS Severe Acute Respiratory Syndrome seems to be
>>>>killing about 5% of those that are being infected. Another
>>>>20% need mechanical respiration. There is also some
>>>>likelihood that Chinese authorities are underrating these
>>>>statistics. There is a panic exodus form China that may be
>>>>spreading the disease world wide.
>>>>The Wall Street Journal Editorial page has called for
>>>>closing borders with China and Hong Kong!
>>>>For this article I advize you to go to the following URL
>>>>because it is extensively hyperlinked to primary sources:
>>>>http://www.vdare.com/misc/pringle_sars.htm
>>>>Do not tolerate public spiting!
>>>>Is Australia ready for the big one?
>>>>[citation of article]
xxxxxxxxxxxxxxxxxxxxxxxxxxxxxxxxxxxxxxxxxxxxxxxxxxxxxxx
b) >>>When this gets to Africa it will finish off what Aids started.
>>>There is a huge immuno-suppressed population and very

>>>little modern medicine. Can you imagine the scale of the >>>disaster that is impending? It is very depressing.

xxxxxxxxxxxxxxxxxxxxxxxxxxxxxxxxxxxxxxxxxxxxxxxxxxx

c) >>Seems that it's Mother Nature and not Saddam who still >>holds the whip hand when it comes possessing biological >>weapons of mass destruction! The worrying thing about it is >>that I saw some professor on TV yesterday saying that he's >>far more alarmed about this particular flu outbreak than he >>ever has been about Aids.

xxxxxxxxxxxxxxxxxxxxxxxxxxxxxxxxxxxxxxxxxxxxxxxxxxx

d) >This could turn out to be *the* big news and not the Iraq war.

xxxxxxxxxxxxxxxxxxxxxxxxxxxxxxxxxxxxxxxxxxxxxxxxxxx

e) I'm not surprised. HIV is only transmitted by swapping blood or semen, and AFAIK [netspeak: As Far As I Know] there are several promising potential cures/vaccines in late-stage testing. SARS has only just been identified and AFAIK can be spread by somebody sneezing on you.

How do these writers signify the seriousness which they attach to the SARS outbreak? The first message here (6a) does so by reproducing an 'authoritative' source text, originating outside of the newsgroup context. This is followed by one which associates the virus with a much better known health problem, HIV/AIDS (6b). This message does not just draw an analogy between SARS and AIDS: it produces an account in which the two diseases are causally related. HIV-infected peoples (that is, the inhabitants of the African continent) are more vulnerable to SARS because the earlier disease has compromised their immune systems. The next two messages (6c and 6d) amplify the seriousness of SARS by framing it alongside the war between the USA and Iraq, suggesting that, counter-intuitively, it is SARS which represents the greater problem. The reference in message (6c) to the opinions of 'some professor on TV' is indicative of an ambivalent or grudging respect for authoritative voices: this particular formulation combining the voice of science with that of the mass media. Finally, the contribution of the fifth message (6e) lies once again in a comparison of SARS with AIDS, but this time the point of comparison is the ease of transmission. By comparison with AIDS, SARS is easy to contract. A simple sneeze will do it.

But not all of the voices in these newsgroup conversations take the gloomy view of the threat posed by the SARS outbreak. Some are altogether more sceptical. Sceptical voices are more likely to concentrate upon the known present than upon the unknown future and in doing so draw attention to low absolute numbers of victims; low numbers in proportion to particular populations (for example, all the residents of Toronto, one of the cities with a significant outbreak); the location of victims globally; the location of victims in particular domains such as hospitals; the low numbers of victims in proportion to other epidemics, for example, the Spanish Flu of 1918; and the low numbers of victims in proportion to other risks such as traffic accidents.

Scale
SARS messages no. 7 (June) on one travel newsgroup

> The SARS risk in Toronto is miniscule. Let's see: 30 people out of 3 million people in Toronto, that's a rate of 10 per million. (Not to mention that it isn't in the general population, just at a few hospitals, and that nobody is known to have contracted it at Toronto's airport.)

Other risks
SARS messages no. 8 (March) on three regional newsgroups

> How many people died from the West Nile outbreak last year? Okay . . . how many people died from alcohol overdose, auto accidents, falling down stairs or accidental electrocution by home appliances? What are the real killers here?

Spanish flu
SARS messages no. 9 (May) on one lifestyle newsgroup

> In any case, SARS is not the Spanish Flu. This is not 1918.

Location
SARS messages no. 10 (April) on one regional newsgroup

> Let's see, you have a 2% chance of dying from it, and probably a 0.0000000000000000002% chance of contracting it here in NZ. So that gives you a 0.000000000000000000002% chance of catching it and dying here in NZ.

Scepticism about the seriousness of the SARS outbreak expresses itself as a reaction against explicit or assumed credulousness – it is, in that sense, dialogic and offered as a corrective to the wrong-headed acceptance of the risk and/or exaggeration of its significance for human health worldwide. Straightforward, rationally argumentative versions of this reaction, as illustrated above, exist alongside more knowing ones which object to the exaggeration and overreaction ('mass hysteria') which they detect in other people and institutions, including of course the mass media, with occasional suggestions about the improper motives for 'hype', as in example 12.

Mass hysteria
SARS messages no. 11 (July) on one regional newsgroup

> Toronto was never a no go area. The only place where you could have possibly got SARS was if you were in a hospital, and there never was a real threat to the population at large. A lot of mass hysteria, but unfounded and baseless.

Media hype
SARS messages no. 12 (April) on one hobby newsgroup

> Another PRIME example of the media overexaggerating risk to scare people and make money through ads.

A significant feature of this particular story was its 'out of the blue' character. The arrival of a new infectious disease on the world stage may not have surprised the experts within the public health community, but it certainly came as a surprise to the mass media and the general public and, especially in the early days, was treated as a mystery to be solved. This uncertainty is certainly reflected in the discourse of the newsgroups, for example, in the following interchange:

SARS messages no. 13 (April) on one regional newsgroup

> >still . . . only 2% of those who get will die.
> xxxxxxxxxxxxxxxxxxxxxxxxxxxxxxxxxxxxxxxxxxxxxxxxx
> Only 99 people out of the 761 who have the disease in Hong Kong have been discharged from hospital. Many of them are on ventilators.

> You are ejaculating prematurely here. No one working with the disease pretends to understand what is going on. It might be a paramyxovirus, it might be a coronavirus, no one knows what causes it. No one knows how it is transmitted. It spread throughout a high rise building in the Amoy Gardens complex, no one knows if it was in the air conditioning or the water. 200 or so people from that complex got the disease. . . .
> This is still a small epidemic, when it gets really loose who knows that the rate of illness and death will be. At the moment it is affecting a predominantly business/travelling class of people. What will happen when it gets into a population of poor, malnourished, more vulnerable people.

In this exchange, one participant berates a previous one for overconfident 'talking down' of the risk. His/her own lack of knowledge is generalized: it is represented as a lack of knowledge with regard to biological facts ('it might be a paramyxovirus'), a lack of knowledge of the narrative of causality ('no one knows if it was in the air conditioning or the water') and finally a lack of knowledge as to the future development of the disease ('when it gets really loose who knows what the rate of illness and death will be').

Associations

People make sense of new information by trying to relate it to something they already know more about. In the case of SARS this leads, unsurprisingly to comparison with other illnesses, particularly other infectious diseases. The range of diseases mentioned by writers includes: Ebola, bird flu, West Nile virus, the Black Death, MRSA, anthrax, Norwalk virus, TB, BSE/CJD, leprosy, hepatitis, monkey pox and hantavirus – but the ones most often mentioned in connection with SARS are flu and pneumonia. SARS may be a type of flu, or a type of pneumonia: if it is not, then it is certainly worth comparing with either or both.

But the analogies and associations that are thought worth making go well beyond the domain of disease. As with mobile phones, one response to this risk is to offer the thought that, to the extent that it is a risk, it is much less so than smoking, driving and other lifestyle hazards of the twenty-first century. On the 'current affairs' side, the connection with bioterrorism was an easy one to make, and so was the connection with the contemporaneous war between the USA and Iraq.

There are things worth saying about the SARS outbreak which connect with such contemporary concerns as racism (are China and the Chinese being scapegoated?); civil liberties and civic order (the rights and wrongs of quarantine); population control (is this Nature's way of regulating the numbers of humans on the planets, or someone other than Nature?); personal hygiene (the spitting habit); civic responsibility (the selfishness of particular kinds of behaviour with SARS 'on the loose'); the safety of air travel; the over-prescription of antibiotics; employers' duty of care, and others. Science fiction parallels were drawn into the mix: newsgroup writers recalled, variously, a BBC drama series called *Survivors*, a Hollywood movie called *Outbreak*, a Stephen King novel *The Stand*, and other fictional work of an apocalyptic or post-apocalyptic character, with and without elements of high-level conspiracy to pursue ruthless ends.

The SARS outbreak started while the USA and its allies were conducting war against Iraq. The fact that fifteen threads out of the 55 could not discuss SARS without also discussing/mentioning Iraq is not surprising, at least on non-specialist types of newsgroup where 'current affairs' discussion of all types is encouraged. Sometimes this occurs as no more than 'topic change' or 'topic drift':

SARS messages no. 14 (April) from a hobby newsgroup

> And while were talking about the news, is anyone else pondering whether the apparent negligence or lack of preparation that allowed the Iraqi national museum to be looted qualifies as perhaps the most serious tragedy of this war?

Sometimes there is an overarching theme to do with the awfulness of life:

SARS messages no. 15 (April) from a hobby newsgroup

> The war is over so now we can get back to the real important news of American Idol and who killed Laci Peterson, what a surprise! ?! I'll just go jump into my freezer now. At least Enron is out of business, so we won't have a blackout tomorrow, so I won't be defrosting prematurely.
> Shit, this country really sucks right now!

One variant of this proposes that SARS may come to be a more catastrophic world event, or story about such an event, than Iraq:

SARS messages no. 16 (April) on four politics newsgroups

> This could turn out to be *the* big news and not the Iraq war . . .

In its character as a 'story' for journalistic purposes, it takes a New Zealander to point out that news values may be different depending on where you are in the world:

SARS messages no. 17 (April) on a hobby newsgroup

> Here in New Zealand it is a bigger story than the war at the moment. Then again, there is a proximity issue. The world rugby championships were held recently in Hong Kong and many NZ residents were there for it (it's possibly a bigger sport to Kiwis than NFL is to Americans of the United States persuasion – people here are absolutely rabid for it) whereas the war in Iraq has little impact here apart from some Kiwi regulars joining with the UN to remove mines and clean up unexploded bomblets.

While a 'media spin' angle proposes, on the back of a proposition that the SARS outbreak is really not that big a deal, that it is being made so for essentially political reasons:

SARS messages no. 18 (April) on a hobby newsgroup

> The reason the story has been propagated as it has is that it is a 'sexy story' – one that sells ads – and also because it deflects attention off of other more important stories, that could be critical of the government, like the war. I find the timing of the unveiling of the SARS crisis (very close to the start of the Iraqi conflict) and the unveiling of the Anthrax crisis (very close to the start of the conflict in Afghanistan) to be very curious. Just like the anthrax threat was massively overblown and managed to deflect from blunders by the US government, so has SARS.

Sometimes parallels are being drawn: China and Iraq behave the same:

SARS messages no. 19 (April) on a lifestyle newsgroup

>the govt of the PRC went to considerable lengths, supposedly
>using panic containment measures, as the official excuse – to
>conceal the real extent of the SARS outbreak. Part of these
>measures included bussing the patients around Peking in
>ambulances during the WHO Inspectors visit at one hospital
>& using a hotel in the grounds of another hospital to re-locate
>the SARS patients to. All conducted under a media restrictions,
>however, to what extent would any Western govt be prepared
>to restrain its media in the event of such a spread of the disease?
xxxxxxxxxxxxxxxxxxxxxxxxxxxxxxxxxxxxxxxxxxxxxxxxxx
sounds familiar. kind of like the why the Iraqis moved stuff around when the UN weapons inspectors were in the area.

The dominant theme in discussions of Iraq before, during and after the war itself was of course the issue of Iraq's possession of weapons of mass destruction: since some of those could have been 'biological' weapons, the possibility that the SARS virus had been deliberately developed to be used in this way comes in for some discussion:

SARS message no. 20 (April) on seven politics newsgroups

http://www.informationclearinghouse.info/article2848.htm
Russian Scientist: SARS Virus Was Created In A Weapons Lab
ACADEMICIAN KOLESNIKOV: THE SARS VIRUS OF ATYPICAL PNEUMONIA HAS BEEN CREATED ARTIFICIALLY
IRKUTSK, April 10, 2003.
RIA Novosti correspondent Alexander Batalin
The virus of atypical pneumonia (SARS) has been created artificially, possibly as a bacteriological weapon, believes Sergei Kolesnikov, Academician of the Russian Academy of Medical Sciences.

Once this idea is on the table so too is the 'other' war – the 'war against terrorism' focused on Osama bin Laden and Al Qaeda:

SARS messages no. 21 (April) on a regional newsgroup

>How long before we're told that the bug was developed by Al
>Quaida in secret labs in Iraq?
xxxxxxxxxxxxxxxxxxxxxxxxxxxxxxxxxxxxxxxxxxxxxxxxxx
When is Bush's next speech?

In this example, the writer is playing with the notion that the American side might well want to claim such a thing, whether true or not, to further their propaganda war against their various enemies. 'Conspiracy' ideas in this material are however generally contested:

SARS messages no. 22 (March) on four regional newsgroups

>>>Paradoxically, the ones who launch mass immunizations (e.g.
>>>for smallpox) are the most likely to be the ones who use it as
>>>a weapon because they are in a position to limit their own
>>>casualties.
xxxxxxxxxxxxxxxxxxxxxxxxxxxxxxxxxxxxxxxxxxxxxxxxxx
>>But that does not suggest that those who immunize are
>>necessarily planning an attack either. Clearly that cannot be the
>>case.
xxxxxxxxxxxxxxxxxxxxxxxxxxxxxxxxxxxxxxxxxxxxxxxxxx
>Necessarily? No. But let us not allow sentimentality to impair
>our judgement.
xxxxxxxxxxxxxxxxxxxxxxxxxxxxxxxxxxxxxxxxxxxxxxxxxx
No. But let us not allow mere jitters to impair out judgement either. A mass innoculation for flu every year does not presage a BW attack via a flu virus. That being the case, there must be some other more useful indicators. Otherwise, we'd be On Guard every time there was a vaccination regiment going on anywhere in the world.

Or, as in example 21, conspiracy is proposed with such complete lack of supporting argument as to suggest that the attitude is either tongue-in-cheek or a knee-jerk reaction. Other attempts to read a political angle into the story are more opportunistic: one thread discusses whether a suggestion from some countries that their citizens should not travel to Toronto until the city be declared SARS free is revenge on Canada for failing to back the military campaign in the Middle East.

SARS messages no. 23 (April) on one lifestyle newsgroup

> I am surprised to hear that the USA, Britain and Australia have apparently issued travel warnings about coming to Canada due to the SARS in Toronto.
>
> . . .
>
> can't help but note that these are the three countries primarily involved in the Iraq war, and wonder if this advisory is a back-door attempt to get back at Canada for stating it will not join a non-UN sanctioned war.

Lexicon

There is a more subtle aspect to the consideration of whether writers are in the business of talking up the SARS danger or of talking it down, and this concerns the lexicon which is brought into play to discuss the topic. The keyword is of course the acronym SARS itself, the initials standing for Severe Acute Respiratory Syndrome. This was the keyword used in the initial search through the newsgroup archive, and its extensive appearance in the database is a consequence of the research procedures.

But the question is not just whether the acronym 'SARS' has made its way from expert discourse into mainstream English usage, or even how it made its way there. The interesting question is how it functions in this particular arena of English usage and whether, in that context, there are patterns of use which feed into the broader rhetoric of talking up and talking down of the danger.

It is fairly clear that the word itself was proposed by one particular research scientist, adopted and claimed by the World Health Organization, who introduced it to the world in their emergency travel advisory of 15 March. From there it was picked up by newswires and reproduced in substantial numbers of mass-circulation Sunday and daily newspapers, as well as by news broadcasting organizations worldwide. This amounts to a global, top-down dissemination process for a lexical innovation, backed by considerable scientific authority. In principle, within its own domains of expertise, science has permission to create names for entities which it discovers, such names then being non-negotiable except from within science itself. However, Leach (1999) introducing his research on the struggle in science over the meaning of the word 'cloning' observes:

> By naming scientific processes and scientific artefacts, scientists attempt to both pin down and construct the objects of their study. But this is never a simple process, and disagreement over scientific meanings is a normal part of the day-to-day communication among scientists. (Leach 1999: 218)

When such names enter popular discourse, lexical drift and further struggles may occur, although popular usage will not usually override scientific authority within scientific communities if they possess sufficient consensus regarding their mastery of reality. Lexical drift can be rationalized as a matter of divergence that has taken place between the 'ordinary meaning' and the 'specialized meaning' of the word in question, ('inflation', for example), although this situation has its own potential for confusion and conflict in any encounters between the discourses of the 'lifeworld' and those of the 'experts'.

There was some recognition within newsgroup discourse of naming as purposive, motivated semiotic activity. At least one writer appreciated that the name could have been other than what it actually became:

SARS messages no. 24 (April) on a lifestyle newsgroup

> They have certainly been clever in their choice of name for the new mystery illness. It is, by definition, Severe as people die from it, and Acute as it comes on rapidly, and tacking on Respiratory Syndrome, because it affects the lungs, produces the catchy acronym. SARS rhymes with Mars and is vaguely suggestive of Star Wars, both of which subliminally hint at SOME ALIEN MANACE FROM 'OUT THERE'. This is certainly a lot more threatening than other possible names that might have included Cars (alluding to its origins as the Chinese Acute Respiratory Syndrome) – or even the Acute Respiratory Syndrome epidemic which would never do – the laughter would be contagious in itself.

Does the 'talking up' of SARS as a threat to human health produce distinctive patterns of use? The answer is yes. SARS is positioned as part of a lexical set in which 'disease' is the ultimate superordinate term, but with some doubt as to its position at the intermediate level – is it a sub-type of influenza or a sub-type of pneumonia?

SARS messages no. 25 (March) on two hobby newsgroups

> I haven't heard of this current outbreak being referred to as any form of influenza, but it is true that most of the world's strains of flu seem to originate in southern China, the same area where this pneumonia was first reported.

Whatever its rightful place in the taxonomy – this, too, being an area where some divergence between official discourses and folk taxonomies might well arise – there is also a need to make reference to the collective social fact that groups of people are suffering from SARS now. On a scale of severity, the three most common words for this are 'problem', 'outbreak' and 'epidemic'.

SARS messages no. 26 (March) on three regional newsgroups

> Tung Shee Wah also tried to hide the truth of SARS problem because it may cause other impact on weaken Hong Kong's economy.

This is relatively neutral, a notch or so below the more common 'outbreak':

SARS messages no. 27 (July) on a regional newsgroup

> So please do come to Toronto. You will find a lot of deals around to help spur the economy, after visitors just disappeared. It's safe. It has always been safe, in spite of SARS. And the SARS outbreak has been contained, and never was significant.

More fearful messages apply the word 'epidemic':

SARS messages no. 28 (April) on two regional newsgroups[4]

> It's sad to hear that HaNoi-Vietnam has about 10% (5 people died/46 case) death ratio in this SARS epidemic. More people will be died on SARS!

There are further options for the fearful, some of them reminiscent of British tabloid newspaper style, mostly involving classification (for example, 'disease') combined with emotionally coloured premodification (for example, 'terrible') or other elaboration:

SARS messages no. 29 (various threads/newsgroups/months)

a) a mysterious disease
b) a life-threatening disease
c) this terrible disease
d) this scary disease.
e) a potentially deadly virus
f) a very worrying infection
g) a potentially lethal and vigorous virus
h) a wholly new and hitherto unknown-to-science viral infection
i) a new highly contagious atypical pneumonia
j) an indiscriminate killer
k) such a scourge

Examples (j) and (k) have been included here as illustrations where classificatory nouns are left behind in favour of others descriptive of the disease's effect on people.

On the other side of the scales, what we find is a range of expressions, with and without the word SARS itself, indicative of a range of sceptical and ambivalent attitudes. There were a considerable number of messages sufficiently doubtful to make use of scare quotes to indicate their distance from the official voices. The word 'SARS' itself gets the scare quote treatment, but so too, from time to time, do uses of the term 'virus', 'disease' and 'epidemic':

SARS messages no. 30 (March) on one regional newsgroup

Doesn't this, alone, suggest that 'SARS' is rather less of a danger than it being blown up to be?

SARS messages no. 31 (April) on one lifestyle newsgroup

The problem with this 'virus' is that it can live for 24 hours outside the host which is unusual for a respiratory 'virus'.

SARS messages no. 32 (June) regional/political newsgroup

This 'disease' is going to kill less people in one year than there are car accidents – just- in Toronto will in one week.

SARS messages no. 33 (April) on one regional newsgroup

I have not yet heard it called an 'epidemic' by anyone. Where did you hear this ? . . . and no . . . I don't think it is (yet ?).

There is even some discussion as to whether 'virus' should be regarded as a technical term:

SARS messages no. 34 (March) from a hobby newsgroup

>> If they don't know what it is then it's a virus? Seriously. 'virus' is
>> a Latin word which I think just means 'poison'. So bacteria are a
>> virus and rogue prions are a virus and rohypnol is a virus . . .
xxxxxxxxxxxxxxxxxxxxxxxxxxxxxxxxxxxxxxxxxxxxxxxxx
>Which is irrelevant, since _virus_ has a very specific meaning
>these days that is not related to its origins.
xxxxxxxxxxxxxxxxxxxxxxxxxxxxxxxxxxxxxxxxxxxxxx
It means 'You're sick and your doctor can't figure out why'.
Or it means 'Something that makes you sick and that doesn't grow by itself in a test tube'.
Or 'A non-living substance X which causes a living body to produce X'. That definition could let prions in.
And while I do see the value of a scrupulous taxonomy of potential pathogens, 'virus' on its own surely is usually seen in one of the first two senses I just gave. When scientists or doctors want to be specific, they seem to talk about 'something-else-latin-o-virus'.

The word SARS, without scare quotes, is also used as a modifier in collocations such as the following:

SARS messages no. 23 (various threads/newsgroups/months).

a) . . . seriously scared by this SARS thang
b) The SARS Disease thing that we are having a problem with

> c) This SARS crap is serious.
> d) This SARS thing does seem to be getting a little complicated, though
> 3) This thing may spread via ventilation ducts. . . .

These general nouns, 'thing', 'stuff', 'crap' are all-purpose lexical substitutes called upon in the absence of more specific or appropriate terminology. In these examples the vagueness comes across in much the same way as the scare quotes. It functions as a kind of distancing device for a speaker who seeks to convey a lack of full understanding for what is happening, maybe even some lack of sympathy for the medical discourse responsible for the term SARS in the first place. Some participants go further than just distancing themselves from the official lexicon: they actively argue with the classification of the disease.

SARS threads no. 35 (April) on five politics and regional newsgroups

> It's just an overhyped cold caught by Chinese malingerers looking to pull a sickie

SARS threads no. 36 (April) on four regional newsgroups

> And have you noticed the politically correct name 'atypical' to me its's pretty typical, it's the Asian flu!

Sources

In these discussions, as with the discussions about mobile phones and cancer, people base their knowledge on a wide ranges of sources, including what they are told by members of their social network. But SARS is different, because it is so new and so little is known, even by sources which claim some authority in this biomedical area. Reference to published sources, including both the print media and the World Wide Web are very much more in evidence, and the patterning of 'textual reference' in this material is somewhat different too. The picture, in relation to the sample, is as shown in Table 5.3: the total is greater than 55 because some threads make use of more than one type of reference.

Table 5.3: Types of reference in SARS threads

Type of reference	Number of threads
Popular/mass media references	48
Science/medicine/health references	
World Health Organization	32
Other science/health/medicine references	18
Governmental references	
CDC[5]	19
Other governmental references	14
Miscellaneous references	12
Commercial (manufacturers of face masks)	2
No references	2

Using and evaluating the mass media. Talking down of a risk often starts from the recognition that someone else has been talking it *up*. The usual culprits for this are either a previous contributor on the thread, or the mass media, or both together. But as in the mobile phone material, mass media references here perform several functions. They certainly function as an 'explanatory factor' for writers who do not think that this disease is anything special, but who recognize that others do; they also function as a source of information both for those who do think that the mass media have a case to answer and for those registering a more fearful or open-minded view on the subject. References to the mass media in this material, when they are of the generic type rather than references to particular articles in the press or programmes/reports in the broadcast media, are almost always of the dismissive, 'media hype' variety. Out of the 55 threads in the sample there are 23 in which reference is made to 'the media' in generic terms: 20 of these are blaming the media for exaggerating the significance of SARS.

SARS messages no. 37 (July) on a regional newsgroup

> You should never have postponed your trip. This SARS thing has been blown so much out of proportion by the media, and it has really impacted this cities economy, especially since the WHO issued a travel advisory, which they have lifted.

Early in the history of the outbreak someone registers the view that the media are not giving the SARS outbreak *enough* attention – in contrast with the coverage of the Iraq war – but this theme does not last for long.

SARS messages no. 38 (March) on a politics newsgroup

This is indeed a rapidly emerging problem. For me, a disturbing one since there has been a case reported in MA (non fatal). I spend much time at Boston Medical center . . . the default hospital for most immigrants including an extremely large Asian contingency. The press for this emerging disease seems to be smothered by the war in Iraq.

One writer is bold enough to counter the 'media hype' line with the view that the mass media are not so influential as they might wish to be and others believe they are.

SARS messages no. 39 (April) on a hobby newsgroup

>In general, masses of people (influenced by the mass media, of
>course) can only react to one threat at a time. If SARS is on every
>front page every day for a month, good luck getting anyone in
>the know-nothing population to think about another risk even
>if it's 10,000 times more important.
xxxxxxxxxxxxxxxxxxxxxxxxxxxxxxxxxxxxxxxxxxxxxxxxx
You are assuming that the media has an influence that it does not have. Very few read the papers, very few watch news programs. Many that do, like me, will believe nothing they read or hear.

Another writer appears to believe that the media have been 'sugar coating' the possible risk to individuals:

SARS messages no. 40 (April) on a health newsgroup

There will be a SARS clinic near you 'call local hosp. 'go yourself with hubby and get tested now do not depend on anyone else. 24 hour delay can be to late for weak immune systems. N95 mask is a must for auto persons when outside until the 39 person SARS medical committee get a handle on this super bug. Check world history of 1918 flu. Today with air travel bugs cover world in less than two days.
I do not wish to scare any of the family, just to say it as it is without media sugar coating.

Within all of this material, people settle upon certain choice phrases to express their dissatisfaction with the media. Here are some examples:

SARS messages no. 41 (various months) on various newsgroups

a) media bullshit
b) newshound sensationalising
c) media hype (×3)
d) media-induced hysteria
e) overhyping of the 'rampant'ness of sars
f) overhyped media sensationalism
g) constant apocalyptic style media coverage
h) media driven scare
i) media over-exaggerating risk

At one level it makes sense to treat all of these as examples of 'the same' reaction to the event; a construction of the SARS outbreak as an event which is either getting more attention than it deserves or the wrong kind of attention. Yet it does not seem to be the case, for the most part, that these writers are thoughtlessly deploying an off-the-peg cliché, such as 'media hype', to index their objections. Although this phrase does occur more than once, and there is no other set phrase to compare with it in this respect, it is the *variation* in the wordings which people use that is most striking here. These wordings – and the context in which they are used – are indicative of different ways of framing the 'problem' of the mass media in relation to SARS. Thus, a reference in one case to 'apocalyptic' coverage suggests an interest in an end-of-the-world-as-we-know-it aspect of the coverage; 'sensationalism' points towards the elaboration of the most dramatic components; 'overhyping of the "rampant" ness' suggests a more specific focus upon ideas about how fast the contagion is spreading and so on; 'media-induced hysteria' and 'media driven scare' are wordings which pay more attention to the effects of the coverage than upon the coverage itself, 'newshound sensationalising' seems to point the finger of blame at the actual journalists.

Using and evaluating the World Wide Web. Another difference between data in this section and that discussed in the mobile phone chapter is the greater extent to which the texts that people quote from, refer to, and invite others to read, are texts available on the World Wide Web and to which the newsgroup message provides a link. Most of these links lead to text on the websites of news organizations. Some of this is on the websites of traditional news organizations such as the BBC and CNN; some of it comes from internet-based news organizations. Thus, the greater use of web links to news sources in this material also reflects the greater availability of such sites in 2003 as compared with the whole of the period 1993–2002.

News media links are not of course the only kind of web links to appear in this material. Another kind which is extremely prevalent is the web link to the sites of 'authoritative' expert institutions. The most common reference here is to the website of the World Health Organization; the next most common, although a long way behind the WHO, takes readers to the site of the Centers for Disease Control and Prevention.

The WHO has considerable authority, judging from this material. The sheer quantity of references to it, and to its website, ought to be some kind of testimony to the trust that people place in it. But the quantity would mean nothing if all of those references were hostile or critical. That is a long way from being the case. The World Health Organization website is offered among newsgroup contributors as a source of reliable information:

SARS messages no. 42 (June) from a travel newsgroup

>How is SARS in Taipei these days? Are there any new outbreaks?
xxxxxxxxxxxxxxxxxxxxxxxxxxxxxxxxxxxxxxxxxxxxxxxxxx
For world health info, see http://.who.org
On that WHO web site, the SARS page is http://www.who.int/crs/sars/en/
On that SARS page there is a link to a Taiwan update notice at http://www.who.int/csr/don/2003_06)17/en

People also pass on WHO advice to one another:

SARS messages no. 43 (April) from a regional newsgroup

>you should remember that the method of this virus being
>transmitted is not clear yet.
xxxxxxxxxxxxxxxxxxxxxxxxxxxxxxxxxxxxxxxxxxxxxxxxxx
Precisely. That's why people should adhere to the advisory. Not only is it the Malaysian government's advisory but also the WHO's advisory.

Some messages just reproduce passages from text from the WHO site in their own messages; others reproduce pieces of journalism which uncritically report information originating with the WHO. The authority of the WHO can also be used to challenge another newsgroup contributor:

SARS messages no. 44 (June) on a lifestyle newsgroup

>the average person is NOT at risk. it's not like the virus is out
>wandering the city streets, waiting to pounce on unsuspecting
>passers-by! and it's hardly an *epidemic* either.
xxxxxxxxxxxxxxxxxxxxxxxxxxxxxxxxxxxxxxxxxxxxxxxxxx
So you think the WHO alerts are unfounded?

The WHO does not claim to be the principal, in Goffman's (1981) sense, for all of the information it purveys. In some matters it knows only what it has been told. This opens the door a little for suspicion and challenge on the newsgroups without necessarily impugning the integrity of the WHO itself:

SARS messages no. 45 (May) from a lifestyle newsgroup

What should be on everyone's mind, is the fact that the govt of the PRC went to considerable lengths, supposedly using panic containment measures, as the official excuse – to conceal the real extent of the SARS outbreak. Part of these measures included bussing the patients around Peking in ambulances during the WHO Inspectors visit at one hospital & using a hotel in the grounds of another hospital to re-locate the SARS patients to.

An important factor here is the fact that the WHO is not just a purveyor of information about the disease, but also an actor in the drama of the SARS outbreak. In this capacity it comes in for some criticism, in respect of its decision to advise people not to visit Toronto during the course of an outbreak there:

SARS messages no. 46 (April) from a lifestyle newsgroup

Some think that the WHO travel restriction recommendation that includes Toronto is wrong – especially people in Toronto. They object to this action by the UN . . . Although the outbreak in

> Toronto appears to have started with a 78 year old Chinese woman who visited relatives in China and was then spread by her 44 year old son, SARS is now not limited to the Chinese population in Canada. In fact, a young girl has apparently carried it from Toronto to Australia. But Toronto is a large city, relatively few people (300 or so?) have gotten SARS (which is not limited to the Chinese population) and mostly only the very young and or elderly have so far died from it. So Toronto probably has a point in objecting to the travel recommendation. It is creating a financial disaster that just might be far larger than the medical disaster.

The strongest form of attack on the WHO combines criticism of the organization both as an actor and as a purveyor of information, finding it, as well as the mass media, guilty of exaggerating the significance of the disease:

SARS messages no. 47 (April) on a hobby newsgroup

> That is amazing that the WHO would want to propagate the myth of this disease. Hell, they already are constructing a new building 'to combat SARS.' Amazing. I guess they gave up on the diseases that are more than 99 per cent more prevalent. Go ahead and read up on the governmental and media reactions to the 1976 Swine Flu 'epidemic' . . . strikingly similar.

There is no evidence – in this material – that the various 'conspiracy theories' being touted implicate the WHO specifically, although there is one message which impugns the integrity of the organization. The thesis of economic self-interest winning out over true public health concerns is instantly disputed within the thread.

SARS messages no. 48 (April) on five health newsgroups

> AIDS and SARS are ways for epidemiologists (e.g., the CDC, WHO, etc.) to secure their jobs and continued funding for their agencies. No new emerging epidemics, maybe no CDC, no WHO, so we've got an infrastructure that REQUIRES the 'discovery' of new, threatening epidemics. And the media pick a new one every year. This year, it's SARS. For the past couple of years, it's been West Nile Virus. Next year it'll be something else.

As for the CDC – it might be expected that such a source would come in for some scepticism as a government body. This is not the case; not in this sample at any rate. Indeed, it comes off even better than the WHO because it is not perceived as an actor in the unfolding story. It is a target in message 48, but as pointed out above, this is both anomalous in the data and contested within the thread. References to CDC and its website as a source of information are numerous (on 19 out of 55 threads in the sample) and they are overwhelmingly neutral or positive in their judgement of its value. The following are characteristic:

SARS messages no. 49 (April) on three politics newsgroups and one regional newsgroup

> Go to these links for complete information:
> World Health Organization (WHO), FAQ
> WHO, current status
> Center for Disease Control (CDC), SARS info
> Canadian Public Health; Don't Panic

SARS messages no. 50 (April) on one health newsgroup

> This has some great info about SARS:
> http://www.cdc.gov/mmwr/preview/mmwrhtml/mm5212a5.htm

Discussion

As the above analysis shows, there is the same roughly equal balance between those who respond to SARS with fear and those who respond with some confidence as there was in relation to the mobile phone debate; and some of the same moves are evident in the management of debate about the issue, notably the tendency of the less fearful to invoke 'the media' in generic not specific terms as the primary agent in the production of a scare reaction in the general public.

The analysis above gives some idea of what a 'global' news event looks like as a subject of popular concern, in the early years of the twenty-first century. The fact that it is a health risk story means that it is something which citizens and consumers have reason to think about in relation to their own lives and behaviour – to travel or not to travel, what personal hygiene precautions to take, whether to avoid certain places and people, the wisdom of particular stock market investments and so on. It is in this respect dissimilar from many global news stories which are about the actions of the political elites. These too affect people's lives, but more remotely and without requiring decisions from those who are affected. Very many threads in the newsgroup material reviewed above include contributions from people who feel their lives to be touched by SARS, even if at 'second hand'. One American expatriate writes 'I AM BORED' from a quarantine room in an unaffected Chinese city, having visited an affected one. Another woman writes that her husband's illness after a visit to China must have been SARS though they did not realize this at the time, and he recovered.

The story, as an event, brings together outbreaks in two continents, North America and Asia, as well as more isolated cases elsewhere; the realm of the World Wide Web brings together websites in Europe (World Health Organization – Switzerland), North America (SARS Watch – USA) and Asia (Wangjianshuo's blog – China). The realm of Usenet involves newsgroups for New Zealanders and Canadians, as well as Singaporeans, Malaysians and Taiwanese – not to mention the residents of the Isle of Wight off the south coast of England who have learned that their island is to be used for quarantine of boarding-school children from suspect areas. The material reviewed here clearly reveals the current bias of internet communication towards the richer, more educated and more computer-literate inhabitants of the world – Africans are strikingly absent except in the third person as victims of AIDS and potential victim of SARS. The theme of international travel is extremely prominent.

But for all that, the subject itself is not a special interest but a general one. Whereas in the mobile phone material most of the discussion took place on newsgroups devoted to cellular phones and radio/wireless communication generally, here, most of the discussion takes place either on regional newsgroups or on newsgroups with quite divergent special interests. Participants in these threads contribute to their newsgroups out of an interest in jewellery-making, ice-skating, sports competitions, Terry Pratchett, raising children and more besides. These primary concerns would not predict 'reacting to the SARS outbreak' as a possible topic of discussion. And while there are personal issue at stake which often explain why SARS comes up as a topic on these groups, such as trying to find out from the grass roots whether it is safe to visit Toronto, these motivations do not account for how the thread subsequently develops. Once the topic has been launched, it usually moves away from the particular and on to the same general issues, themes, source references, associations and arguments, in groups as different as 'misc. survivalism' and 'alt.design.graphics'. Within Usenet the 'global audience' of the internet is fragmented into distinct interest groups, unaware of each other's particular concerns, and each potentially very small in the total number of individuals reached. But this apparent parochialism is misleading. Global events do touch the affairs of these enclaves, and in their discussions of such topics they manage and display resources of understanding which are not very different from group to group.

6
MMR and Autism

The letters 'MMR' are short for 'Measles, Mumps, Rubella'. Since the 1980s in the United Kingdom it has been possible to provide immunity to these diseases for a majority of newborn children via vaccination, and national policy to try and achieve this result. This is national policy in other countries too, but the specific vaccine, which combines all of the antibodies into a single product involving a single injection (plus a 'booster' after a few years) is less controversial outside the UK. This health risk issue (with autism and related conditions as the possible harm – see below) shares with the mobile phone issue the element of personal choice, but in a complicated way. First, the choice is made not in respect of the individual but in respect of her child: many parents will be more cautious on a child's behalf than on their own. Second, the personal choice is compromised: if I choose not to vaccinate I am resisting official pressure. Vaccination, with MMR, is the default option. Third, vaccination is offered as a positive health *benefit* in the first instance, so parents also have to think of the consequences if their unvaccinated child should contract measles, mumps or rubella. Some parents may have come to believe that single vaccines offer a way out of the dilemma. This chapter discusses what is at stake in the MMR debate, then explores websites and Usenet discussion on this subject.

The story of MMR

Measles, mumps and rubella are three infections traditionally contracted in childhood, from which, if the child recovers, he or she should have developed antibodies in the course of fighting the disease. The antibodies give protection against subsequent infection. Measles is, according to the WHO, 'the most infectious disease known to man'

(WHO 1999) and is not treatable by antibiotics. Vaccines were developed in the 1960s and vaccination programmes were instituted in industrialized western countries. By the 1970s it was possible to combine the antibodies for all three diseases into a single product and this has been the preferred form of immunization since that time. Many developing countries do not routinely vaccinate and suffer the consequences in terms of infant mortality and blindness as a complication of measles (WHO 2003b).

Where countries have a policy of vaccination, this is not generally compulsory or universal. There are contra-indications for vaccination in certain cases, and parents may choose not to vaccinate. Yet there are pressures to conform. In Britain, with its publicly funded National Health Service, the official policy is thus provided and administered in the main by a state institution. The voice of the government and the voice of the National Health Service and its employees are the same thing, although individual doctors may, 'off the record' in conversation with their own patients, dissent from the official view. The immunization policy specifically requires that immunization for measles, mumps and rubella be achieved through the use of the MMR vaccine and not, for example, through the use of separate vaccines for each disease, administered separately on different occasions. This form of immunization is possible but the onus is on parents to find a doctor who will agree to provide vaccination in this way, if their own family doctors will not, and also to pay for this treatment rather than accept the free provision of MMR.

In the USA the pressure to conform is felt in a different way. State by state, there is a requirement that children be certified vaccinated against the three diseases in order to be enrolled in a kindergarten or elementary school. MMR may be the preferred method for achieving that end within the medical establishment in the USA, but with something more like a consumer relationship between patient and physician in the United States context, there is less difficulty than in the UK in choosing an alternative schedule of vaccination, involving multiple vaccines. The obligation to demonstrate immunity from measles, mumps and rubella is a leaky one, with possibilities for opt-out under certain conditions which vary from state to state, such as religious objections.

The controversy about MMR in Britain developed as follows. Prior to 1998 there were anecdotal accounts from concerned parents of autistic children that the onset of the autistic symptoms coincided with the administration of the first of the MMR vaccination shots. (MMR also involves a second, booster shot in the year that children start school.)

There was little or no scientific support for the suggestion that the vaccination caused the autism in these cases until the publication, in February 1998, of an article in *The Lancet* (Wakefield 1998) which described in a particular set of twelve autistic children with a (possibly associated) bowel condition, the existence of traces of measles virus. Wakefield suggested that this was a link which deserved further exploration. The discovery gained a degree of media attention and fuelled the pre-existing anxiety about the MMR vaccine. Most scientific opinion continues to dismiss the causal hypothesis. The Wakefield study was criticized for its scientific weaknesses; better-designed studies have failed to produce any evidence of a link between the vaccination and autism. But Wakefield's supporters still offer lists of research besides his to support their position, and criticize the negative studies for *their* methodological weaknesses.

Some alternative medicine discourse promotes the idea that all vaccination is an unnecessary and damaging form of therapy within conventional western medicine, with its enormous vested interests in the shape of the pharmaceutical companies, and includes MMR within this general critique, an economic and political as much as a medical one.

The policy of universal vaccination in industrialized countries has the additional goal of providing 'herd immunity'. If a sufficient proportion of the population is immune to measles then most of them will also be incapable of passing the disease on to the small proportion which is not immune. That proportion will not contract the disease either, if the plan works, so the entire population will be protected and some individuals can be free-riders. Herd immunity arguments do not persuade parents worried about autism in their own children, since this would require them to put the public before the private good.

In Britain there has been some research into mass media coverage of the MMR debate, focusing upon press rather than the broadcast media. Lewis and Spears (2003) undertook a content analysis of the national press during the period January–September 2002, along with two national surveys of 1000 adults each in April and October 2002. They found that press coverage, in adopting its usual approach of balancing views in conflict, gave the misleading impression of a research community equally divided over the issue of risk. The truth is that most published research has found no evidence of risk. The researchers found that the incorrect 'equally divided' message (and not any of the finer detail of media reports) had successfully been conveyed to the British public. The press had also been successful in conveying the idea of single vaccines as a safer alternative to MMR, even though this was supported by no research evidence and had merely been suggested by Andrew Wakefield at a press conference. But the single vaccine option *did* receive media coverage, and was duly remembered by the public.

In the autumn of 2003 there was another moment of 'bad media' for the supporters of MMR when *Hear the Silence* was broadcast. The Oscar-winning actress Juliet Stephenson took the role of a mother in this television production, which dramatized a fictional case history in a manner sympathetic to an anti-MMR position. But the pendulum started to swing back again in the following February when *The Lancet* drew attention to the compromised nature of Wakefield's involvement with autistic children and even further on 3 March 2004 when the press announced that ten of his co-authors had withdrawn their support for the suggestion of a link between MMR and autism.

On the internet

Having access to the internet, especially the World Wide Web, ought to make matters more complicated for parents seeking guidance on this topic. The low level of regulation means that bizarre and extreme materials can coexist with carefully considered accounts from responsible bodies and individuals. The good news is that the wilder accounts to be found on the web are often unprofessional in presentation and styling and less than coherent in content, thereby undermining their potential credibility. The bad news is that, for some readers, the fact that a given site is on the fringes as far as its opinions are concerned is not necessarily going to count against it. Fringe positions usually offer a critical frame for the re-reading of mainstream accounts. A reader influenced by such an account may come to understand that everything reassuring she reads is likely to be putting some or all of the following considerations ahead of the need to prevent autism:

- The need to reassure parents before vaccination
- The need to stave off and defend against litigation after vaccination
- The need to ensure the continuance of the programme for the sake of herd immunity
- The need to avoid the extra cost of providing alternative forms of vaccination
- The need to avoid confessing mistakes

With this in mind it is important to discover just how easy it is to find the anti-MMR voice on the World Wide Web and in Usenet.

Exploring the web

The most popular search engine at the present is Google. Google explains the efficiency of its software thus:

> PageRank relies on the uniquely democratic nature of the web by using its vast link structure as an indicator of an individual page's value. In essence, Google interprets a link from page A to page B as a vote, by page A, for page B. But, Google looks at more than the sheer volume of votes, or links a page receives; it also analyzes the page that casts the vote. Votes cast by pages that are themselves 'important' weigh more heavily and help to make other pages 'important.'
>
> Important, high-quality sites receive a higher PageRank, which Google remembers each time it conducts a search. Of course, important pages mean nothing to you if they don't match your query. So, Google combines PageRank with sophisticated text-matching techniques to find pages that are both important and relevant to your search. Google goes far beyond the number of times a term appears on a page and examines all aspects of the page's content (and the content of the pages linking to it) to determine if it's a good match for your query.

A web search on Google, 5 March 2004, for 'mmr' 'autism', produced 46,400 hits in total. By Google's own criteria the best-quality links should be the ones nearest the top of the list. Before discussing what the software regards as the best-quality links in this case, it is important to say something about categorization. Even before encountering actual websites and web pages, some software-produced discrimination has been exercised. A distinction is made between 'news', 'sponsored links' and the main links. 'News' links – two or three only – are clustered at the top of the page under the header sections. These go to such sites as the BBC web page, the *New Scientist* web page, the Reuters web page – the 'brands' of news in the internet marketplace. Google also offers a 'recency' indicator alongside each entry. 'Sponsored' links, one in the header section and five in a right-hand column, are part of the commercial apparatus which keeps Google profitable. But they are distinctive on the page. A reader concerned about bias has been warned . . .

On 5 March 2004 the fissures over MMR were reproduced within this structure. The theme of the news links is good news for the defenders of MMR:

Controversial MMR and autism study retracted – New Scientist – 21 hours ago
MMR Doctors Reject Own Autism Link Report – Reuters – 3 Mar 2004

The underlying theme of the sponsored links is less good news. Three of them are from health organizations in the private sector (outside the National Health Service) offering single vaccines as an alternative to MMR for parents who want the immunity but not on the terms it is being offered by the government.

On balance, however, the defenders of MMR would feel reassured by the results of this exercise in relation to the main links themselves. The 'top ten' main results produce seven 'hits' on the mainstream, pro-vaccine side of the argument. Of the remaining three, only one was unequivocally anti-vaccine. This page came in at position 8 on Google's quality list. It took the form of a paper by a writer with letters after his name (Yazbak 2002). Yazbak, MD, FAAP, invites readers to be suspicious of mainstream reassurance:

> Given that the CDC has yet to look into the medical illnesses of children with late-onset autism, it is more than likely that the CDC hierarchy was aware of the anticipated results of the study – to exonerate MMR – before a decision was made to co-fund it.

Two of Google's top-ten results were even-handed. One presents hyperlinks to other sites on both sides of the debate but without any commentary to steer the reader one way or the other; another is from a local newspaper, in a story where the voice of a pro-vaccine expert is set against the voice of concerned parents.

Of the seven pro-MMR results, one was on the CDC website, two were on the websites of reputable academic journals (*Nature* and the *Medical Journal of Australia*); one was on the site of the non-profit making Institute of Medicine in the USA, one was on an autism-related information service, the Autism Biomedical Information Network, and one was on a specialist 'headline' web news service for the medical profession. This accounts for six of the seven pro-MMR results: the seventh is on the web page of BUPA, an organization which provides private health insurance and health care in the UK. BUPA could make money from single vaccines if there was a demand for them. But the link was to a BUPA story headlined: 'MMR/autism link is unlikely'.

The defenders of MMR can also take comfort not just from the imbalance in favour of the pro-vaccine view, but also from the fact that even the commercial sites, with considerable thought for their legal position as well as their interest in promoting single vaccinations for concerned parents, are hardly doing so in a strident fashion:

> The causes of autism or inflammatory bowel disease (for example Crohns Disease) have not yet been fully elucidated. By offering the single antigen vaccination course, we are not implying that there is any proven link with these conditions and the combined MMR vaccine. We do not know of any guaranteed way to prevent these devastating illnesses. (Directremedies.com 2004)

> **Are the single vaccines safer than MMR?**
> Choice Healthcare Services do not advise on the safety of the single vaccines over that of the MMR three in one vaccine. However, in the light of some reports about the possible diseases and mental disorders that have been identified after the MMR has been administered, we are here only to offer you the ability to make informed decisions about your child's health, and to choose a method for protecting your child that you feel is suitable.
> (Choice Healthcare Services 2004)

The wilder side of the web

'Whale'[1] is the kind of website that causes people to worry about the web's role in the circulation of ideas so far beyond the mainstream as to be dangerous as a source of popular understanding – taking on the kind of role that 'superstition' used to play in contrast with modern, rationally grounded beliefs (Vincent 2000). The problem with the web from one perspective is the amount of rubbish, masquerading as factual and truthful, which exists alongside and in an apparently equal relationship with more responsible and reliable sources of information.[2] The equality of access to the medium for text-producers does not necessarily result in equality of product. Websites maintained by individuals on the whole have a different look and feel from those maintained by organizations with the resources to pay large design teams to create and maintain their complex, multi-service sites. Even the sophisticated software now available to bloggers cannot entirely overcome the limitations of resources in this respect, and many of them would not need to. They are not in the same business as organizations. There is also the issue of commercial support via online advertising, which can be used to generate revenue for site producers and thus give them more to invest in site design.

For science/health related public websites the opportunity exists, notwithstanding the limitations mentioned above, to promulgate views which are (according to the judgement of readers) unorthodox, unconventional, eccentric, alternative, fringe, bizarre, crackpot, insane and perverse – within the limits of whatever jurisdiction is able to exercise legal control. This is one of the web's great strengths and virtues, but it comes at a cost. The cost is the burden it places upon readers who wish to exercise discrimination in their encounters with web resources. How can readers, knowing so much less than writers about the topics they are exploring, hope to be able to give any particular site a 'credibility rating' when they are all saying such different things, and saying them using similar rhetorical strategies, citing research literature and basing arguments upon the findings therein?

As I have indicated in the SARS chapter above, there is some evidence via the newsgroup material of a branding effect – evidence that, other things being equal, readers will trust the websites of organizations they have heard of and which have an established reputation in their field. If this is true then sites which are not thus branded will to that extent lack credibility, even when their scientific knowledge is good and their argumentation robust.

To avoid too much prejudgement of the validity of anything offered on Whale it is prudent to begin by assessing it as merely 'unconventional'. Many of its critics (these will be discussed later in the chapter in relation to the newsgroup material) would go much further than this.

It is unconventional at a number of levels. In the first place, it does not carry a brand label. Its title, Whale, has no self-evident connection with the range of topics discussed on the site and if it is symbolic, the writer does not offer an account of the symbolism as he sees it. The absence of a brand name is compounded by the absence of an authorial attribution. Readers do not know the name of the person responsible for the site. Even the email address is anonymous. Plenty of contemporary texts, including websites, do not publicize the names of authors. Sometimes this is because there are too many people involved for the traditional idea of 'author' to make much sense; sometimes it is because of the convention that, in a commercial context, all authorship rights are subordinated to the corporate purpose, as with contemporary advertising for example. These are copyright issues. Nevertheless, within the context of an 'unbranded' web page, the absence of any way to identify an author is unusual and potentially damaging to its persuasive project.

Textual structure and design

The design of the site is essentially a simple one: there is a 'gateway' or home page and a set of related pages accessible via hyperlinks from the gateway page. There is extensive cross-linking between these secondary pages. The design of the gateway page itself is tripartite: a header section at the top, a central section, and a footer section at the bottom. In the header section we read the title, 'WHALE', large font, centred, and we see figurative images of two whales symmetrically posed to the left and to the right of that title. The background page colour is peacock blue, the title section features black text on a white background superimposed over the blue. The central section is in tabular form: a fifteen-cell grid, five columns, three rows, with breaks between the rows. The footer section has two email functions, one for sending a message to the writer and one for forwarding the page to a third person. There is also a site search engine in the bottom right-hand corner.

Hyperlinks

Within the fifteen cells of the central table, all but two are filled with hyperlinks to other pages on the site. Thus, some cells have no links, some have one link, and some have more than one. In adopting this grid principle, and placing hyperlinks accordingly, the suggestion is that items clustered together within any given cell are related, and are distinguished from items in other cells. The clustering principles used by Whale are not completely transparent simply from inspection of the gateway page itself. Some of the clusters do make sense at this level. For example, one cell (top right) reads:

Articles
Interviews
Quotes
Testimonies
Books, videos, tapes

This cluster makes sense as a grouping based upon some sort of 'text-type' principle. In contrast, the adjacent (mid-left) cell reads:

Animal Health
Child Health
Women's Health

This cluster also coheres around the theme of 'affected beings' – animals, children, women. So far, so satisfactory. But other cells are more awkward from a classification perspective. The cell which is at the start of the probable reading path (Kress and van Leeuwen 1996) at the top left reads:

Cancer
Vaccination
Pharmaceutical drugs
The diseases
Medical citations

Understanding the principle for this cluster is more problematic. It appears generally to be a substantive cluster, that is, focused upon areas of medical concern – in contrast with the text type cluster on the right-hand side. But on this basis 'Medical citations' is the odd man out. It seems to belong better in that right-hand cell, with other text types, except that that cell already has an entry for 'quotes' and another for 'testimonies'. So maybe we're dealing here with a metonymic (proximity) rather than metaphoric (similarity) relationship. *These* medical citations will all relate to cancer, vaccination, pharmaceutical drugs and the diseases. The similarity of items in the cluster is unsatisfactory in other ways. Cancer is a separate list item from 'The diseases' even though cancer is a (set of) diseases and thus subsumable within the latter category. Why separate it out in this way, and not, say, 'arthritis'? Neither of the other two entries are diseases. They are usually classified as therapies, though for Whale they are problems, not solutions.

Cells with a single entry have a problem of overlap rather than of internal coherence. One cell, bottom centre, contains the single link, 'Quotes'. 'Quotes' is also one of the entries in the text-type cell at the top right. It shares territory with 'Medical citations' from the top left-hand cell. Another cell features the single entry 'Banking & EU', which lacks any obvious thematic connection with the overarching 'health/medicine' theme, while indicating (along with entries in some other cells, for example, 'Mind control/Shadow Government'; 'Medical Politics'), an agenda broad enough to take in politics and economics as well as medical science itself.

In short, this site lacks coherence on a superficial examination, for example, by a reader who is only interested in a single topic. Perhaps further exploration of the detail is required to see what it is, if anything, that makes the site cohere.

Content

The material on this site is not limited to discussion of the MMR vaccine and its possible link with autism. There are links which mention other kinds of harm which might occur as a result of this vaccine. There are links which mention harm from other kinds of therapy such as pharmaceutical drugs, radiotherapy, chemotherapy. There are links to pages of quotes from published works; there are links to media stories about different kinds of health issues including MMR and autism. There are links to accounts offered by individuals who believe they or their children are victims of one of these conditions, whether or not the medical profession accepts liability. To a very large extent, these are 'internal' links: mass media stories have been cut-and-pasted into the site. There is a page on the site about the webmaster where he describes himself, in the third person, as:

> a 49 yr old (UK) father to 6 kids, the last two (5 & 8) being unvaccinated. He started to look into cancer therapies when he came across a copy of Nexus Magazine, where he discovered the suppression of cancer therapies (something his father died of after surgery & radiation therapy). He then started on vaccination 8 years ago after being handed a copy of Walene James book on vaccination by the Naturopath Kiki Sidhwa

This, with other comments on the page, is sufficient to establish (a) a personal rather than a professional interest in health and medicine, and specifically in the areas of cancer treatment and vaccination, and (b) an alignment with alternative rather than mainstream medicine. There are of course degrees of alignment with alternative medicine as well as a scale of 'alternativeness' with some therapies gaining more mainstream acceptance than others, and some practitioners within the mainstream more open-minded than others to new ideas and criticism of accepted practices. The problems of some practices – prescription of antibiotics for minor infections, for example – are now very widely accepted as storing up trouble for the future. Whale is not frank about its own position within this spectrum. A close investigation of the site reveals contradictory signs. The site has many pages of attributed quotations. There is no commentary by the webmaster to say how far he agrees/disagrees with the sentiment expressed, but the general tendency of the quotes is supportive of an 'alternative medicine' perspective. On particular issues such as the MMR/autism link, the only material provided does indicate belief in such a link. References to work disputing the link are critical ones. For example, Whale publishes the testimony of Bernard

Rimland, PhD (who was a consultant on the film *Rain Man* because of his expertise in the field of autism) which criticizes Taylor et al. (1999) – an epidemiological study which found no link between MMR and autism. No space is given for voices in support of Taylor et al. while the converse is true of the earlier research by Andrew Wakefield and his colleagues (Wakefield 1998). Although this research was extensively criticized, on this site it is defended.

The webmaster's preference for quotation without commentary does not mean that he has no position. He is after all responsible for the selection of the various fragments brought together and assembled here. Nothing he selects is supportive of vaccination in general or of MMR in particular. But while some of his selections support a case against MMR because of its link with autism, others support a case against MMR because of links with other conditions, or indicate opposition to vaccination generally because it compromises the development of immune responses via encounters with 'wild' bacteria and viruses. Further selections on this site indicate a philosophically grounded critique of western medicine as a project; others suggest that western medicine's ideals are fine, but compromised by the profit motive and the large drug cartels. There is no 'worldview' in which all of these lines of argument can be supported without contradiction. The 'God as Modern Medicine' page is the furthest away from orthodoxy. It offers the following undated quotation from Mahatma Gandhi:

> I was at one time a great lover of the medical profession . . . I no longer hold that opinion . . . Doctors have almost unhinged us . . . I regard the present system as black magic . . . Hospitals are institutions for propagating sin. Men take less care of their bodies and immorality increases . . . ignoring the soul, the profession puts men at its mercy and contributes to the diminution of human dignity and self control . . . I have endeavoured to show that there is no real service of humanity in the profession, and that it is injurious to mankind . . . I believe that a multiplicity of hospitals is no test of civilization. It is rather a symptom of decay.

That the webmaster includes this quote is no evidence that it represents his opinion as well as Gandhi's. It is published on the same website which also offers texts that seem to approve the processes of peer review which originally allowed Andrew Wakefield's research past the gatekeepers of scientific reliability/integrity (Wakefield's integrity was only much later, in 2004, called into question by his publisher). *The Lancet* operates firmly within the medical establishment as Gandhi would have perceived it – a perpetuator of sin, a symptom of decay. Whale's chosen discourse fragments do not cohere epistemologically: the coherence is 'confrontational' or agonistic. There is space for a quote or an example or a testimony if it goes against official views. There is only space for an official voice when embedded within the voice of someone taking issue with it.

Newsgroups and MMR/autism

The material

The data reviewed for this chapter cover a similar but slightly shorter period than the data examined in connection with mobile phones. The earliest message was 1 October 1995 and the most recent (the cut-off point) was July 2003. Table 6.1 gives a crude picture of the amount of Usenet traffic (counted in threads) for this period.

The figures for 2001–2003 in Table 6.1 (shown in italics) are *projections*, based upon the rate of growth of the Google 'hit list' with the same search parameters as for the previous years. The hit list produces too many messages to examine one by one, including vast numbers of single-message 'threads', threads which are off-topic more than they are on-topic, cross-posted threads and other complications. These estimates exclude all threads of fewer than three messages.

The distribution of these threads across different types of newsgroups can also be offered, though only for the years 1995–2000 (Table 6.2).

A subset of these threads was compiled for the purposes of closer analysis. Threads were chosen on the basis of their relevance to the

Table 6.1: Usenet threads about MMR and autism, 1995–2003

Year	Threads	Messages
1995	1	6
1996	9	42
1997	9	73
1998	27	441
1999	24	349
2000	48	1053
2001	*110*	*2750*
2002	*200*	*4000*
2003 Jan–July	*90*	*1800*
Total	**518**	**10514**

Table 6.2: Distribution of threads on MMR/autism by newsgroup type

Newsgroups	Number of threads	Example
Support groups for specific conditions, including autism.	50	alt.support.autism
Children's health and parenting	60	misc.kids.health
General health groups	8	uk.people.health
Science/medicine groups	4	sci.med
Regional groups	4	soc.culture.malaysia
Politics groups	1	alt.politics.british
Other groups	5	uk.rec.competitions
Total	**132**	

Note: Cross-posted threads have been double-counted.

topic, their spread across different types of newsgroup and their spread across the eight-and-a-half years of the period. Four hundred and forty people contribute messages to these 58 threads on the subject of MMR and autism – although 39 of these are off-topic. The highest number of on-topic contributions from any one participant is 55. Two hundred and twenty-six people contribute just one on-topic message.

Confidence and doubt

Table 6.3, admittedly a crude measuring instrument, is based on a classification of every message in the sample according to whether it talks up the risk, talks it down, expresses ambivalence by putting both arguments or doing none of these. It shows a degree of balance between negative and positive opinion on this subject.

Table 6.3: Orientation to risk in MMR threads

Orientation to risk	Number of messages	(%)
Talking up of risk	291	19
Talking down of risk	330	22
Putting both sides, i.e., ambivalent	47	3
Putting neither side, e.g., asking a question without presupposition	535	36
Total	**1203**	

'Confidence' and 'doubt' are not really the same thing as 'talking up' and 'talking down'. Talking up and talking down are two different kinds of confidence: confident belief that the vaccine is dangerous to children vs. confident belief that it is not dangerous. 'Doubt' is different from either of these. In this material, it is the position of most parents, not convinced either way substantively and thus influenced in their judgement, to vaccinate or not to vaccinate, by considerations which go beyond the medical science, such as a personal commitment to the precautionary principle for the non-vaccinators or faith in the authorities on the part of the vaccinators.

Here are examples of the voices of confident defender, the confident detractor and the doubter:

MMR messages no. 1 (2003) from a health group

> It has been with us years and there is not a link to autism nor to an 'overload' of the immune system.
> ARCHIVES OF DISEASE IN CHILDHOOD No evidence for immune system overload after triple jab MMR [Bacterial infections, immune overload, and MMR vaccine 2003; 88: 222–3]
> http://www.mmrthefacts.nhs.uk/news/newsitem.php?id=42
> Independent review for WHO finds no evidence of link between MMR and autism. http://www.mmrthefacts.nhs.uk/news/newsitem.php?id=41

MMR messages no. 2 (2002) on a support newsgroup

> If I had known then what I know now, my children would have never had immunizations. 'They' try to tell us that there is no connection to autism but I am totally convinced.

MMR messages no. 3 (1998) on a support newsgroup

> Just as we learned from the 89–91 outbreak, there are things about the vaccine that we just don't know. We didn't know the immunity would not last a life time. We don't know what measles virus can do in every case to every *body.* I want the research to continue.

In practice the two kinds of 'confident' voice are less absolute than the above characterization suggests. Each side has to qualify its position. Confident detractors qualify themselves in recognizing that not all of those who receive the vaccine will become autistic, and that the treatment is intended to be positively beneficial to health, in protecting the individual and the herd from infectious diseases. The confident defenders qualify themselves in recognizing that the MMR vaccine can be dangerous in other ways besides the specific risk of autism which is the focus of concern in the public debate. As with other vaccines, MMR may be 'contra-indicated' in certain circumstances.

How much reading and information seeking any of these newsgroup participants has done is impossible to know, and so too is the quality of the sources they have read, from a scientific or a public information perspective. But people represent themselves as well-informed or ill-informed. The avowedly well-informed may nevertheless still diverge in their support for MMR vaccination, and may even present themselves, after looking into the issue, as more confused than they were to begin with.

Associations and comparisons

This was the third of the case studies to be researched, and in starting to examine the material there was strong sense of déjà vu. It was very much a case of 'the usual suspects'. For those wanting to play down the MMR/autism link the formula was a comparison with other lifestyle hazards, especially driving a car.

MMR messages no. 4 (2002) on a children/parenting newsgroup

> Reason #4 [against the substitution of MMR by three separate injections]: The extra trips by car to the doctor's office will increase by at least 100% the exposure the child has to the largest killer of children – auto accidents.

Another rhetorical strategy which sometimes accompanies the strongest form of risk denial is that of the 'ludicrous comparison'. Fear of autism from the MMR vaccine makes as much sense as fearing attack from a pack of tigers:

MMR messages no. 5 (1998) on a children/parenting newsgroup

> By being inside the doctor's office for the amount of time required to receive the vaccine, you are sparing your child the slight theoretical risk that a pack of tigers could rush down the street during that time.

Denying that MMR is safe because those who say so have only established no evidence of risk, is captured in the following vignette:

MMR messages no. 6 (2002) on a children/parenting newsgroup

> If you were running in from a hailstorm and made it into a hotel lobby and someone said, 'Whew, we'll be safe in here,' would you reply, 'No, a chandelier or something could fall on us inside! Or there could be a terrorist attack or a robbery in here?' No, you'd know what he meant and shut up about it.

Those in the rhetorical business of talking up the risk opted for comparisons with smoking, using thalidomide or eating beef. These comparisons focused not on risk statistics but on the role of government and its agencies in purveying reassurance:

MMR messages no. 7 (1999) on a support newsgroup

> On radio 5 last week there was a lady doctor representing the government who was earnestly assuring us how safe the vaccine was & that individual vaccines were not available & were not effective.
>
> She finished off by assuring us that she had had her own children vaccinated, this is shades of the agriculture secretary feeding his own children beefburgers on national TV at the height of the BSE scare.

MMR messages no. 8 (2002) on a miscellaneous newsgroup

> My mother was offered thalidomide as a cure for morning sickness when she was pregnant with me. Thankfully she refused it. The medical profession don't always get it right.

MMR messages no. 9 (2002) on a miscellaneous newsgroup

> I can of course see your point – however, in the 50s there were another bunch of scaremongerers, who, at the time, insisted that 'smoking was potentially dangerous' – they were of course rubbished for the lack of evidence at the time.

The general theme is that of the unreliability of government speech:

MMR messages no. 10 (2003) on a miscellaneous newsgroup

> I would dearly love to trust the government experts who say MMR is safe, that CJD is not related to BSE, that there were weapons of mass destruction in Iraq all set to destroy us in 45 minutes, that genetically modified crops can be safely tested with only 20 metres separating them from commercial crops. Really I would, but there is plenty of evidence to suggest that we're told whatever is expedient to be told.

One dimension of comparison works differently here than in the other two cases. Because vaccination is, in intention, beneficial to individuals in helping to protect them against the diseases of measles, mumps and rubella, and the potential further consequences of these diseases such as sterility in men and foetal abnormality in the unborn babies of women, parents have to weigh the extent of their fear of autism against the extent of their fear of the diseases. Such is the advice offered to parents confronting this decision, and also by parents themselves:

MMR messages no. 11 (2002) on a children/parenting newsgroup

> There is no reliable evidence that the vaccine causes autism. It is almost impossible to 'prove' that something is safe so this may be as good as we ever get here. There is lots of evidence that Measles can cause death and disability. Hence if your choice is MMR or nothing then MMR is the way to go unless your child has exceptional medical circumstances.

MMR messages no. 12 (2002) from a children/parenting newsgroup

> Whether there is any link between autism, Crohn's and MMR is (to me) still unproven. However, even if there is a link you have to consider the comparative risks. 6/1000 children suffer from ASD – only a fraction of those lay the blame at the door of MMR. 1/100,000 children suffer a severe reaction to MMR, the majority with no long-term effects. However, 1/20 children with measles will catch pneumonia, and 1/1000 will develop encephalitis. 1/1000 children who catch measles will die.
> To me, the risks of autism were far outweighed by the risks of the MMR [sic].

In weighing these factors, parents do not always conclude in favour of MMR:

MMR messages no. 13 (2002) on a health newsgroup

> nobody can really help you make this choice. I made the choice not to let my children have the MMR or single vaccines as I felt that I could not live with artificially induced damage to my children. As a result they have had all their childhood illnesses and come through very healthy. I could only make that choice because I felt fairly certain that as well nourished children they had the best chance of getting through without complications (compared to children in the third world). I made a different choice when it came to polio and tetanus.

Arguments

Newsgroup discourse about MMR and autism is not just concerned with the arguments about the risks, ethics and politics of the debate. Some part of it is also for sharing knowledge and advice. In the British context for example, one parent may help another to find a doctor willing to administer single vaccines rather than the combined MMR one, and in the American context, parents suggest ways around the requirement that children be certified as vaccinated in order to enter school.

MMR messages no. 14 (2001) on a regional (local) newsgroup

> Try News web sites like BBC, search on stories of GPs who offer single doses, and then try search on their names, or try to get their practice contacts from a central authority.

MMR messages no. 15 (1999) on a support group

> you could have your child screened to see if he is already immune to measles mumps and rubella, and if so, you can forgo the mmr shot. Prior to this I had never known you could do this. I may not have had my son vaccinated if I'd known.

Yet there is, on balance, more disagreement/argument than there is support of this kind, and it can be vitriolic. As in the other case studies, when Usenet participants discuss MMR their disagreements can be extremely combative. Flaming is common, and includes a lot of name calling and abuse, as well as criticism of other people's views which tends towards the blunt.

MMR messages no. 16 (1999) on one children/parenting newsgroup and one science newsgroup

> In direct response to a post which includes citations and abstracts of studies that show MMR is not related to autism, all you can offer is a paraphrase of a 'study,' and then you pretend you won't post the citation because we're supposed to be delighted to find it ourselves. The usual tactic of a defenceless know-nothing such as yourself.

In terms of politeness theory (Brown and Levinson 1987), many contributions would be best characterized as 'bald, on-record' performances of the face threatening act of disagreeing:

MMR messages no. 17 (2003) on a regional (local) newsgroup

>I'm not a doctor, or a parent, but, what if you are playing Russian
>Roulette by not having your child treated to NHS & WHO
>standards.
xxxxxxxxxxxxxxxxxxxxxxxxxxxxxxxxxxxxxxxxxxxxxxxxxxxx
I AM having him inoculated, he will have the three covers. So, no you are wrong to say it is not to WHO standards. As for the NHS, a group now based upon cost downs, not the best service. The only reason for the triple jabbing pushed by the NHS is the cost line.

This degree of bluntness is not universal: there are many messages in which disagreement is mitigated by negative or positive politeness. People may disagree about the merits of vaccination but work to find common ground in the principle that parents have to make their own decisions:

MMR messages no. 18 (2002) on a children/parenting newsgroup

To me, the risks of autism were far outweighed by the risks of the MMR [sic]. Both my children are vaccinated, after much deliberation and soul searching. I don't think that the separate vaccines are much better – the studies I have read indicate that it is the measles component that is most often blamed for this alleged link, not necesarily having the triple vaccine.
Good luck with your decision.

Disagreements among people in their role as parents and thus with a very personal stake in the argument are less confrontational than arguments between participants who are not currently personally involved. There is a degree of mutual respect for the 'responsible attitude' of taking the decision seriously. The following message comes after earlier ones from parents who did vaccinate:

MMR messages no. 19 (2001) on two children/parenting newsgroups

Not wanting to start a debate, but I chose not to immunize my two children, they are now 4 years and 2 years, very healthy and very rarely sick, in fact my 4 year old had his first tummy bug a week ago and was very frightened when he vomited as he had never done this before, Anyway my view on it is I am neither for or against it as the evidence on both ends of the stick is so variable, but chose not to as in my view the risks of a reaction were too high, versus, no immunization, no reactions, just a childhood illness that can be treated if caught early.
No offence anyone

But even among concerned parents, arguments can become hostile when the discussion focuses more upon interpretation of research findings, or on to the possible effects of promoting one particular view:

MMR messages no. 20 (2003) on one health newsgroup

>>Some may even be driven to find out _HOW_ it is possible for
>>any vaccine to be used on every toddler in the country before
>>all ingredients have been rigorously tested and justified.
xxxxxxxxxxxxxxxxxxxxxxxxxxxxxxxxxxxxxxxxxxxxxxxxxxxx
>Stop spreading your fears on others xxx. You are deliberately
>endangering other people's children by propagating such
>unfounded rubbish. We can only hope that a child is not harmed
>by your advice.
xxxxxxxxxxxxxxxxxxxxxxxxxxxxxxxxxxxxxxxxxxxxxxxxxxxx
Perhaps xxx can tell us where, when and for how long MMR was tested prior to licencing?

The free-rider – who does not immunize whilst everyone else does – can come in for criticism too. Whatever his or her motives, if the herd is immune the unvaccinated benefit. The vaccinated (or their parents) may object:

MMR messages no. 21 (2002) on a children/parenting newsgroup

> Considering that my child will be fully immunized and yours not and because vaccines are not 100% effective, your child poses a risk to mine. I don't like that. Do you think it's fair?

Threads become hostile too when a participant is suspected of writing as the mouthpiece of some lobby:

MMR messages no. 22 (2000) on one health group, one science group and one children/parenting group

> xxx, the point is simple, if someone does a study that shows that vaccines are safe, you, and your bleating and braying chorus, would whine that it was prejudiced, as the findings do not support your idle conjecture.

In message 22 it is the opponents of MMR who are seen as a collective, but the opposite also occurs:

MMR messages no. 23 (1999) on a children/parenting newsgroup and a science newsgroup

> Know-nothing defenders of the medical establishment are out in force with either ridiculous non-sequitur arguments (comparing autism with teething fevers) or relying on the fox to investigate the hen house (establishment med group juggles statistics to come up with the same pro-MMR pronouncement they made before the study).

Some parents recognize that there are vested interests on both sides:

MMR messages no. 24 (2000) on a children/parenting newsgroup

> So far, I have found lots of information published by 'firmly planted' people – the government firmly insists that vaccines are safe, the Autism Research Institute firmly believes there's a link. Who do I believe? Myself, when I've looked good and hard at their numbers.

The idea that, where there is dispute, the voices of many experts ought to outweigh the lone voice of a single expert does not necessarily sway readers towards majority opinion. A critic can always say that the majority are simply ignoring that which does not fit their paradigm.

MMR messages no. 25 (1998) on a support group

> Childhood vaccination against measles, mumps and rubella (MMR) is not linked to autism and bowel disease, a panel of medical experts said Tuesday. Thirty-seven doctors and scientists who gathered in London for a one-day meeting to discuss the latest research said there was no proof of any link between the triple MMR jab and the disorders, nor any reason to change vaccination policy. The Medical Research Council, an independent charity, convened the meeting of experts at the request of Britain's chief medical officer after research suggested a MMR vaccination could be associated with the illnesses.
>
> Comment: To these doctors I say BAH HUMBUG! They think they won the battle but don't realize the war is over with (just beginning). Wait till they start seeing the upcoming articles coming out. Parents, Keep your eyes on the Lancet at: http://www.thelancet.com
>
> I wonder why these guys don't call for further research instead of denying this research that has come out by Dr. Wakefield. Could it be they are afraid to look into it? Hummmm.

Sources

In these discussions, as with the previous case studies, people base their knowledge on a wide range of sources, including what they are told by members of their social network. The picture, in relation to the sample, is as in Table 6.4; the total is greater than 58 because some threads make use of more than one type of reference.

Table 6.4 comes with the usual reservations about the widely divergent types of 'reference' which it encompasses. The majority are references to specific web pages, scientific papers, research articles and so on. Some are vaguer references in the style of 'I saw a report recently . . .' without more information, and some are generic references to the unworthiness of 'the media' in their treatment of this issue, or comments to the effect that 'Science has shown . . .' It does show that the World Health Organization does not play nearly as high-profile a role

Table 6.4: Type of reference in MMR/autism threads

Type of reference	Number of threads
Popular/mass media references	54
Science/medicine/health references	
World Health Organization	10
Other science/health/medicine references	30
Databases (Medline)	11
Governmental references	
CDC	22
Other governmental references	18
Support/lobby groups and other non-governmental organizations	31
Commercial (drug manufacturers)	15
Miscellaneous, including personal web pages	4

in relation to this issue as it does in relation to the SARS debate: undoubtedly this is because of the very central role that the WHO played as both a participant and a source of information in relation to SARS, such that most secondary reports were necessarily drawing information from the WHO anyway. The CDC in contrast retains a prominent role, and so too do support/lobby groups and other non-governmental organizations: this category includes, for example, the NVIC (National Vaccination Information Center) in the USA, largely sceptical about vaccination in general; JABS (Justice, Action, Basic Support), a campaigning organization in the UK, as well as Whale.

Using and evaluating the mass media. References to the mass media as a source of information are more prevalent for this case study than for either of the other two. References to 'the media' in general, or to particular kinds of media, or to particular programmes/newspapers, or to particular episodes/articles, occur in almost every thread. This is not surprising – the topic has been as 'high profile' as SARS, although not in such a concentrated way and over a much longer period of time.

Although it is often difficult to tell which country someone is in when they post to a newsgroup, the fact that many of these groups have 'uk' as part of their name, the fact that many participants talk about their GP rather than their physician or paediatrician, and mention the NHS in their messages, does help in assigning people to countries. On that basis, UK contributors seem to be as well represented in this material as US contributors, or better, with contributors from other countries very much marginalized by comparison, although a few Australians and New

Zealanders also feature in the material. This supports Lewis and Spears' (2003) claims that the British are responding to mass media attention. From the USA there are complaints about *lack* of media attention to important developments:

MMR messages no. 26 (1998) on a support newsgroup

> I don't know anything about Dr Wakefield's study. Why is there nothing in the media, why is there nothing to read, does this study even exist??? It really makes me wonder, because I've been trying to find out what Dr Wakefield said. And there's nothing. Is it just a rumour???

Lewis and Spears credit the mass media with popularizing the idea of the single vaccine as a safer alternative to MMR. Certainly, the single vaccine option is much discussed in this material, both favourably and unfavourably, in comparison with MMR. But this discussion takes place not only among British newsgroup participants, who have been subjected to high-profile mass media coverage, but also by participants writing from the United States where there has been much less public concern about the combined vaccine. It is likely that in the USA there is more of a 'grass roots' network, protesting and avoiding the MMR vaccine in favour of single vaccines, and sensitized through this network to pay attention to what media coverage there may be, even if it is not much, or not sustained – as in example 30 below.

MMR messages nos 27 (2003) and 28 (2002) from British contributors on a variety of newsgroups

> a) So given two alternatives, one to toe the government line that 'it is safe' and hope like hell my child isn't one of the rare cases who presents with regressive autism after MMR, or find out about separate vaccinations and the concomitant risks and go that route, knowing that if sometime in the future it turns out there IS a causative link, at least I've done what I can to mitigate the risks, then we chose to 'play it safe' as we evaluated it. We weren't 'taken in by this charlatan', we saw the same numbers (which the IOM and the UK MCA don't refute) and saw the same possibility of at least an association.

xxxxxxxxxxxxxxxxxxxxxxxxxxxxxxxxxxxxxxxxxxxxxxxxxxxx

b) People have every right to be able to choose single vaccines for their children if they wish to, without the State forcing them to have triple vaccines to save money.

MMR messages nos 29 (2002) and 30 (2000) from American contributors on support groups

a) I think I may possibly do things a little differently should we have another child, like start at 15 months, and have the shots given separately. Just to be on the safe side.

xxxxxxxxxxxxxxxxxxxxxxxxxxxxxxxxxxxxxxxxxxxxxxxxxxxx

b) I am putting off the mmr until my xxx is 2 and then she will get it in 3 separate doses. There was a spot on 60 minutes that interviewed the British researcher who has done the research. He spoke about his findings, and there does seem to be a correlation between the mmr and autism. He really believes that the mmr would be safe if given in 3 separate doses, that it is the combination that makes it unsafe.

There is a generalized critique of 'the media' as a source of misinformation working alongside a pragmatic reliance, by detractors, defenders and the doubtful, upon the mass media as a source of information:

MMR messages no. 31 (2001) on two children/parenting newsgroups

>many people think that Measles is a fairly innocuous disease, but
>it can be a killer. About 3 in 1000 cases result in death (higher
>in children), and while most survive unscathed a number will
>suffer permanent side effects, which can include severe brain
>damage.

xxxxxxxxxxxxxxxxxxxxxxxxxxxxxxxxxxxxxxxxxxxxxxxxxxxx

my newspaper (express) yesterday said 1 in 5000 for children

The generalized critique is most often mounted by the defenders of the vaccine:

MMR messages no. 32 (2003) on a miscellaneous newsgroup

> What I object to is newspapers hyping this to sell copy and causing people who can't afford single jabs to not have any vaccinations at all.

But those who are convinced that the vaccine is unsafe in this respect, or who are sceptical of official reassurance, will also find ways to blame the media:

MMR messages no. 33 (2001) on a local newsgroup

> I should imagine you are a Daily Mail reader, so probably have never read anything by Paul Foot, in my view Mr Foot has a somewhat less compromized view of the MMR situation, than many of the other media commentators, charged with regurgitating, gov press office pr nonsense.

What this last example also illustrates is that it is possible for newsgroup participants to offer some discrimination when talking about the press, even while finding it reprehensible overall. Paul Foot wrote for *Private Eye*, a satirical fortnightly magazine of some notoriety for its efforts in exposing scams. It is often in court doing battle in libel cases. The *Daily Mail* is a mid-market daily tabloid with a right-wing approach to politics. To see it as both right-wing and as supportive of the current (2003) British government is also to see that government as right-wing.

Using and evaluating the World Wide Web. There are in the region of 200 website links in this material, though some of these are off-topic. With the passage of time many of the specific links have disappeared – the web is a highly unstable textual environment. Sometimes entire sites disappear, sometimes it is just particular pages which vanish. For example:

MMR messages no. 34 (2000) on a science newsgroup, a health newsgroup and a children/parenting newsgroup

> 'We commissioned an OPV Vaccine Report and started making all kinds of other inquires. The OPV Vaccine report that we received was

a shocking report. It covered a recent period a little less than 5 years and the following is the summary for that period: The number of Vaccine Associated events that occurred: 13,641 . . . . The number of events resulting in death 540.' – The Polio Connection of America http://idt.net/~w1066/poliov1.html.

The idt.net site to which this link points still exists – it is a telecommunications company providing a wide range of services and products. One of its services is 'web hosting', that is, providing server space for other organizations. The 2002 quote indicates that one of the organizations which it hosted at that time was the Polio Connection of America. That too still exists, but in March 2004 its web space is now provided by 'geocities' (part of the Yahoo! enterprise) at http://www.geocities.com/w1066w/. However, anyone seeking to trace this quote back to its source would be frustrated even on finding the new site, lacking as it does a 'search engine' or an clearly identified archives section.

The best represented types of website are very conventional in character. Those belonging to national governments and their agencies are very well linked in: this includes the most referenced site of all, the CDC (Centers for Disease Control and Prevention) in the USA. In addition, online news organizations (particularly the BBC), the websites of non-governmental and campaigning organizations, such as JABS (Justice, Action, Basic Support) in the UK and the National Vaccine Information Center (NVIC) in the USA are strongly represented via hyperlinks in the newsgroup material.

Less well represented, although not overlooked, are commercial sites such as those maintained by drug companies manufacturing vaccines (Merck), search engines (Google, Yahoo) and databases (Medline). There are also web links to sites of a kind which seem, like the blogs discussed in the previous chapter, to owe their existence and function to the World Wide Web. One of these is the Whale site, discussed earlier in this chapter. It is the best referenced of all the websites in the newsgroup material. Of the 200 website links in this material, 27 of them are to this site. In contrast, there are six hyperlinks to the BBC website, and 14 to the CDC. Yet this does not mean that 'whacky science' is exerting excessive influence on popular opinion via the web. The important facts to note about this vast series of references to Whale are these: first, that the references are on a comparatively small number of threads – on seven threads out of 58. By contrast, the 14 hyperlinks to the CDC website are spread over 11 threads, and the six hyperlinks to the BBC website over five threads. In the second place, all but one of the references to Whale are introduced by the webmaster himself (the email address matches the address of the website). And in the third place, every contribution by this participant is robustly contested by other participants on the thread. Rarely are there any like-minded participants on these threads: those who do contribute are also challenged.

MMR messages no. 35 (2000) on two children/parenting newsgroups

>Disintegrative psychosis is recognized as a sequel to measles
>encephalitis. Viral encephalitis can give rise to autistic disorders,
>particularly when it occurs early in life. *Wing L, The autistic
>Spectrum London Constable, 1996>pg 68–71
>http://www.whale.to/Vaccines/encephalitis.htm
xxxxxxxxxxxxxxxxxxxxxxxxxxxxxxxxxxxxxxxxxxxxxxxxxxx
Warning: The whaleto site sited above is a site that has poor quality information in it. The author even refuses to put his name on the site.
However, xxx does make a good point. If you prevent encephalitis from measles, you may DECREASE the incidence of autism. However, this would be mere speculation, just as xxx's claims are mere speculation.

There are other warnings against Whale as well, including this unsolicited one:

MMR messages no. 36 (2003) on a children/parenting newsgroup

Anyway, I'd check out the CDC web site. Ignore the 'whaleto' web site; it's chock full of mythology masquerading as science.

And another contributor describes the site as 'this anecdotal research blurb-form of cyber-terrorism disguised as heroic charismatic pop-sci'.

These are 'generic' criticisms of Whale, but there are some more specific points of critique as well. When the link to Whale is posted accompanying a quotation from someone else arguing the MMR/autism link, the objection is made that the reference is no more than an 'opinion' when what is needed is facts, or, as below, 'data':

MMR messages no. 37 (2000) on a children/parenting newsgroup, a health group and a science newsgroup

>'They claim that autism naturally occurs at about 18 months,
>when the MMR is routinely given, so the association is merely
>coincidental and not causal. But the onset of autism at 18
>months is a recent development. Autism starting at 18 months
>rose very sharply in the mid-1980s, when the MMR vaccine came
>into wide use. A coincidence? Hardly!' – Dr Rimland
>http://www.whale.to/v/rimland.html
xxxxxxxxxxxxxxxxxxxxxxxxxxxxxxxxxxxxxxxxxxxxxxxxx
Again you post a link to an opinion. You post that the incidence of autism rose sharply in the mid 80s. Where are the data that demonstrate that the population incidence rose sharply – not the uptake, not the diagnostics, but the actual incidence? Those are the data I am interested in, not some obviously biased individual spouting off about what he or she 'knows' to be the truth.

On all threads where this site is introduced, there is strong polarization of opinion of an often abusive character on both sides. Less committed voices mostly bow out of the discussion and leave it to the antagonists. Whether or not they continue to monitor discussion as 'lurkers' cannot be known.

Discussion

For many people writing about contemporary risk the real problem is *uncertainty*: not knowing whether a particular activity is risky or not and not knowing who to trust when some say one thing and some another. The difficulty about who to trust includes the mass media, which are as ever in the middle: they too are in the business of 'trust assessment', mediating trust by including/excluding particular voices; giving the same or different amounts of space to particular contributors and choosing different linguistic modalities ('say' versus 'claim' and so on) to report particular speech acts.

Uncertainty is certainly an issue in respect of the MMR scare. Lewis and Spears (2003) claim that aspects of mass media coverage contributed to that uncertainty, made it worse than it should have been. But at the same time they believe the mass media to be responsible for an inference on the part of the public that was *insufficiently* uncertain. There should, they believe, have been more emphasis given to the fact that *single* vaccinations were untested in respect of the autism risk. If the evidence on MMR was dubious, the evidence regarding single vaccines was nonexistent. The general public (in Britain) never understood that because they were never given the resources to do so by the mass media.

Let's imagine that people had been given the message 'single vaccines are untested' much more than they were, that they understood it and that it contributed to their construction of the issue. Would they then have allowed this *greater* uncertainty than in respect of MMR its full power to turn them against single vaccines as they had (in some degree) turned against MMR? If they had, then they would have been a step further along the road which leads to the land of Whale. Doubts about MMR are the first step, then come doubts about the single injections, then doubts about other injections (and other risks), then doubts about immunization programmes in general, then about pharmaceuticals in general, and eventually about the entire philosophy and practice of western medicine.

But as the Lewis and Spears study suggests, and mine strongly reinforces, very few people have gone all the way along this road and most have held quite a long way back, in a 'comfort zone', dependent upon western medicine and expecting it to 'work' most of the time. In Lewis and Spears' study, most people did not embrace doubts about the safety of single vaccines.

So what about the citizens who go 'past' the mass media for information about MMR and autism and seek as well (or instead) to use the internet? Are such people more likely to conclude that the single vaccine option is just a 'holding plan' without much intrinsic merit except to stop people worrying more? Will the web and other internet resources suggest to them that single vaccines are an answer to a non-problem? Or will the complexity and incoherence of the internet simply add to generalized confusion?

Generalizations are impossible while there is such a range of materials online but on balance the supporters of MMR probably have little to fear from the internet. Consider the evidence:

- Those who *actively* use the net to seek information and opinion about the safety of MMR in respect of autism have already gone beyond the 'misleading' mass media versions, suggesting their disinclination to trust such sources. Such people would be in a minority, so there is not necessarily any inconsistency here with Lewis and Spears' find-

ings which indicate a degree of real influence on the part of the mass media in respect of this issue.
- The search engine 'test' above uncovered more sites supportive of MMR vaccination than critical of it.
- The 'anti-MMR' websites are rather unconvincing, judged on design characteristics in relation to content.
- In Usenet groups, where the voice of the MMR critic can be a loud one, that voice almost always encounters challenge and resistance on the thread.

There is another side, which is the strong presence, here as in Lewis and Spears' material, of the view that single vaccinations are the solution to the problem. Not only is this option mentioned in many newsgroups' threads, it is often mentioned so as to *presume* the greater safety of the single jabs over the multiple one, as in threads asking where a parent should go to find a practitioner willing to administer the jabs separately. The Google search engine too fed into this parental strategy: some of the *sponsored* links on the first results page were from organizations offering single vaccinations for a price. This may be taken as further evidence of the power of the mass media.

To be sure, the 'pro-MMR' discourse on the internet cannot be guaranteed to make those who are uncertain more trusting of the vaccine, let alone altering the views of those who 'know' that MMR is dangerous. As this book has shown, and not just in this chapter, uncertainty can resist a lot of counter-discourse, especially if the harm which is the downside of getting it wrong is of an especially fearful kind. The point however was not so much to establish the persuasiveness of 'pro-MMR' discourse on the net, but rather to show that, quantitatively and qualitatively, the 'pro' case is well represented there, and has the potential, when mass media are found wanting, to act as a corrective. The persistence of the single vaccine solution indicates though that the mass media are not found wanting as much as they should be.

7
Constructions of Risk: Change, Conflict and Trust

The three case studies discussed above have some important similarities. Each involves an element of uncertainty. Each has been responsible for major news events; each has involved accusations that the mass media bear some responsibility for an unjustified level of public concern. Each involves issues about the responsibilities of national governments in protecting citizens from harm.

There are also significant differences between the three cases. In the case of SARS there is a very clear and obvious health effect. The deaths and illnesses caused by the new virus were communicated around the world. The mystery centred upon the biological nature of the disease organism (the pathogen), how it had come into being, how it had spread from victim to victim, what the future course of the disease might be. In the other two cases there are practices – using a particular technology, submitting to a particular medical intervention – and possible consequences – brain cancer, autism – but dispute and confrontation about whether there is any relation between the two. These two studies, although similar, also have differences. There is no obligation to use a mobile phone, but there is an obligation for children to be vaccinated against measles, mumps and rubella, although no absolute compulsion. Vaccination against these diseases is for the positive benefit of the individual, and is also good for the population as whole, helping to contribute to the eradication of the diseases within whole populations. Using a cellphone is a convenience not a therapy, even though there are circumstances where its health benefits may be considerable – calling an ambulance in an emergency is an obvious case of this.

These differences do have consequences for the ways in which the three issues are variously constructed through the World Wide Web and Usenet discussion. Again, the distinctiveness of the topic of SARS stands out in contrast with the other two. SARS as a news story erupted suddenly, without prior warning, during a period when the headlines had been otherwise preoccupied by another globally significant event – the war in Iraq. Usenet response to the news was very fast, on a very large scale, intense, and took place among online groups of widely disparate kinds. World Wide Web resources, apart from SARS Watch and the WHO resources, lagged a little bit behind the newsgroups. In contrast, the level of Usenet attention to the other subjects was more moderate in quantity, more sustained over time and conducted within narrower boundaries of interests. Usenet discussion of MMR in particular mostly takes place within rather obvious contexts such as the 'parenting' newsgroups. A little spills over into other groups, mostly when there are mass media stories to provoke it.

World Wide Web and health risks

Types of website

Each of the topics is quantitatively well served by the World Wide Web. Three important types of website with resources devoted to this subject are web-based news sites, official sites and unofficial sites. Web-based news sites offer news reports and include the websites of established news organizations like CNN and the BBC from the world of broadcasting, or the *New York Times* and the *Guardian* in the world of print journalism. Alternatively, web-based news reports might be posted by organizations like Yahoo News, restricted to the web alone for output, drawing on the same newswire copy as the traditional organizations, as well as on the output of those organizations. Both streams of web news are sustained in whole or in part by advertising revenue unless, like the BBC they are prohibited from doing so.

Official sites are the sites of organizations which have a specific remit in relation to the topic. These topics are all health-related, so the most obvious kinds of official site to show interest in SARS, in mobile phones and cancer or MMR and autism are those of institutions in the public health business. Apart from the World Health Organization, most of these institutions are national bodies with government funding (including their scientific branches), although there is also a respectable 'web presence' for non-governmental organizations. Commercial organizations also add to the available resources on the web. Aegisgard tries to make money by advertising its radiation protection shields online; Choice Healthcare Services advertises single-vaccine alternatives to MMR. But for legal reasons they have to be extremely circumspect in what they say about the potential of harm from the 'risky' product and the scope of the protection offered by their own. The purveyors of single vaccines in particular take their stand on the principle of 'parental choice' rather than engaging in any more explicit forms of promotional discourse.

Unofficial sites can vary enormously. In this material they are represented by the cellphone FAQ, Electric Words, SARS Watch, Wangjianshuo's blog and Whale. The cellphone FAQ can be regarded as unofficial, since it is the responsibility of a single individual. But this individual is an employee of an academic institution, the site carries the logo of that institution and its reputation, as well as that of the webmaster, is at risk if the information on the site is flawed. SARS Watch moves one more degree in the 'unofficial' direction. It is an individual's site, and designed on blog principles, that is, by date, but much of its information is drawn from the more official sites, especially that of the World Health Organization. The remaining three sites are even less official, but in quite different ways. Electric Words and Whale are, respectively, the respectable and the outrageous face of critique. Both of them set their face against the current majority/official view. But where Electric Words provides a reasoned though impassioned critique of that view, and restricts the critique to specific topics, Whale offers an eclectic collage of textual fragments to support an ethos of opposition to orthodoxy in medicine, to vaccination and to the MMR vaccine. Wangjianshuo's blog is not at all in the business of critique. It is the role of the individual also to offer the voice of experience, the view from the lifeworld. This lifeworld (as also in the newsgroup material) is not just a matter of recording daily experiences, but also of expressing *opinions* – without having the kind of responsibility that other voices do to turn those opinions into ones that readers can or should share.

The web clearly does provide a congenial channel of publicity for extreme voices of all kinds, surpassing anything available prior to the arrival of the internet. However, the evidence from these three studies overall suggests that the voice of orthodoxy and the mainstream view continues to maintain a much firmer web presence than any rival views. In some cases – for example, the Electric Words site – the rival view and the mainstream view share a considerable amount of their beliefs. If the Stewart Report is seen as belonging to the mainstream, its recommendation to keep children away from mobile phones until more is known is quite consistent with the precautionary approach promoted on this site. The MMR case study showed that the non-mainstream voice was struggling to make an impact online.

In coming to this conclusion it is important to remember that even if the defence of MMR has both quantity and quality on its side in respect of the World Wide Web materials, this is no guarantee that the sites defending MMR will be the influential accounts as far as readers are concerned. The problem is one of trust. If readers have reasons for not trusting the voice of government, of industry, of science, of the mass media, then it does not matter what those voices are saying (see Langford, Marris et al. 1999 on public health and trust). To explore the limits of trust it is necessary to examine the voices of those who watch television, listen to the radio, read newspapers and consult the World Wide Web. Some of these people are participants on Usenet and their accounts will be revisited below.[1]

Stability and change

In examining what the web makes available to its users, it is only possible to take a snapshot of provision at a given point in time. The fluidity of the web and the limited amount of public-access archives for superseded web resources means that accessing earlier versions of texts can be difficult or impossible. The question of editing/updating is one that confronts individual webmasters. On the one hand, times change and websites need to change with them; on the other hand, earlier material is not necessarily made redundant by newer information and ideas, and in any event, editing can be labour-intensive and a chore – it is worthwhile, particularly for sites maintained by individuals, to minimize the upkeep effort.

Some sites are designed so that newer versions of the same text need involve only clearly-identified additions, no substantive changes or deletions. Blogs (diary-style sites), discussed in Chapter 5, are of this kind. Thanks to this it is possible to see exactly when SARS Watch began (29 March 2003) and was 'mothballed' (8 June 2003):

> I've spent time researching what little is known about SARS, and I am alarmed about how little attention is being paid by the government and the media to the SARS epidemic. I've **written about it**, perhaps a bit hysterically, to several people who have much wider audiences than I do, hoping that they would focus in on it. They have declined to do so.
>
> Well, I have some time, I've been looking for an excuse to play with a new piece of **software**, it looks like there is a real need for getting more information about this epidemic more widely disseminated, and it seems like an opportunity to turn my formerly useless

> knowledge to some good. So I'm launching **www.sarswatch.org.** 29 March 2003.
>
> While I am grateful to the many people who contributed financially to SARS Watch Org, I have not received enough contributions to make working on SARS Watch Org full-time a reasonable proposition. Also, in spite of all the protests the last time I suggested closing SARS Watch Org, it is clear that the original impetus for the site, the lack of good sources of information about the disease, is no longer a reasonable concern. Finally, it is clear that the SARS epidemic is winding down, although it isn't clear how much this can be attributed to the public health efforts of the Chinese authorities, and how much to the seasonal life cycle of the virus. So I have decided to mothball SARS Watch Org. I will leave the site in as is, so it can serve as a historical record if anyone is interested in how the epidemic started. The links should still be useful, and the automatic **news** and **weblog** section will still be updated daily, but I am not going to read and write about SARS every day any more. June 8th 2003.

There are materials on this site other than the dated entries and if these have been changed during the life of the site, the editing has left no traces.

The World Health Organization deals with the problem of the past by maintaining a distinction between current materials and the searchable archive. It is someone's responsibility in Geneva or wherever the site is maintained to decide when a text has lost currency to the point that it can be assigned to the archive and becomes accessible only through that point of entry. This is not so very different from the blog approach, except that the principle of 'currency' which keeps particular links on the front page of the site is not the same as the arbitrary relentless procession of calendar dates. It is a more relative principle: an item's currency depends on relevant changes in the world. Two documents created on the same day may lose currency at different times thereafter. A report from a particular committee remains current until after the next committee meeting, while announcements about the nature of the pathogen depend upon the speed with which the scientific teams can establish new findings.

Another manifestation of the change/stability dynamic is apparent in the case of the cellphone antenna FAQ. This, like SARS Watch, can be seen as a text which allows additions but not deletions. Given the design principles of the site, around 'Frequently Asked Questions' concerning cell phone antennas and health risks, there is less reason for a non-deletion, non-change rule. In the case of a blog with entries tied to dates, the dates and their entries pass into history. In the case of an FAQ with entries tied to questions, it is possible to imagine questions changing as well as the answers to those questions. But it is easier and more revealing to add continuously rather than to edit. This also has the advantage of revealing research to be a process, cumulative in its findings, showing how one study follows on from a previous one. This particular FAQ begins with a 'What's New' section devoted specifically to the changes since the previous version. 'What's New' is a set of hyperlinks: the 'new' material itself is found within the main text. Typically a new item is a brief report on the findings of a piece of relevant research. Each such addition is placed within the FAQ in relation to the particular question which it helps to answer. Unlike a blog therefore this approach requires two edits of the text: one within the FAQ proper and one within the 'What's New' section. In the following version of a 'What's New' section from January 2004, only one of the bullet points indicates editing which involved changing text: all of the others involve addition to the previously existing text.

> What's New?
> v6.0, Jan 2004:

- Some out-dated references were removed and Q19C was reorganized.
- A fifth letter to the editor [216C] concerning the 2002 Utteridge et al report [197] that the 1997 mouse lymphoma study of Repacholi could not be replicated.
- A report [166] that mobile phone RF radiation had no effect on immune function in humans.
- A report [243] that mobile phone RF radiation had no 'substantial effects' on immune function in mice.
- A report [244] of subtle changes in the brain function (EEG) of mobile phone users.
- A report [245] that mobile phone RF radiation had no effect on learning in rats.
- A report [246] that mobile phone RF radiation had no effect on melatonin levels in rats.
- A report [248] that exposure of mammalian cells to RF radiation did not produce or enhance genotoxic injury unless the SAR exceeded 50 W/kg.

- The international committee working on revision of the IEEE C95.1 RF radiation standard published a set of 13 'white papers' that review the relevant biology and epidemiology [247].

The permanence of older material in the FAQ has a different rationale from the permanence of older material on SARS Watch. In a diary-style composition, entries remain because the past does not change. Each entry belongs to its moment in the past and always will. In the case of the FAQ, time is not the point. Entries persist not because of their place in history, but because they have been added to the permanent knowledge-base for this particular topic. For example, one much-cited study in this research is the Repacholi or Adelaide Hospital study of radiation-induced cancer in lymphoma-prone mice. The significance of this study for the debate is now fixed in the assessment of this webmaster, who has no need to rewrite his own comments on it thereafter. When other researchers try to replicate the results of the Repacholi study and fail, this too is recorded in the FAQ but as an addition: no revision of the earlier entry is required.

Usenet and health risk

SARS was by far the most popular of the three topics on Usenet, followed by MMR and then by cellphones. For the SARS study a month would have been long enough to assemble the 1000 messages required for the sample. For the other two studies, the collection period necessarily spanned years rather than months.

Quantifying the degree of interest is of some value but only when accompanied by an assessment of what people were saying and how they were saying it. They were asking questions, answering them, offering opinions and arguing, coming to the topic from something different, and moving off the topic when struck by other ideas. They joked, teased, pontificated, shared personal information, abused, expressed sympathy, and passed on relevant news from other sources. This is normal enough for any kind of conversation, online or otherwise. Much of this has had to be ignored in the present context, in order to focus upon what is of most interest for the present research: the range of opinion which is possible upon each of the topics, what happens to an expressed opinion in this interactive context, the range of information sources which are acknowledged by participants and the terms on which different sources are accorded the trust or distrust of Usenet participants. Two themes are explored below, one focuses upon divergence and dispute within Usenet and one focuses upon sources and trust.

Opinions in conflict

A survey questionnaire about people's opinions concerning the risk of autism from MMR might start with a proposition: 'children injected with the MMR vaccine are at greater risk from contracting autism than children who are not. Do you agree?' and offer three possible answers, inviting respondents to pick either 'yes', 'no' or 'don't know'. In the context of Usenet, it is possible to examine materials where people spontaneously offer their views on this and equivalent questions for the other topics, and where they do so in their own words. To classify these people, or these messages, as 'yes', 'no' and 'don't know' positions is much harder than with the simple 'check boxes' of the survey questionnaire. There is ambiguity and equivocation alongside more emphatic expression, as well as many contributions where the question is not relevant, and many where it is relevant, but tangential to the participant's central focus in his or her contribution. What looks 'messy' from a survey point of view is also where its value lies as a point of entry into the discourse of SARS, MMR and mobile phones. Rather than viewing messages simply as answers to a question along the lines indicated above, it is possible to examine them as speech acts, in the rhetorical business of 'talking up' or 'talking down' the postulated risk. And since the context is interactive, it is also possible to examine what happens in the encounters between divergent positions.

Accordingly, the preceding three chapters began by assessing the proportions of sampled messages which were engaged in talking up the risk or in talking it down. In each case the figures suggested about equal proportions of fearful voices and complacent ones. Perhaps this is not surprising in an interactive medium (people have more to say when there is something that they disagree about than when they are in accord) not to mention a medium which is thought to be congenial to confrontation.

Whether talking up the risk or talking it down some very similar strategies are adopted for each of the topics. Among those inclined to think that there is little or no risk of the proposed kind, 'blaming the media', generically, for its exaggeration of the danger is one of the most striking. The participants discussing SARS include many who wrote about 'the media' blowing the new illness up out of all proportion to its real significance as a disease – in comparison with major flu epidemics, with AIDS, with deaths from road traffic accidents and so on. Many of the participants discussing mobile phones wrote about the lack of scientific understanding for microwave radiation displayed by 'the media' in general (and sometimes by particular programmes or articles). Many of those discussing MMR wrote that, so far as the science was concerned, Andrew Wakefield's hypothesis *had* been refuted – it was only 'the media' which could not let go of such a controversial, newsworthy possibility. At the same time, in all three cases it is the mass media that people, on either side of the argument, rely on for their information, and in each of the studies, newsgroup participants constantly refer one another to the websites of news organizations for up-to-date input on the relevant topic. Much news citation is uncritical: but citation of specific *non-news* media sources (TV dramas, current affairs programmes, documentaries; in print, features and editorials) introduces a critical note.[2]

Another key similarity between the 'talkers up' and the 'talkers down' is in their preferred points of reference and comparison. The proportion of people who die and suffer injury in car accidents compares 'favourably' with the proportion at risk from injury by mobile phone, SARS infection and MMR injection for those disposed to play down the risk in each case; 'favourably' in the sense that the numbers are much, much higher with road traffic accidents than with these other 'risks'. In contrast, the relevant comparison for those disposed to take the opposite view is not just a matter of contrasting statistics: it involves, specifically, cases where the voice of authority (the government and/or the medical establishment – probably in affiliation with some industry) had proved itself untrustworthy in its reassurances. The 'reference event' function varies as between Britain and the USA. In Britain, the key reference event is the BSE/CJD affair of the 1980s and 1990s. In the USA it is the much longer history of the fight to establish smoking as a dangerous activity.

There is a real risk at stake in Usenet discussion, albeit one of a very different kind from those which are the substantive focus of the study. The real risk is the risk of loss of face. To express an opinion (in a face-to-face context) is to challenge the integrity of an interlocutor who disagrees with you and to risk loss of face yourself when you are confronted with their opposition. The invisibility of the actual face, not to mention most other attributes of personal identity in CMC has been an important research theme in this field of study. This invisibility may be one of the factors inducing more confrontational discourse – more 'flaming' – in CMC than in equivalent face-to-face exchanges. Even in Usenet however, disagreement need not be expressed agonistically. It can be managed with a show of politeness and mutual respect. Parents disputing the effects of the MMR vaccine were often respectful and laid considerable emphasis on the principle that the decision to vaccinate or not to vaccinate was ultimately a personal one.

Example no. 1 (2000) on a parenting newsgroup

I believe the measles vaccine has changed since xxx had it and I know the age at which it is given has changed. Lets make it crystal clear for the flame-throwers out there – I am not suggesting that you do not have your child vaccinated. I am not suggesting that MMR does cause Diabetes – I am simply saying that this is the experience I have had with my children. You have to decide what is best for your child but do so after getting all the information and advice you can get from various sources and then – whatever your decision – stick to your guns. Certainly if you decide against you may have to defend your position quite vigorously.
Best of Luck

Nevertheless, confrontation is very common in this material, descending into abuse in 45 per cent of all 195 threads. The following is characteristic of the most abusive end of the spectrum:

Example no. 2 (2003) from a miscellaneous newsgroup

>>SARS is being overhyped. It's only got a 4% fatality rate,
>>apparently, doesn't seem to be particularly contagious,
xxxxxxxxxxxxxxxxxxxxxxxxxxxxxxxxxxxxxxxxxxxxxxxxxxxxx
>BULLSHIT roomfuls people in the fucking emergency rooms
>were getting sick because one person with SARS happened to be
>sitting in the room. One SARS patient infected TWELVE
>DOCTORS and many other healthcare workers in a Chinese
>hospital. A woman traveled home from China with sars and
>infected her son when she got home and they both died. Don't
>make ridiculous claims like it's not 'particularly contagious'. IT'S
>CONTAGIOUS AS A MOTHERFUCKER THAT'S WHAT.
xxxxxxxxxxxxxxxxxxxxxxxxxxxxxxxxxxxxxxxxxxxxxxxxxxxxx
Go hide under you bed.
If you take a flashlight, the bogeyman might not come and get you.

Some abuse is not even provoked by disagreement between participants: someone asks a question and another participant finds the questioner so ignorant as to deserve insult:

Example no. 3 (2001) on a cellphone newsgroup

God u must be so stupid! Or are you just thick? Or just incredibly gullible? Didn't u ever go 2 school?

Disagreements on these threads tend to begin at the general level of whether there is or is not a health risk of the kind proposed. Some groups have sufficient expertise among the participants to allow them to take the debate on to a scientific and technological level:

Example no. 4 (1999) on a cellphone news group

>Actually, buried somewhere in that study released a couple years
>ago is a portion which noted higher tissue heating and higher
>possible genetic changes with digitally modulated signals, as
>opposed to analog modulation. Sorry, can't site the specific part
>of that study.
xxxxxxxxxxxxxxxxxxxxxxxxxxxxxxxxxxxxxxxxxxxxxxxxxxxx
This doesn't make any sense. I am an electrical engineer working in communications, so I have some input that contradicts that statement. Digital transmission is much more resilient to noise than analog transmission. Therefore, a digital transmission requires less signal power than analog. It is the transmitted signal that people fear could cause 'tissue heating' and 'genetic changes'. This is the main reason that the dual band phone show 2–3 times longer battery life in digital mode than analog.

'Informed dissent' of this kind usually puts an end to argument. No further protest is heard from the original contributor in this case. But the 'science' needed to produce this effect is *canonical* science/technology. It gets more difficult if participants attempt to draw upon science-in-the-making to support their arguments, especially if the science in question is epidemiological:[3]

Example no. 5 (1993) on a science newsgroup

>There seem to be several questions floating around here and
>getting mixed up. First is the question of whether non-ionizing
>radiation can have a carcinogenic effect.

>The evidence here seems to be piling up: the original
>Wertheimer-Leeper study has been confirmed a number of times
>(Tomenius, Savitz, London, Feychting, Folderus [occupational
>but ELF], a new Danish study [Olsen]) and a good sample of
>occupational studies, mainly of case-control design for brain
>cancer or leukemia. Then comes the question about particular
>emf exposures like cellular phones. Since there probably is a
>window effect for frequency and amplitude, I agree that the ELF
>studies do not necessarily implicate cellular phones. HOWEVER,
>most occupational and environmental carcinogens were first dis-
>covered by astute clinicians who saw something unusual. In this
>case I believe there was also a neurologist.
xxxxxxxxxxxxxxxxxxxxxxxxxxxxxxxxxxxxxxxxxxxxxxxxxx
Stuff seems to be piling up, but is it evidence? I assume that all of these are epidemiological studies with low incidence and various confounding factors?

In this case both participants display some expertise on the subject. Yet the question of 'evidence' is not restricted to participants on science newsgroups or who claim expertise in the manner of the second participant in example no. 4. In its many forms it is *the* issue across all of the material in the mobile phone and MMR case studies: a kind of 'pre-technical' debate informed by 'circumstantial' knowledge of science more than knowledge about particular studies and their methodologies. Here are some of the forms that it takes:

- Asking someone to provide evidence when someone makes a strong 'risk' claim, often with the implication that they can't – because there is none.

Example no. 6 (2000) on a cellphone newsgroup

>there is a non-thermal effect that is poorly researched, and
>that any risk is proportional to exposure. You don't dispute
>any of my assertions.
xxxxxxxxxxxxxxxxxxxxxxxxxxxxxxxxxxxxxxxxxxxxxxxxxx
Well I do. What is this 'non-thermal effect' and what evidence do you have of its existence?

Example no. 7 (1999) on a parenting newsgroup and a science newsgroup

>If you had attended the 'Biological Treatment of Autism
>Conference' a couple months ago in Orlando, you would have
>learned first hand from world class researchers and MDs how
>these vaccines, especially when given in triads, relate to
>autism and autoimmune diseases.
xxxxxxxxxxxxxxxxxxxxxxxxxxxxxxxxxxxxxxxxxxxxxx
Cites, please to the peer-reviewed, published studies of these 'world class researchers' showing a statistically robust, reproducible link between vaccine triads and autism.

- Telling someone that the evidence they are citing is unsatisfactory – usually because it is 'anecdotal' or else because it is a citation of an 'opinion' not of 'facts'.

Example no. 8 (2002) on a cellphone newsgroup

Anecdotal evidence is very unreliable, someone thinking a phone (or whatever) made them ill does not necessarily make it so. None of these claims have been substantiated and large scale studies have shown no evidence of damage. If the anecdotal evidence was plentiful _ and _ it was true the results would be measurable, they are not.

Example no. 9 (1999) on a children/parenting newsgroup

>>This view was endorsed by editorials in both of Britain's
>>leading medical 'journals. The hypothesis rests on clinical
>>anecdote [that is, Dr Wakefield's description of 12 cases]
>>rather than an epidemiologically sound base (statistics),'
>>observed Dr Angus Nicoll in the British Medical Journal,
>>adding, 'Chance alone dictates that some cases [of autism]
>>will appear shortly after vaccination.'
xxxxxxxxxxxxxxxxxxxxxxxxxxxxxxxxxxxxxxxxxxxxxx
>It is amazing how these experts can say with a straight face,
>when confronted with evidence, that there is no evidence.

xxxxxxxxxxxxxxxxxxxxxxxxxxxxxxxxxxxxxxxxxxxxxxxxx
There is 'evidence' of twelve anecdotal reports. However, to derive a cause and effect relationship, one needs far better evidence than that. Twelve cases could occur by random chance, considering how many kids are vaccinated.

Example no. 10 (2000) on one parenting newsgroup, one science newsgroup, one health newsgroup

>'They claim that autism naturally occurs at about 18 months,
>when the MMR is routinely given, so the association is merely
>coincidental and not causal. But the onset of autism at 18
>months is a recent development. Autism starting at 18 months
>rose very sharply in the mid-1980s, when the MMR vaccine
>came into wide use. A coincidence? Hardly!'–Dr Rimland.
>http://www.whale.to/v/rimland.html
xxxxxxxxxxxxxxxxxxxxxxxxxxxxxxxxxxxxxxxxxxxxxxxxx
Again you post a link to an opinion. You post that the incidence of autism rose sharply in the mid 80s. Where are the data that demonstrate that the population incidence rose sharply – not the uptake, not the diagnostics, but the actual incidence? Those are the data I am interested in, not some obviously biased individual spouting off about what he or she 'knows' to be the truth.

- Offering the proposition that 'no evidence of risk' is not the same as 'no risk'. This is the argument favoured by those in the business of talking up the risk.

Example no. 11 (2002) on four politics newsgroups

'At the moment, there is no scientific support for introducing any sort of limitation either on use of mobile phones or setting new safety limits.'
They are trying to tell us that lack of proof of damage is the same thing as proof of no damage.
They can say that no dangers were found – because they haven't looked!

Example no. 12 (1999) on a children/parenting newsgroup

Public health officials unblinkingly aver that there's no 'proven' casual [causal] relationship between vaccination and death. *Literally* correct, perhaps; the pivotal word being' proven.' What ISN'T stated, however, is that there's also no proof (i.e., it hasn't been 'proven') that vaccines DON'T cause death.

- Conceding that 'no evidence of risk' is not the same as 'no risk', or that 'you can't prove a negative', while protesting that 'evidence of no risk' is an impossible demand.

Example no. 13 (1995) on one science and one cellphone newsgroup

This is why us microwave types get nuts at the cries of fear and danger. We can't rule out an *unknown* effect, but the known effects ARE ruled out, and the level of evidence for some unknown process are pretty lousy small.

Sometimes this line of argument is converted into a *reductio ad absurdum* form. Since you cannot prove a negative, you can also not prove that 'milk' does not cause autism – or even 'breathing' – so the parent who is operating on the logic of avoiding everything where risk has not been completely eliminated as a possibility must, to be consistent, avoid those too.

Example no. 14 (2002) on a children/parenting newsgroup

>My son is 3 years old and as yet has not had his MMR vaccine,
>I have had several conversations with my doctor, and they
>still say he must have the vaccine and they wont give it
>separate. The reason is that two young children in my direct
>family (cousin's) have had the MMR vaccine and both has
>been diagnosed with Autism, one is in primary 4 now but has
>been to several special schools, I do not want to take the
>chance that my son could end up with Autism.
xxxxxxxxxxxxxxxxxxxxxxxxxxxxxxxxxxxxxxxxxxxxxxxx
Have they both eaten peanut butter sandwiches and drank milk? Better avoid those too just to be safe. Oh yeah, and whatever you do – don't let them breathe, everyone with autism breathes.

Newsgroup discourse can be used to explore not just overt disagreements, such as the above, but also aspects of conflict which are 'below the line' and which contribute in a different way to construction of meaning, as discussed in the cellphone chapter in relation to the use of the 'brain frying' image and in the SARS chapter over the legitimacy of the term SARS itself and its place in the lexicon of disease (see also Launspach 2000; Hellsten 2003).

The limits of trust

The vast majority of people who have to make decisions one way or another about their own behaviour in relation to a particular 'risk' do not have the technical knowledge to assess the available research evidence on its own terms. So it is not surprising that much discussion and debate turns upon which sources are worthy of public trust and which are not.

The MMR issue and the mobile phone issue are similar in that both have become structured as an opposition between a majority/mainstream view and a minority/fringe view. The mainstream view is broadly confident of the safety of the technology: the fringe view is the sceptical one, although the boundary line between mainstream and fringe is hard to pin down. What this structure produces is a perspective in which the majority view comprises voices from industry, science, government and the medical professions which are seen, collectively, to form a unity, with the same information to convey:

$$\text{There-is-no-evidence-of-}\left\{\begin{array}{l}\text{cancer-}\\ \text{autism-}\end{array}\right\}\text{from-}\left\{\begin{array}{c}\text{mobile-phones}\\ \text{MMR vaccine}\end{array}\right\}$$

Does this unity, this 'Medical Establishment', also include the mass media? Not necessarily. Mass media accounts may be represented and used as the chink in the armour of orthodoxy. Hence the attacks on 'the media' by proselytizers for the majority/mainstream view: hence also the penchant for citation of sympathetic media accounts by risk promoters. To attack the mass media is to perceive them as having voices in their own right, rather than acting as a channel for other voices. This distinction is not a firm one since one way in which mass media can exercise power is in the way that they include/exclude particular voices and amplify or downplay those which they do include. Whether citation in the mass media detracts from or adds to credibility is an issue in its own right.

The pillars of orthodoxy are susceptible to representation as a 'They . . .' whose interests make them culpably blind to the rationality of the fringe account. What 'They' say cannot therefore be trusted. One (MMR) participant puts up the following resistance to a newspaper report on a scientific study, the report and the study being both generally anti-risk:

Example no. 15 (2001) on a politics newsgroup

What a load of bull, I know what to believe, would not trust these people that say there's no connection.
Our government have a lot to lose by admitting there's a correlation.

Usually the wording in most messages where the risk is 'talked up' is less vague than this. The government, the industry, the medical profession, the scientists, are independently 'named and shamed'. The heavy reliance by doubters and critics upon the BSE and smoking analogies, discussed elsewhere, points the finger of suspicion principally at the government. Governments take their responsibilities to the profitability of industry more seriously than their public health responsibilities; industrialists wield (economic) power over governments and not the other way around. There are also numerous messages claiming that particular research, or all of it, is not independent but has been paid for by the industry, and cannot be trusted for that reason.

Example no. 16 (1995) on one science and one cellphone newsgroup

>A recent court case in FLA was settled when studies confirmed
>that there are no detectable affects on human tissue caused by
>cellular radio waves. You might check the biology news groups
>for more info.
xxxxxxxxxxxxxxxxxxxxxxxxxxxxxxxxxxxxxxxxxxxxxxxxxxxx
Studies conducted by who and for what organization? These kinds of studies require a much more flexible methodology than the hard sciences (i.e. physics, chem.) and hence can usually be manipulated to confirm a multitude of hypotheses. E.g. in the 70s the tobacco industry was producing 'studies' that showed there was no relationship between smoking and cancer and the Power companies have done the same. So if these so-called 'studies' were paid for by the Cellco and telecom manufacturers, I'd look at some work from an independent agency before making any strong conclusions.

Example no. 17 (2001) on a local newsgroup

> Sadly most of the 'research' concerning MMR has been carried out by (or sponsored by) drug companies directly involved. This type of 'research' is how the rBST genetically engineered hormone treatment, for cattle got approval in the USA (and here now maybe). He who pays the piper calls the tune perhaps?

There is also, especially in relation to mobile phones, a lot of argument in which scientific facts and findings are discussed on their own terms. This exercise would lack any purpose if either of the arguers believed that scientists were simply producing the results which their paymasters had bought from them. This applies rather less to the SARS case study than it does to the other two because of the different components which were in the public domain in this case.

There is further evidence in this material against the existence of a widespread conspiratorial or radically sceptical frame in the fact that the doubters as well as the defenders on the MMR issue and the mobile phone issue are interested in pulling 'science' on to their side of the argument. In both cases this is an unequal struggle because the weight of opinion and argument favours the defenders of mobile phones and MMR vaccine. But there is extensive belief in the *possibility* of scientific truth so long as scientists are truly independent, and resources are provided for research to continue. The following illustration shows how far the conspiratorial line can be pushed.

The subject line in one MMR message reads: 'I think this is great news' and the message that follows offers a hyperlink to a news report of an epidemiological study in California with more evidence against the idea of an MMR/autism link. This message is posted to an autism support newsgroup in 2001, where participants have spent many years trying to get the link taken seriously. Unsurprisingly therefore the 'great news' spin is resisted by applying a sceptical interpretative frame:

Example no. 18 (2001) on a support newsgroup

> Why, I think it isn't [great news]. . . .
> What they are missing in their cute little denial studies is the genetic predisposition to problems. If your family has depressed folks, Alcholics, ADD, ADHD or dyslexia of any kind, DON'T let the next generation get all the shots at once.

While writing as a parent who 'knows' from experience alone that MMR can cause autism, what she also 'knows' is that this is because the genetic makeup of certain children will result an adverse reaction to the combined vaccine. She may have gone beyond the evidence, but she has produced a hypothesis capable of scientific testing, and her contributions in this message and elsewhere align her with a view not that science has become so compromised that it is *incapable* of producing the evidence she requires, but that non-scientific agencies, that is, governments, are likely to prevent the research being conducted.

What this example shows is that a participant can't just offer 'cute little denial studies' as the limit of her response to a study which does not say what she would like it to say. Here is a further selection of messages from the cellphone corpus and from the MMR corpus, with discussion, to illustrate aspects of how participants articulate the relations between the various interested parties.

Example no. 19 (2000), on a health support group

>Almost certainly nothing to worry about. No evidence that radia-
>tion is relevant to tinnitus and certainly not from cell phones.
xxxxxxxxxxxxxxxxxxxxxxxxxxxxxxxxxxxxxxxxxxxxxxx
No evidence! perhaps, but the British Govt has decided that a health warning is to be put on the box, use them sparingly is the best advice.

As this example shows, one way for governments to win over public trust is to express a cautionary rather than a confident view. If they do this it constitutes evidence that they are *not* aligning themselves with the industry, which would presumably prefer more robust support. The British government is not really in a position to express a 'cautionary' view in relation to MMR. Whereas popular opinion, via the mass media, has caught on to the idea that 'caution' would take the form of substituting single vaccines in place of the joint vaccine, there is in fact no evidence, no research, that this might be a safer option than MMR while producing the same result – immunity from these childhood diseases. There is no caution in a line of action which refrains from any vaccination: this line of action is the one that leads back to widespread disease. (Some parents, though not the government, are prepared to countenance this on the grounds that the diseases are not *very* serious, and that it is better for children to develop 'natural' immunities through minor suffering than artificial immunities leading to other kinds of health issues. This remains an extreme position among parents from all countries contributing to the Usenet debate.) Nevertheless, Usenet parents seem poised to trust the present British Labour government more if it would only provide them with a choice between MMR and single vaccines.

Example no. 20 (2003) on a miscellaneous newsgroup

> So it might cost more to offer single jabs, but if the govt's first priority is maximum uptake of the vaccine, instead of being so bloody insistent that MMR is the only option they should offer other options. I'm sure if they hadn't been so suspiciously insistent, a lot more people would've thought 'there is no ulterior motive' and gone for the triple jab anyway.

There is also scope for a position which puts trust in the regulatory agencies such as the IEEE (Institute of Electrical and Electronic Engineers in the USA) and the CDC, viewing these indeed as part of the government apparatus but a part which in good faith seeks to ensure that industries work within guidelines which have public interest at heart. This is an official model of how governments should operate in relation to industry, and many people express faith that the model really does what it says on the tin.

Example no. 21 (2001) on a cellphone newsgroup

> does anyone REALLY believe, that any manufacturer for that matter would be allowed by the authorities to market a phone which did not comply to these requirements – I don't think so.
> . . .

What is also very important about relations of trust in this form of discourse is that they are expressed within an interactive context, in contrast with the mainly monologic framing of the web pages discussed previously (SARS Watch stands out in this respect as the website which has gone furthest in the introduction of dialogic characteristics). Just as participants take issue with one another's representations of facts in physics and biology as well as in general knowledge, they also take issue with one another's placement of trust. Consider the following message sequence from the mobile phone material.

Example no. 22 (2003) from a miscellaneous group

>>>>Brain cancer statistics have risen steadily the past decade or
>>>>so, and a recent study on the subject shows that business
>>>>men above 40 [in Sweden] (who were the first to use
>>>>cellphones on a frequent basis) are more likely to develop
>>>>brain cancer than other groups.
xxxxxxxxxxxxxxxxxxxxxxxxxxxxxxxxxxxxxxxxxxxxxxxxx
>>>What study is that? The one I quoted earlier* was published
>>>by the Swedish Radiation Protection Authority in 2002. It
>>>examined several years worth of studies and found no link
>>>between cancer and cell phones [full citation] . . .
xxxxxxxxxxxxxxxxxxxxxxxxxxxxxxxxxxxxxxxxxxxxxxxxx
>>I don't know if it's published online yet. . . .
xxxxxxxxxxxxxxxxxxxxxxxxxxxxxxxxxxxxxxxxxxxxxxxxx
>I would be interested in reading the study if it really did find a
>risk of cancer associated with phone use.
>The FAQ I mentioned in a previous post discusses this a bit in
>questions 13 and 14:
>http://www.mcw.edu/gcrc/cop/cell-phone-health-FAQ/toc.html#13
xxxxxxxxxxxxxxxxxxxxxxxxxxxxxxxxxxxxxxxxxxxxxxxxx
I would be cautious of these studies coming out of Sweden for one very strange reason. I have seen and heard of these studies for years, and they seem to be carefully done. Then there is no independent backup from the rest of the world. Hence I am not sure of their general applicability. I know this is strange, and I am NOT saying that the Swedish scientific community is not capable. This area though is really borderline science and the results so far worldwide look like a null effect.

The attempt to use 'science' to support the anti-phone position is weakened because other participants have not heard of the study and have heard of other research with which it is in conflict. The final contribution hints at problems of a methodological kind with studies coming out of Sweden, implicitly rejecting the alternative interpretation of the anomalous finding which would be to hypothesize some uniquely Swedish vulnerability on the part of the population studied.

'Don't trust the businessmen' is a proposition that both defenders and detractors of mobile phones can sign up to.

Example no. 23 (1998) on one science newsgroup

>I don't trust the businessmen when they say mobile phones are
>safe. I just started a course in EM theory and I don't feel safe
>about the phones.
xxxxxxxxxxxxxxxxxxxxxxxxxxxxxxxxxxxxxxxxxxxxxxx
You shouldn't trust businessmen about RF safety, because they don't know much of anything about it.
xxxxxxxxxxxxxxxxxxxxxxxxxxxxxxxxxxxxxxxxxxxxxxx
>Can the experts assure me about its safety?
xxxxxxxxxxxxxxxxxxxxxxxxxxxxxxxxxxxxxxxxxxxxxxx
RF safety experts can tell you that there are no known hazards unless you use one while driving a vehicle.

There are however, two groups of 'businessmen' (that is, industrial interests) in this particular topic. As well as phone manufacturers there are also the makers of 'protection devices'. Some fearful consumers rely upon information from these sources.

Example no. 24 (1998) on a health support newsgroup

There is also Microshield Industries PLC in the U.K. at http://www.microshield.co.uk They make a cellular phone cover that they say reduces the amount of energy absorbed by the head. I recall they claimed 90% attenuation. There is some good general information on their Web site.

More characteristically though, uncritical references to information from this branch of the industry are very quickly challenged, by participants with a more robust view of the safety of mobile phones, for preying upon the fears of consumers with products based upon disreputable 'science'.

Example no. 25 (1999) on four cellular newsgroups

>Are Cellular phone hazardous to health?
>And if you think Cellular phones are hazardous to health, would
>the use of Radiation Shields like the one sold at the URL below
>alleviate the problem?

>Please see the URL below for details:
>http://www.goaegis.com/aegisguard_phone_radiation_shields.html
xxxxxxxxxxxxxxxxxxxxxxxxxxxxxxxxxxxxxxxxxxxxxxxxx
Total con Job, Because the phone has to transmit more power to overcome the power that is absorbed by the shield. If you are truly worried (And you should not be.) get a Hands free Kit. Again see part of the report on.
http://www.newscientist.com/nsplus/insight/phones/mobilephones.html
xxxxxxxxxxxxxxxxxxxxxxxxxxxxxxxxxxxxxxxxxxxxxxxxx
Don't you get it? Acunet is trying to plant the doubt and get you to go to the website and purchase the shield!

However, when a similar critique of 'promotional discourse' was offered in respect of a contribution which suggested that MMR might not be safe, it was robustly challenged. A site called 'Thinktwice: global vaccine institute' at http://www.thinktwice.com/mmr.htm which associates itself with the sceptical view is extensively quoted by one participant in a 2002 thread on a health newsgroup. This produces the following response:

Example no. 26 (2002) on a health newsgroup

A sales hype site.
If anyone thinks that this site is a source of information to make medical decisions for their children, then read the hype regarding their polio book.

But whereas on mobile phone newsgroups such a reaction was generally sufficient to terminate this line of argument, in this case it is not, and the original contributor defends the site:

Example no. 27 (2002) on a health newsgroup

This is a source of information and many shared their concerns.
The drug company that makes it has an extensive list of adverse reactions.
Why is that? Are they lying? Why would a company selling the product have such a LONG list?
Saying the MMR is perfectly safe is simple not true.

The industry itself, as represented on the Thinktwice website, is, for this participant, a source of information about the *bad* effects of vaccines, including MMR. Where an industry, with so much at stake, can acknowledge a risk, it must be trusted. This is the principle of: 'They wouldn't say that unless they had to' – and what they have to say, must be true. On the specific issue of *autism* however, no risk admission has yet been made from within the industry, whatever it may say about other possible hazards and contra-indications.

There may be scepticism about what manufacturers *say*, since this can always be framed as mere promotional discourse, like claiming that sugar is good for you because it gives you energy, while ignoring its other health effects. In some cases this can be played off against what they *do*.

Example no. 28 (2001) from a radio hobbyist newsgroup

> I note that recent cell phone ads promise to include an ear piece free. You need not wonder why.

Stability and change

SARS

SARS as a topic on Usenet began with three messages on 15 March, the day of the WHO travel advisory. All of these started by providing information via references and citations, and two of these added their own comments which linked SARS with other global news stories:

Example no. 29 (2003) on a health support newsgroup

> Don't know about you but I find this distinctly more scary than Saddam Insane

Example no. 30 (2003) on a hobby newsgroup (science fiction)

> Well, 9/11 was nasty, but this looks like it could be much worse.

By 26 March there was more reflection on the implications of the outbreak and the wider political/medical context. One thread sought to initiate discussion on the overuse of antibiotics, another on the secretive tendencies of the Chinese government. By the 29th the 'backlash' had begun, with the first of the threads complaining of 'media hype'– although this was not allowed to pass uncontested in the thread. What also began at this point was the use of newsgroups by participants to improve their information on the subject for personal reasons. Concerned individuals addressed questions to groups likely to have decent local knowledge.

Example no. 31 (2003) on three local newsgroups

> What's the current situation for SARS in Beijing and Hong Kong? I'm in Taiwan and travel groups to China are all canceled. Hong Kong dimsum stores have no patrons. Companies stop sending people to China for meetings. Any info? This affects my friends from China and affects my schedule.

Circulation of news via reference and citation continued through the subsequent months. At the end of March, for example, someone used the groups to circulate a story about the shortage of face masks in Toronto; in early April there was a story about chlamydia and SARS and later that month, one about SARS in Baltimore. In May *The Lancet* published its first epidemiological study of the spread of the disease and references to this took place on Usenet threads; in June one of the stories was of a second SARS outbreak in Canada.

Cellphones

By contrast with SARS, discussion of mobile phones and health on Usenet is more of a 'slow burn', beginning in the era before the massive expansion of internet access and of Usenet itself (not to mention the massive expansion of mobile phone use), continuing and growing throughout that era, spreading into a range of newsgroups which did not exist in the early period, and persisting into 2003, just as Usenet began its relative decline. The earliest Usenet message on this subject was a question, evidently provoked by mass media attention:

Example no. 32 (1993) on a science newsgroup

> I've missed the news regarding the claims of cancer being linked to cellular phones. Could anybody fill me in and comment?

This message went on to invite a particular named individual to respond – which he did. This fits with the idea of newsgroups as 'communities', acquainted with one another via their use of the medium – although it is also consistent with the idea of pre-existent networks and communities using the medium as an additional communicative resource. Whichever it is, it is a form of 'intimacy' which does persist in the later years but alongside much more attenuated and anonymous relationships, with extensive use of nicknames rather than 'real' names for online identities. There was one other example in the material where a possible 'lurker' on the thread is addressed directly – it occurs in 2002:

Example no. 33 (2002) on two regional/hobby newsgroups in the cellphone sample

> Are you listening, Lord Ponce-boy? Could be right up your (or any other idiotic conspiracy theorists) alley.

'Lord Ponce-boy' is a sarcastic corruption of an online pseudonym. No such person contributes on the thread, though he (the chosen nickname suggests a male not a female participant) does contribute on other threads within the same group. Clearly he is 'known' to the group as a promulgator of 'conspiracy theories' and despised by this contributor at least for that reason.

Through 1994 and 1995 the only newsgroups to take much interest are either scientific/medical ones, or else about cellphones on the technical side. Even in 1996 this pattern continues, although with one exception (in the sample) in a newsgroup classified as 'miscellaneous'. This marks the point when the topic seems to take on a 'general interest' character:

Example no. 34 (1996) on a miscellaneous newsgroup

> I do not wish to do any scaremongering, but I read a brief article in the British press yesterday (Mon 15th April) about Mobile phones causing cancer.
> How the heck can a mobile phone do any damage? I have a phone myself, but I am not familiar with the science of it . . . is it from the radio waves? (in fact what do mobile phones use – radio or microwaves?)

A newsgroup called 'alt.cellular' began in 1994, but did not feature any threads about health risks until 1996. By 1998 there were newsgroups devoted to particular models of mobile phone – Motorola, Fido, Sprint PCS, Ericsson and so on – as the technology became a genuinely mass market commodity. Interest in the health issue spread to these groups, while continuing on the 'older' groups, where it sometimes provoked the reaction 'Not this again!' as time passed and more people joined in the conversations. 'Cancer' groups became interested from 1994; other health-related groups focused upon particular conditions such as tinnitus joined in by 2000. The image of mobile phones 'frying the brain' was not restricted to any particular type of newsgroup or excluded from any: it occurred on threads at the technical end of the spectrum right through to 'misc.consumers'. It was used each year between 1997 and 2001 ('boil your brain' occurs in 1996) and although in the sample there are no 2002 or 2003 examples, the usage certainly continued during this period.

Example no. 35 (2002) on a cellphone newsgroup and a regional newsgroup

> We have had overhead pylons for decades and only now are people/organizations recognising the health threats; we have had tobacco since the days of Walter Raleigh yet only now are US big and fat corps being forced to pay out; and we have been casually warned for many years that excessive use of a mobile phone can fry your head, oh and by the way, don't use them in petrol stations because they can cause sparks and a very nasty incident.

The 'double voice' of concern on the one hand and reassurance on the other, in response to the 'don't knows' who are just looking for information, was there from the beginning of the story in 1993 as these two messages on that early thread both show.

Example no. 36 (1993) on a science newsgroup

> I appreciate the comments about non-ionizing exposures and cancer induction. It is quite a public-relations time out there for radiation-related folks. My concern hasn't been about thermal effects. It is the non-thermal effects, which would occur at possibly very low exposures. For microwaves and RF these would include general malaise, anxiety, headache, but, cancer induction is not one of them. Or could it be?

Example no. 37 (1993) on a science newsgroup

> As for nonthermal effects of RF/MW; there is evidence that such effects exist. I don't find the laboratory evidence for nonthermal effects very convincing, but in any case most of the evidence for nonthermal effects does not point to a human health risk.

By 1994 the pro-risk voice was a little stronger:

Example no. 38 (1994) on a cellular phone newsgroup

> The danger is real, but don't start to panic. The best way you can protect yourself is with moderation. If you're on the phone continuously, for huge periods of time, your chances will increase. A normal 3 watt carphone antenna has the waves travel through your rear window, rather than drilling through. Now, if it can easily go through your glass window, how easily can it go through your skull? The good thing about that is that handhelds are only .6 watts. Also, switch ears often. With these careful hints, you shouldn't have anything to worry about.

The tone of dispute was still polite at this early stage: other participants on this thread take issue with the wording 'the danger is real' but only to substitute something more like 'the jury is still out, let's not panic before we have to'.

Example no. 39 (1994) on a cellular phone newsgroup

> IMHO [netspeak: In My Humble Opinion], I would say that until the jury is in, be cautious, but not worried. Your advice about moderation, as I said, makes sense to me. But your statement about 'danger' did not.

There was nothing that could reasonably be regarded as abusive, or even impolite, when this issue was discussed on Usenet until 1996, when it was provoked by a description of mobile phone technology as 'unnatural'. The abuse took the form of ventriloquistic mockery for a 'Luddite' worldview.

Example no. 40 (1996) on a telecommunications newsgroup

> What a load of bloody rubbish you have written ! Oh dear, those steam cars, they're not natural ! I saw one go 6 miles an hour yesterday – that was faster than the man with the flag !

1996 was also the year when the first really emphatic 'no risk' messages appeared, in contrast to the earlier 'no evidence of risk' ones.

Example no. 41 (1996) on two science newsgroups

> There is no known physically plausible mechanism whereby non-ionizing electromagnetic radiation such as the radio waves from cell-phones could cause cancer. Such radio waves do =NOT= have sufficient energy to =directly= damage anything in a cell, nor do they resonantly interact with anything that we know of existing within a cell. There is simply =NO= physically reasonable mechanism that could possibly justify the claim that cell-phones can cause cancer.

This was politely contested (no *known* mechanism, but there could be an unknown one): the contestant was a lone voice and was mocked for his efforts. Discussion of 'protection devices' (radiation shields, stickers, hoods and so on) – much of it scornful – also began in 1996. The exception is the hands-free kit, which essentially got the thumbs-up from 1996 and throughout the rest of the period, even from people who wanted to reassure more concerned participants: their line is 'use hands-free if you're worried'. There was a blip in this following the publication of the *Which* report, but it did not do lasting damage to the reputation of the hands-free kit as a safety precaution. In a few threads from 2003 which were also examined, all of the trends and patterns established in the earlier phases of the story were present: voices for and against the idea of risk, in more or less equal balance, recommendations to use hands-free kits, discussion of the value of particular studies, citations of the cellphone antenna FAQ and so on. But there was less animosity in 2003 than in the earlier years which may suggest that although the indeterminacy is still there, it is at a level and of a type that the public has learned to live with.

MMR

As it develops over time on Usenet, the MMR story was more like that of mobile phones than it was like that of SARS. But there are important differences. Although the MMR corpus covers almost as long a period as the mobile phone debate (from 1995 as compared with 1993), and although it captures what seem to be the earliest online message on this topic, there was actually very little traffic, comparatively speaking, until the publication of the seminal paper by Andrew Wakefield and his colleagues in 1998. That there was any discussion of the MMR/autism link prior to 1998 at all is of interest. The earliest message wrote of having 'read some discussion' about this – but probably not on Usenet. A curious feature of this thread is that after the first two messages in 1995, the thread 'went to sleep' like Rip Van Winkle until 1997, and then again until 1998, when it became very active. Two other early threads comprised just six messages between them. It seems that there was just not enough 'happening' to fuel extensive discussion in these forums before 1998. All of this changed radically after February 1998. The support groups where the topic began were joined by general health groups and children/parenting newsgroups. For the most part this cluster of groups kept the topic to itself until 2001, when there was some broadening out into regional newsgroups and politics newsgroups. This broadening out continued through 2002, which also brought in a range of more miscellaneous groups. When the topic broadened out across a wider range of groups, the proportion of participants who were already parents of autistic children declined as a proportion of the whole: parents contemplating vaccination for their healthy children then became the most active participants, especially from 2001 onwards, alongside those for whom the issue had become a 'cause', whether or not they had this kind of personal interest in it.

The low profile of the MMR/autism discussion prior to 1998 does not mean that it is also a discussion without conflict at that early stage.

Example no. 42 (1996) on a science/medicine newsgroup

>I will reprint an ad from the American Parent's Magazine in 1994,
>taken out by Merck, a vaccine manufacturer about the measles
>vaccine and then, I'll dig through and forward a few articles that
>I have on measles for you to read.

. . .

>What they don't mention is that measles vaccine can cause, MS,
>diabetes, autism, ADD [Attention Deficit Disorder], ADHD
>[Attention Deficit Hyperactive Disorder], Guillian-Barre paraly-
>sis, ocular neuritis and subacute sclerosing panencephalitis as
>well as many other disorders (Crohn's Syndrome, ulcerative
>colitis – the list goes on!)
xxxxxxxxxxxxxxxxxxxxxxxxxxxxxxxxxxxxxxxxxxxxxxxxxxxxx
How do we know that it can cause any of these? The rest of your post provides zero evidence.

One of the support groups where this issue is discussed did not exist prior to 1998. This phenomenon, of discussion moving on to newsgroups as and when they come into existence (if the topic is relevant), was very marked in relation to the cellphone debate, thanks to the development of all of the brand-specific mobile phone groups. It is less prevalent in this debate which is also a more restricted one in terms of the range of newsgroups involved.

As with the early years of the mobile phone debate there is some indication in the early years of the MMR debate (including the pivotal year of 1998) of a 'community', sharing some degree of online mutual acquaintance, for example via references to conferences which some of them have attended and others will know about.

From 1998 advice was offered and requested not just about whether to vaccinate or not, but also about how to avoid it in the USA where it is normally a requirement for school entry, and where to go to get individual jabs instead of MMR in the UK where only the triple vaccine is available on the National Health Service.

Discussion

This chapter has identified some significant similarities between the three topics. Substantively, the topics are similar in the overall bias towards orthodox/majority views, as well as the consistency with which the mass media are both decried for sensationalism and relied on for basic information amongst newsgroup participants. Formally, all topics produce websites from a variety of sources with greater or lesser institutional backing, and varying styles for appropriating the literacy practices which have developed around this new medium. In Usenet as well, the three topics are similar in the proportions of texts which make use of practices such as flaming and metalinguistic terms such as 'troll' – the distribution remains fairly constant over time as well.

Where there are differences across these three topics online, it is principally in relation to substantive changes over time: the three topics each have different patterns of 'uptake' which the retrospective analysis of Usenet materials was able to capture. The web-based analysis is much less relevant here, thanks to the tendency on the web to replace 'past' materials with more recent ones.

The considerable common ground shared by these three topics in respect of their 'web presence' may have something to do with the nature of the particular topics chosen. It would be valuable therefore to undertake comparable analysis on other kinds of health risk topics. In particular, it would be important to examine at least one topic with less of a mainstream versus fringe structure, something where opinion was more evenly divided between the arguments for and those against the risk in question.

8
The Internet and the Public Interest

This short chapter is divided into two main sections. The first section discusses the significance of this research for the study of computer-mediated communication, drawing out the implications of approaching CMC as public discourse. Four aspects of communicational 'publicness' have been touched upon in this research: communication in the public domain; communication for the public; communication by the public; and communication which is in the public interest. It is the last of these which is the focus of discussion here. The second section discusses the implications of the research for the study of the social construction of health risk.

Computer-mediated communication as public discourse

The research presented above has shown that there are advantages in linking the study of online communication to the study of offline communication in some circumstances. In the present case, with the focus on the internet as a forum for public communication, it was important to draw out these connections, distinguishing websites and newsgroups from email and other kinds of restricted communication managed over the net, while linking it with the study of the mass media, which used to have more of a monopoly in the public communication field. This does not mean that within a new field of 'public communication studies' the differences between broadcasting, print media and internet-based forms of communication should be elided. On the contrary; the focus should be very much on comparisons between the affordances, the semiotic potentials, of different media for similar purposes. Audio-visual media are able to achieve things which primarily text-based media cannot, and vice versa. Notwithstanding the rhetoric of 'convergence', at the time of writing, the TV screen is still the best place outside the cinema to encounter 'moving image' audiovisual text, not the computer or telephone screen, and print newspaper sales have not collapsed despite the availability at no cost of the same text online.

At the same time the public communication perspective is also one within which the migration of particular kinds of content from their traditional forums in print and over the airwaves to the net can be subjected to analysis. In this research a large number of messages gave the web addresses of the sources that they referred to and a high proportion of these were to news websites. What is also interesting in the age of the internet is that individuals are able in some cases to refer one another 'past' the news media, back to a deeper level of the discourse, in the form of the source texts which the journalists themselves have used in compiling their reports. There is some evidence of this as a practice in the research presented here. For example, the WHO website was extensively referenced by newsgroup participants during the SARS outbreak. If the underlying question is whether the coming of the internet is a good thing or a bad thing for the state of public communication then trends like this weigh in on the 'good' side.

A primary concern in research concerned with the public character of computer-mediated communication has to do with the extent to which it is possible/desirable to protect all or part of the 'electronic commons' (Goggin 2000; Starr 2000; Dyer-Witheford 2002; Murphy 2002) from the encroachment of private (that is, commercial) interests or market forces.

To the extent that the internet does offer such a virtual commons, in whole or in part, other researchers have addressed themselves to what this offers, potentially and actually, to democracies concerned for the quality (for example, rationality) of public debate (Spears and Lea 1994; Schneider 1996; Dahlberg 2001; Slevin 2000). In this context, the question of regulation is an issue, not just at the 'macro' level but also in research concerned with the *self*-government of online forums, by which attempts are made to restrict individual behaviour for the good of the group as a whole (Kollock and Smith 1996; MacKinnnon 1997). The general theme here is that of whether the coming of the internet is or is not likely to make a positive contribution to democracy (Arterton 1987; Golding 1998; Oblak 2003).

Seen from a different angle the publicness of CMC is not so much a question of access, regulation or privatization, but a question of the interactive profiles of the communicative forms on offer. From this angle, one-to-one communication is 'private' whereas any mass medium (one-to-many) is 'public'. Some aspects of CMC invite comparison with mass media, with CMC users being regarded as 'audiences' for this purpose (Morris and Ogan 1996; Roscoe 1999; Livingstone 2004). From this perspective too, the interest of CMC lies in the fact that any of us can in principle be 'the one' who addresses 'the many'.

The 'many' of traditional mass media is addressed by the 'one' as a multiplicity, indeterminate in size, of unknown individuals. For the second half of the twentieth century, especially for the broadcast media, these have been national audiences. Most CMC researchers believe that audiences for internet communications are *not* best understood in national terms. The glory of the internet is its global reach.

The mass media version of the 'one-to-many' profile has other problems in relation to the interactive forms of CMC. It is not just that everyone here can be the 'one' but also the feeling that the 'many' is not the same kind of 'many' as it is for broadcasting and the press. In particular, so the argument goes, the 'many' of these various interactive online forums are not indeterminately large multiples of unknown individuals. They are something different – *communities* (Rheingold 1993; Baym 1995c).

Unfortunately, as researchers have come to appreciate, this approach has had flaws too (Rheingold 2002). In the first place the meaning of 'community' has not been sufficiently stable either in everyday usage or in academic research. In Benedict Andersen's work for example, nations *are* communities, and it is the contribution of the daily national press which has helped to make them so (Andersen 1991). Furthermore, the idea of addressing a multiplicity as a community seems to entail the idea of mutual *acquaintance* among at least a critical mass of the individuals who constitute that multiplicity. This raises questions about just how much and what kind of prior knowledge of online others is (regarded as) sufficient to underpin a claim of mutual acquaintance, as well as about the balance between sociability and information-seeking purposes in relation to use of online forums (Bakardjieva 2003). A further complication is that on any given thread on any given forum, particular messages will be directly addressed not to 'the many' at all, but to a particular individual, a previous contributor. Yet this is still not 'private' or restricted communication since anyone can read it (and add subsequent messages of their own if they wish). This can be compared with the situation in broadcasting, where the remote audience (and the studio audience if there is one) are ratified participants (Goffman 1981) even where they are not directly addressed, for example, watching and listening to an interview between a host and a guest. Their virtual and actual presence influences the conduct of that speech event. Such broadcast discourse is *designed* for an overhearing audience (Heritage 1985). Interactive CMC in public forums can likewise be regarded as designed for an invisible overhearing audience. One-to-one direct address overlays a persistent one-to-many construction in which the role of the one fluctuates.

Perhaps it does make a difference to the styling of an online message according to whether the overhearing audience is construed as a grouping of the mutually acquainted (Baym 1995b, c, 1996, 1997, 1998) or as 'the public'. McLaughlin and her colleagues were certainly conscious of this difficulty back in 1995, talking about the fact that flaming is sometimes challenged online on the grounds that it creates a bad impression to others, characterized here as 'lurkers'.

> . . . one could argue that lurker-conscious posters reflect not an inclusive view of the community membership but, rather, an alternative conception of Usenet as a magazine or publication medium; that, however, is an argument our data do not currently allow us to resolve. (McLaughlin, Osborne et al. 1995)

The research in the present book does not indicate a conclusive answer to this question either. Nevertheless, it has proved useful to construe Usenet groups as publishers and publics not communities, partly to resist the tendency elsewhere in the literature to reject this option without much discussion, if any. But it is important also to recognize that even if individuals do not design their *particular* messages for a public readership, the system has done this for them, by creating these maximally open conditions of access.

So far most empirical media studies research is either in mass media studies or in the study of the new media. Research relating these to one another is uncommon. An important exception to this rule is Livingstone (2002) who examines the use of media technologies by young people circa 2000–2001. This multi-method approach with a strong ethnographic emphasis is interested in lifestyles and how new and 'old' media as well as other ways of using leisure time are articulated in different types of household.

The present research differs from Livingstone's even though both seek to integrate aspects of traditional media studies with aspects of new media studies. Livingstone's approach connects with the ethnography of home and leisure, and with the work of people like Morley (1992), Silverstone (1992) and Lull (1990). The public communication perspective promoted in the present research is less concerned with circumstances of actual encounters with media texts and technologies, and more concerned with the nature of communicative form and address. Another branch of ethnography, Hymesian 'ethnography of communication' (after Hymes 1972), which includes some research on the ethnography of writing (Basso 1974) takes on board such questions. But the most significant figure in understanding such matters is Erving Goffman (see especially Goffman 1981), whose concepts are insightfully applied in much sociolinguistic work. Public communication can also be approached from a more socio-political direction, via Habermas and theorization of the 'public sphere' in modernity (Habermas 1989/1962; Dahlgren 1995). These two strands come together in the 'critical discourse analysis' of Norman Fairclough (Fairclough 1992, 1995), while for those who object to the pervasiveness of media *criticism* in the CDA project, there is always Scannell (1996), with a much more positive view of the public functioning of mass media, and Corner (1995, 1996). So far, little of this has fed through into *new* media studies, although research on the contribution of new media to political life is plentiful. The political communication literature here though is more likely to be concerned with channel and content than with form and address.

Public address and public interest: the World Wide Web

Most of the web is de facto public communication, available on global public access. Finances and political regimes permitting, anyone can contribute to the web at little cost, although maintaining a complex multi-purpose website may now be beyond the technical abilities and resources of the home computer user. Websites are sustained, economically speaking, in a number of ways. Some are sustained by public funding via taxation. In Britain the TV licence fee helps to sustain the BBC's website, with the main problem being the number of 'free-riders' – since the BBC site is on global access it is also available to millions outside of Britain who pay no fee (Naylor et al. 2000). Some are sustained by voluntary public subscription direct to the webmaster (SARS Watch, discussed in Chapter 4, is of this kind). Some are sustained by donation to the charity which owns the site (although the donations may be general rather than specifically for the website). Some sites are sustained by advertising and sponsorship money. Universities which maintain websites allow individual members of staff web space for their own work-related purposes. Finally, some sites are sustained privately as a kind of vanity publishing for individuals.

These differences may affect the public address of websites in a variety of ways, but the most important one is the separation of sites which feature commercial advertising/sponsorship from those that do not. Advertising and sponsorship puts a large number of websites into logoland: in those sites without commercial relationships, logos (apart from any belonging to the site itself) are conspicuously absent and the absence may even be a source of pride. To people living in countries accustomed to a public service broadcasting tradition alongside a commercial tradition, this differentiation is a familiar one adapted to a new media context.

The websites examined in this research are mainly on the 'unsponsored' side of this divide. The Google search engine produces 'hit lists' which always include some website addresses from organizations which pay for the privilege (see Chapter 6 above). Such sponsored hits are clearly differentiated from the main list. The absence of the sponsor or advertiser's pitch may enhance the authority and trustworthiness of these sites as ones which are not compromised by commercial considerations: not just examples of 'for-the-public' (compare Chapter 3, above) public communication but also 'in the public interest'. Certainly it is not hard to imagine what it would do to the credibility of the World Health Organization if they suddenly started mounting advertisements for painkillers on the site. On the other hand, the absence of advertisements in some cases will send a meta-message that the site is simply not popular enough to deserve a share of the money which advertisers have at their disposal.

All of the websites examined in this research have some concept of operating in the public interest. The least civic-minded is Wang's personal blog. Its version of public address is on a human interest level, engaging its readers outside China with the details of an exotic life. It takes on a public interest aspect during the SARS outbreak because Wang is in a position to add local colour to the story of SARS while it is still a prominent global news story. As the least civic of the contributions, it is the least likely to be compromised by commercial relationships if these were to be made available to him.

Given that five out of the six sites are maintained by individuals – a university scientist, two freelance writers, an IT specialist and another whose working life is not made public – this degree of civic responsibility is interesting. The reluctance, except on the two blog-style sites (SARS Watch and Wangjianshuo's blog) to incorporate a dialogic element into the site itself, accompanies in each case a degree of assertiveness as regards the rights and wrongs of the issue under discussion. The World

Health Organization speaks with the voice of institutional authority, even though it sometimes has to say (authoritatively) that 'we' do not know the answers to important questions about SARS. The webmaster of the cellphone antenna FAQ speaks with the voice of the research scientist surveying the field: his is also an authoritative voice when it comes to assessing the significance of particular research findings. The journalist responsible for Electric Words uses the site polemically, conscious of speaking in opposition to a more mainstream view. Whale, in its inchoate and indirect way (mainly via quotations from other people), likewise constructs an oppositional position for itself.

These are the different kinds of online voices that can be found on the web, constructing and deconstructing health risks with their visual and verbal textual materials, making very different choices regarding the best ways of presenting what they want to share with their readers, from the heavily footnoted FAQ of Moulder, through to the conversational address of the blogs, via the extravagantly multivocal discourse of Whale and the healthsite-of-record properties of the WHO. It is hard to make many generalizations about this range of material, which in any case only represents a small selection of what is available online. There is one characteristic that is shared among those sites with a public interest project: all of them are rhetorically committed to the view that the truth, whether it is known or still to be discovered, is not paranormal truth but scientific truth, however much it is currently obstructed by ill-will, conspiracy, ignorance, commercial interest, prejudice, media sensationalism or government cover-up. Even the fringe views of Whale are buttressed with support of the conventional kind where this seems to be available. Across all the variation there is a substantial level of appeal to shared rationality grounded in the scientific enterprise.

Public address and public interest: newsgroups

Usenet newsgroups are public (in the public domain) and always were. Prior to the collation of major archives, first by DejaNews and in the present decade, on an even larger scale, by Google, that public character may not have been fully appreciated by all users. In the very early days there were simply not enough people online to sustain a strong idea of publicness and only a small number of newsgroups for them to participate in. The growth of the 'system' throughout the 1980s and 1990s changed this, although the group-based arrangements distributed the millions of participants into smaller communicational enclaves for practical purposes. Numerically speaking, newsgroup discourse is not mass communication, but it shares some characteristics with broadcast communication. It shares the characteristic that all messages sent are sent out indiscriminately to 'the group', which means to an indefinite number of people comprising unknown as well as known users.

The public address nature of newsgroup messages is clearest to see in relation to the first messages which start new threads.

Example no. 1 (April 2003) – SARS

> A course I played at had no drinking water on the course this week, apparently because of fear SARS contamination.
> Anyone else experience this?

The 'anyone' here refers to 'anyone who might be reading this', with the expectation that they will be fellow-golfers, since this is a golfing newsgroup. Broadcast address is not so clear for subsequent messages because these are, at one level, designed as responses to earlier ones. The 'you' in example 2 below refers to the person who asked the question in example 1.

Example no. 2 (April 2003) – SARS

> In what area are you playing? Beijing?

After the first message, 'conversations' appear to narrow down so that they only involve the active participants. But others can join in at any time, and when they do, their active participation at that point also confirms their prior passive participation. They were 'there' for the conversation before they chose to 'speak'. As others have pointed out there is no way of knowing how much of a thread any given participant has experienced, or how many readers are reading messages without contributing any.

Talking to a newsgroup is a kind of broadcasting and like broadcasting, designed for an overhearing audience (Heritage 1985). Even if the overhearing audience is in the tens rather than the hundreds or thousands, the fact that it is indefinite in number and unidentifiable to those exchanging messages is sufficient to give it this quality. This quality of audience design is systemic, independent of the intentions of the contributors, who may not find it easy to come to terms with this property. In one long and very acrimonious thread in my material, a contributor at one point says that he is 'leaving'. After this message, two participants who have been actively arguing with him and directing their messages to him in the second person, start talking about this contributor in the third person. One of them says: 'I'm going to miss xxxx's comments'. But he bounces back, with another insult and a message along the lines of: 'this time I am REALLY going'. He makes four more contributions after this. In his final message he writes; 'I guess you just won't drop the subject', in response to a message critical of something he had written. The tension between talking to one another and talking to the wider audience at large is much more awkward in newsgroup material than it ever is in professionally managed broadcasting, because the participants have to manage this for themselves, and with no obligation to get it 'right'.

The exchange of individual newsgroup messages does not take place on the basis of shared commitment to public interest. It is not out of concern for *public* welfare that a parent writes to a newsgroup asking where to go to obtain single vaccinations in place of the alarming MMR vaccine. Nevertheless the collective existence of newsgroups does have a public interest function to the extent that the system serves as a kind of communicational commons in cyberspace (compare Kollock and Smith 1996). Despite the 'flaming', it is the sharing of information and of interpersonal support which sustains newsgroups, and there is nothing else quite like this system, on or offline, with quite this mixture of public and private communicational dynamics, and independent of particular institutional apparatuses such as those offered by AOL and other internet service providers. Resistance to 'trolling',[1] even more than resistance to flaming, can certainly be seen as resistance to the abuse of the commons principle. The content of 'troll' messages is not the issue: it is the perceived motivation, as a desire to provoke, to stir things up, to create pain for the group which is found objectionable. Trolling is in the eye of the beholder and so disputes can also break out as to whether any particular message is a troll or not.

Example no. 3 (2001) – mobile phones

>>>Troll.
xxxxxxxxxxxxxxxxxxxxxxxxxxxxxxxxxxxxxxxxxxxxxxxxxx
>>xxx, you calling somebody a troll is like Rush Limbaugh calling
>>somebody a fat-ass.
xxxxxxxxxxxxxxxxxxxxxxxxxxxxxxxxxxxxxxxxxxxxxxxxxx

>No. You *are* a troll. You refuse to discuss the issue, and instead
>deflect attention away from debate.
xxxxxxxxxxxxxxxxxxxxxxxxxxxxxxxxxxxxxxxxxxxxxxxx
xxx, that is exactly what you did in the latest round with me when I actually was agreeing with a number of your points – go back and read it.

The special interest enclaves represented by particular newsgroups can be seen as particular publics, as distinct from the 'general public'. Certain kinds of messages seem to indicate the existence of a public-spirited motivation with respect to these more limited publics. There is a class of message which takes a story from the news media and draws it to the attention of the group, thereby claiming for that story some relevance to the group's core concerns. A large number of such messages (not studied in the present research) go no further: no thread ever develops out of the first and only message. Some are attacked in one or two subsequent messages as trolls. But others are taken up and discussed; their value is appreciated and the contributor's public-spiritedness is given support.

With such messages the public-spiritedness of the individual newsgroup contributor seems not unlike that of other individuals who have taken the further step of launching websites to put information into the (general) public domain. Some participants indeed engage in both kinds of online communication, and two of them are represented in this study; the webmasters of the cellphone antenna FAQ and of Whale. The difference is that on newsgroups the information offered is subject to contestation and re-evaluation by other voices; this contestation is itself on public view, and the contributor is vulnerable to loss of face. Cyberspace conditions provide some protection, to the extent that it is the online persona who suffers, a persona which can if required be set at a distance. The predominantly monologic discourse of the web creates less vulnerability for their webmasters since whatever criticism comes their way does not have to be made public.

The social construction of health risks and the role of the internet

If we take on board the view that health risks are indeed socially constructed, in discourse (in the sociocultural sense), we then need to ask *which* discourses are the powerful, effective ones in this construction. What is the relationship between scientific discourses, political discourses and lifeworld discourses in establishing the kinds of behaviour which are to be regarded as 'risky' in a negative way?

Many different kinds of behaviour could be constructed as 'risky' but only some of them are, and this applies to health risks as it applies to any other kinds of risk. In some cases public authorities take a lead in trying to instate some behaviour as problematic (such as bad dietary habits); in other cases, public opinion or parts of it run well ahead of what the authorities are prepared to allow, as happened with the scare over the MMR vaccine. There is a sense in which risks which are not discussed in public are only potential risks. Maybe all bananas distributed for consumption in Britain during 2000 carried a microbial infection which in some cases but not all will cause food poisoning. I ate a banana every day in 2000 but I never suffered the symptoms of food poisoning during this period. Was I taking a risk? In one sense, yes. The facts are such that sickness was a real possibility, albeit one I did not succumb to. In another sense there was no risk because I did not know, nor could I have known, about the microbe, hence there was no way that such knowledge could have influenced my conduct. The real-life equivalent of this relates to the victims of v-CJD whose sickness and death was due to the infected beef which they unknowingly consumed before anyone understood that this was a dangerous thing to do. Some parents of autistic children fear that they too are in this situation because they unknowingly allowed these children to be given the MMR vaccine. In all these cases there was, or there could have been, harm, and something which caused, or could have caused, that harm. But to use the word 'risk' seems either to be prematurely accepting the truth of the causal relationship (as in the MMR scenario) or else to be examining the past with the benefit of hindsight (in the banana and the v-CJD scenarios).

In the literature that discusses the social construction of risk (for example, Kemshall 2002, 2003) a distinction is drawn between a modernist discourse of risk as calculable chance (the probabilistic discourse) and a late modern/post-modern discourse of risk as uncertainty. The view is taken that there is currently a tension between these two discourses. Comparisons of one risk with another (dying of tobacco-induced lung cancer versus dying from eating beef infected with BSE, where the former is very much more likely than the latter) belong primarily to the probabilistic discourse while appeals to the precautionary principle belong to the uncertainty discourse (since no one really knows, why take chances?). In the analysis chapters of this research it is very easy to identify each of these kinds of argument.

Comparative risk
Example no. 4 (1999) – mobile phones

> If you think Cell phones are hazardous, then do not drive your car. Cars can kill you. I have yet to see one person die from a Cell phone. Also, do not eat anything. All the vegetables are loaded with pesticides and the meat has hormones and nitrates in it. If you eat you will get cancer and die. This could happen before the Cell phone or Car kills you.

Precautionary principle
Example no. 5 (2000) – mobile phones

> I will try and find stuff on non thermal effect on net, I have no evidence at all, nor claimed it. But I have heard many references to it, and just think it's best to adopt the precautionary principle.

Example no. 6 (April 2003) – SARS

> In any case, I bought a couple of cartons of 3M N95 respirators. Better to be safe than sorry, and masks won't wear out.

Example no. 7 (2002) – MMR

> Treating child health issues with such contempt as not to afford them the precautionary principle speaks volumes of the value of children to adults in this country. With such standards no one can claim that any new vaccination today is for the benefit of children and do so with sincerity.

What this underlines is that although newsgroup participants are expressing their opinions 'in their own words', they are doing so within the parameters of discursive frameworks which are widely shared, and not just 'in tension' but actually in real conflict in some cases. In example 8 the right to observe the precautionary principle is strongly asserted against an insistence, deriving from a more actuarial position, that precaution is demonstrably unnecessary and thus irrational:

Example no. 8 (2001) – mobile phones (note the 'intercutting' in the response to the second message, marked by single > characters)

>>I don't need a mobile phone to enjoy my life so why risk short-
>>ening it?
xxxxxxxxxxxxxxxxxxxxxxxxxxxxxxxxxxxxxxxxxxxxxxxxxxxxxx
>That's your prerogative *[continues below]*
xxxxxxxxxxxxxxxxxxxxxxxxxxxxxxxxxxxxxxxxxxxxxxxxxxxxxx
EXACTLY WHAT I HAVE BEEN SAYING. It's my choice not to take the risk, but will they leave it at that. No. I think they have some weird desire to get me to say the opposite.
xxxxxxxxxxxxxxxxxxxxxxxxxxxxxxxxxxxxxxxxxxxxxxxxxxxxxx
>[*continuation from above*] but the jury is still out, and I think you
>will be surprised at the outcome. If RF was truly a problem just
>about every RF engineer would be a cancer magnet.

At one level exchanges like this can be read as evidence confirming the reality and power of the two discourses. This is fine, but it leaves one further loose end: what happens to the idea that the newsgroup material represents people speaking about risks in their own words? Have we now started to suggest that these are not the participants' own words at all but are, rather, pre-assembled for deployment in discursive interchange? This is reminiscent of 1970s-style theories of ideological reproduction, and not very satisfactory. It does not do justice to the wide variations in how individuals realize (express) the competing discourses, nor to the processes of negotiation which may be required when one 'discourse' confronts another. But the details are as important as the big picture. Consider, for example, what happened to the word SARS in the discourse(s) of risk, from March 2003. A top-down lexical innovation, backed by the authority of medical science, very quickly became assimilated into English writing about this subject, and not just in technical reports. The news media adopted it, and so too did the 'people', or at least those people with internet and newsgroup access. But there was also resistance to it, and ways of coding that resistance via the use of scare quotes and vague language.

Conclusions

The work presented in this book has attempted to span several distinct academic specialisms, notably the study of computer-mediated communication, mass media research on health and risk, and the public communication of science. Through particular case studies, I have attempted to explore some of the publicly-available resources on the internet that are being used for communication in the general area of health risk. The rationale for such an enquiry lies in the fact that, given the importance of health to people's lives, people might well be motivated to look to the internet to address their concerns.

Among the substantive points which can bear repetition here I would include, first, the considerable similarity of the three topics. The theme that the mass media cannot be trusted and are to blame for engendering fear within the general public is one aspect of this similarity; another is the extensive reliance, notwithstanding this scepticism, upon mass media for core information. A third aspect is the parallelism in the use of particular argumentative moves: comparison with tobacco smoking for those who are disposed to take the fearful view; comparison with automobile acccidents for those on the other side. A second notable point concerns the overall bias towards 'conservative' and/or mainstream resources online (see especially Chapter 6 above). On the web, this conservatism manifests itself in the greater prominence of orthodox resources compared with unorthodox ones; in Usenet it lies in the fact that unorthodox views are routinely contested within threads. Although Usenet contestation can be less than rational in the way it manifests itself, involving flaming and personal abuse, this is not an invariant feature of the material. There is also much evidence of disputes between the heretical and their critics over factual accuracy and/or logical consistency.

More important, perhaps, than particular conclusions, such as those outlined in the previous paragraph, is the approach that this work takes towards the analysis of online materials. What I have tried to do throughout this book is to construe online discourses about health risks as encounters with *particular* texts and text-types, and consider the implications of these encounters for the social construction of health risks. There are things that people want to *know* about cellphones, MMR and SARS, as well as about many other health issues. There are also things that people want to *say* about such topics. There are online resources which permit them to do either of these. When they access the internet with the aim of finding information that they do not have, or contributing information and opinion for others' benefit, they encounter, engage with and contribute to very specific kinds of text, including web pages and discussion forums comparable to the ones analysed in this book. In online discourse, as in all text, form and content influence one another. It is important to take this into consideration when trying to investigate what is available and what kind of communicative purposes it can serve. Questions about the credibility of online resources, for example, must be sensitive to the actual forms of discourse through which information is mediated. This includes the kinds of social relationships which are possible in particular cases. The social relations enacted through Usenet newsgroups are clearly very different from those enacted through websites. Yet in both cases there is scope for variation: the impersonality of presentation on the World Health Organization website constructs a very different relationship with its audience than does the first person address of SARS Watch, and Whale is different again. In newsgroups, those which allow or even encourage flaming have a different communicative ethos from those which do not.

There is scope for further research along the lines presented above. It would be interesting to determine whether the conclusions I have drawn are the result of choosing particular topics for case study purposes, or whether they can be generalized to other health risk issues. In some issues, such as tobacco smoking, the risk in question has official support; in others, such as the debate about genetically modified foods, the health risk angle is only one of the elements making the topic controversial. Whether and how such differences result in differences as regards internet materials on these subjects is certainly worthy of exploration. Changes are under way with respect to the internet and to the communicative possibilities which it has enabled. Some resources, including Usenet, are declining; others, like instant messaging, are expanding; the ethos of large parts of the World Wide Web has become predominantly commercial. Developments like these will impact upon the kinds of public discourse which will be possible online, and should certainly be monitored for their impact on the social construction of health risk.

Notes

1. Introduction

1. Although changes are under way, the potential 'universality' of the internet is still restricted to the wealthier countries of the world (Ngini, Furnell et al. 2002). Within 'wired', western countries the large proportions of people online – 68 per cent in the USA as of December 2003 (Pew 2003b), 58 per cent in the UK as of October 2003 (Office of National Statistics 2003) – mean that the technology has spread well beyond the most affluent social sector (or school/workplace access), although there are still concerns about the 'digital divide' between the haves and the have-nots. There is also the issue of the language of access. From the beginning, the English language dominated the internet, though as access has spread beyond its original base in the USA, to non-English speaking developed nations and thence to the rest of the world, this has changed. See Danet and Herring (2003) for discussion of the multilingual internet. For online statistics by language, see Global-Reach (2004), which put the English language online population at 35.8 per cent in March 2004. The next biggest online group by language was Chinese at 14.1 per cent, followed by Japanese at 9.6 per cent and Spanish at 9 per cent. All statistics of this kind come with serious caveats with respect to when and how the data was collected.
2. AIDS stands for Acquired Immune Deficiency Syndrome, a condition which compromises the body's immune responses. HIV stands for Human Immunodeficiency Virus. This is the virus thought to be responsible for AIDS. The website of the Terence Higgins Trust is a useful source of information on this subject (Terence Higgins Trust 2004).

   v-CJD stands for 'new variant Creutszfeldt-Jakob Disease'. This form of the disease, attacking people of all ages and not just the elderly, is the form which has been specifically associated with the eating of meat products from cows suffering from BSE – Bovine Spongiform Encephalopathy.

   SARS stands for Severe Acute Respiratory Syndrome. This disease, a form of pneumonia, emerged in 2002/3, originally in China and spread worldwide in April and May of 2003. The spread of SARS is now thought to be largely contained. Chapter 5 in this book is about SARS on the web.

   MMR stands for measles, mumps and rubella, three traditional diseases of childhood bracketed together as the name for a specific form of vaccine which is effective against all three.
3. In Britain, by contrast, government-sponsored research on the uses of the internet (PublicTechnology.net 2003 summarises information from the Office of National Statistics) does not indicate that the search for health information is a particular concern of the British. The different forms of health care provision in the two countries may account for this difference, or it may just be that the survey did not specifically ask about health. For

relevant, related research on the use of the net for medical and health information, see Harris (1995), Eastin (2001), Dolan, Iredale et al. (2004) and Rogers and Mead (2004).

4. Miller and Macintyre (1999) observe that most discussions of 'risk communication' tend to take the perspective of just one participant in the process, rather than paying attention to the entire circuit, including various branches of the government as well as institutions outside government, such as the mass media, public relations agencies, lobbying organizations and so on. Miller and Macintyre are specifically concerned with the kind of risk communication which has a top-down character. Some 'risk discourse', of course (such as the MMR/autism issue, discussed in Chapter 6), seems to start at the other end, moving 'upwards' in the direction of state institutions. Miller and Macintyre are right to stress the importance of recognizing that the trajectory of any 'risk story' does involve a range of participants, though aspectual approaches such as the present research may still have a part to play.
5. There are some 'key references' for internet/new media research, although these vary according to the research perspective adopted. Included amongst the most-cited works, are the following: Hiltz and Turoff (1978), Bolter (1991), Postman (1993), Rheingold (1993), Negroponte (1995), Turkle (1995), Castells (1996), Cherny and Weise (1996) and Hauben and Hauben (1997). The negative view of 'what it all means' is represented by Postman and Castells and parts of Cherny and Weise; the other authors adopt a more celebratory perspective. Cyberculture studies now has its own historians too (Silver 2000).
6. 'Blog' and 'blogging' are recent additions to the English language. The word 'blog' is short for 'weblog'. It is typically a kind of public online journal, easily updated by the owner, usually an individual, and not necessarily 'professionalized' in the way that corporate websites are now required to be (though there are software tools designed to facilitate the production of user-friendly blogs). A popular format for blogs involves hyperlinks to other sites, quotes from those sites and comments upon them. For a recent discussion of blogs in the context of new media research (focusing on their role in political activism) see Kahn and Kellner (2004).
7. Cottle (1998) offers a useful attempt to give an account of the risk society thesis, concentrating on Beck rather than on Giddens, which relates it to the concerns and findings of mass media studies. He agrees with Lupton (1999) that Beck is inconsistent as between a social constructionist and a realist view of the nature of 'risk', and therefore unclear as to whether the mass media 'represent' risks or, more powerfully, contribute to the 'construction' of them. Cottle concludes that 'Beck's discussion of the mass media has, however, been found to be uneven, underdeveloped and often contradictory' (Cottle 1998: 25), and ends by calling for further theoretical elaboration, conceptual precision and empirical support. Similar difficulties of this macro kind, beyond the scope of the present research, exist in relation to the 'new media'.
8. From one perspective, the present research can be regarded as treating the internet as a source of 'data' for an enquiry into something other than the new media themselves. There are precedents for such an approach: see,

for example, Harrington (1998), Illingworth (2001), Robinson (2001) and Roberts (2002). At the same time, it is also an attempt to deepen and extend the study of computer-mediated communication by focusing on the use of particular online resources – websites and Usenet newsgroups – for particular communicative purposes.

2. Computer-mediated communication and language

1. Because of the instability of the web, a new research enterprise has developed, concerned with the archiving of web pages on a permanent basis for research purposes. For discussion of some of the issues, see Lyman and Kahle (1998).
2. Although the internet is in principle congenial to public online interaction, it is not a very prominent characteristic, nor is it easy to find the interactive spaces, other than the Usenet groups now archived by Google. See Wouters and Gerbec (2003).
3. The idea of online 'community' is revisited in Chapter 8, in connection with discussion of publicness in online discourse.
4. Crystal discusses Netspeak as a set of conventions and forms which can be used interactively online. Some of the forms he examines are not specific to group communication, but can be used also in email on a one-to-one basis (for example, sig files). Others, including the acronyms of electronic discourse (such as FWIW standing for 'For what it's worth', and AFAIK for 'As far as I know'), usable in synchronous as well as asynchronous group discourse, are amongst the forms used in text messaging by mobile phone, and may even be spreading beyond the electronic domains. In the data collected for the present research, between one-third and one-half involved flaming. More than 80 per cent of all threads featured the use of signature files, and about half featured the use of smileys/emoticons. Other forms and practices of Netspeak ('snipping' of previous messages; using 'smileys'; using special email addresses to block spam messages, and using new lexical items such as 'newbie', 'netiquette', 'troll') occurred in fewer than one-third of the collected threads. There were no significant variations between the three topics and no significant variations over time (between 1998 and 2003) in these proportions. There were too few threads from before 1998 to make comparison worthwhile in respect of the earlier years.

   In the present research, most of the threads collected are from 1998 onwards. For Usenet generally, 1998 does not represent the high-water mark of its growth, though it is very high up the growth curve.
5. For more discussion of the ethics of online research, see Thomas (1996), Scharf (1999), Mann (2000) and Danet (2002). For methodology of online research more generally, see Mann (2000), Jones (1999a, 1999b) and Williams (1988).

3. Public discourses of risk, health and science

1. Theories of risk and society can be positioned according to where they stand on a realist-constructivist spectrum (Lupton 1999: chapter 2). Those at the

realist end of the spectrum examine the calculability of particular risks and are concerned about public misperceptions of risks, seeking to address the social and psychological factors which cause such misperceptions (as in the 'psychometric' tradition). Those at the strong constructivist end of the spectrum take the view that nothing is a risk in itself: 'what we understand to be a "risk" (or a hazard, threat or danger) is a product of historically, socially and politically contingent "ways of seeing"' (Lupton 1999: 35). At all points on this continuum, there are questions about the representation of risk. For the most realist orientations, the prevailing perspective measures technical representations (as the best possible judgement, using the best possible analytic instruments, on the nature and probability of the risk) against non-technical representations which are judged on how well they measure up to the technical ones. For constructivists, technical and non-technical representations differ in their social power, not in their truth value, and interpenetrate: strict separation is impossible and undesirable.

Empirical studies of risk representations have more affinity with constructivist approaches than with realist ones, and the present research is best viewed as 'weak constructivism', as Lupton defines it;

> Risk is an objective hazard, threat or danger that is inevitably mediated through social and cultural processes and can never be known in isolation from these processes. (Lupton 1999: 35)

2. Kilroy's show endured for many years but was finally cancelled in 2004 when the host, Robert Kilroy-Silk, was found to be in breach of BBC regulations concerning the publicizing of political opinions on the part of broadcasters with a responsibility of remaining publicly neutral. He has since obtained political office as a Member of the European Parliament for a fringe party advocating the withdrawal of the United Kingdom from the European Union.

4. Mobile phones and brain cancer

1. A well-known version of the precautionary principle (the Wingspread statement) was formulated and publicized in January 1998 and reads as follows:

> Precautionary Principle: When an activity raises threats of harm to human health or the environment, precautionary measures should be taken even if some cause and effect relationships are not fully established scientifically. In this context the proponent of an activity, rather than the public, should bear the burden of proof.

There is no official published source for the Wingspread statement though it has been widely circulated and is available on many websites, for example, on that of the New World Agriculture and Ecology Group, Alliance for a Healthy Tomorrow, iGreens, Our Stolen Future and so on.

For a polemical account of resistance to this principle, see Rampton and Stauber (2002); for an account of some conceptual as well as political difficulties with the concept itself, see Runciman (2004).

2. Bovine spongiform encephalopathy, a degenerative disease of cows, was not officially deemed a health hazard to humans until March 1996. This was the moment of crisis in the story. Conservative government reassurance at that time, that beef was safe because of earlier measures taken to eradicate the disease and prevent infected meat from entering the food chain lacked credibility. A Labour government was elected in 1997 and used the precautionary principle when it banned the sale of beef on the bone, 'just in case' it might harbour the infective agent, when research indicated that bone tissue was more prone to carry the agent. For a fuller account, see Gregory and Miller (1998: 173–80).
3. Thalidomide was a drug prescribed to some pregnant women in at least 46 countries during the late 1950s and early 1960s to prevent morning sickness. It later transpired that this drug caused foetal abnormalities. As a result, a considerable number of babies were born with deformities of their limbs, in varying degrees. The individuals concerned were a very visible and shocking sign of the causal effects. For a fuller account of the thalidomide story, see (CBC On Air, no date).
4. The NRPB website can be found at http://www.nrpb.org/.
5. The FCC website can be found at http://www.fcc.gov/.
6. The WHO website is at http://www.who.int. There is more about this site in the next chapter.
7. This website can be found at http://www.mcw.edu/gcrc/cop/cell-phone-health-FAQ/toc.html. It is updated several times a year, so the version accessible to readers of this book will not be the same as the versions accessed by me during the course of writing it.
8. Motorola's home page can be found at http://www.motorola.com/.
9. The home page of Aegisguard can be found at http://www.goaegis.com/.
10. In the HTML source code, the keywords for Fist's site are given as: 'on line, on-line, online, dictionary, reference, encyclopedia, encyclopaedia, companion, school, university, multimedia, IT, information technology, telephony, telecommunications, politics, economics, economic rationalism, Australia, Australian, liberal, agnostic, social, cultural, cellphone, mobile phones, radiation, junkscience, junk-science, corruption, science, distortion'. In the code for Moulder's site they are: 'analog, ANSI, antenna, base, broadcast, brain, cancer, cell, cellular, commission, communications, damage, density, digital, DNA, electromagnetic, EMF, EMR, environmental, epidemiology, exposure, frequency, FAQ, FCC, federal, field, FM, gain, guideline, hazard, headache, health, human, ICNIRP, IEEE, laboratory, leukemia, lymphoma, magnetic, microwaves, miscarriage, mobile, modulated, MW, NIR, non-ionizing, pacemaker, PCS, phone, portable, power, questions, radiation, radio, radio-frequencies, radiofrequencies, radiofrequency, radiowave, research, RF, risk, safety, SAR, science, siting, standard, station, tower, TV, wave'.

5. SARS

1. The URL for the SARS section of the WHO site is http://www.who.int/csr/sars/en/.

2. The URL for SARS Watch is http://www.sarswatch.org/index.php.
3. The URL for Wangjianshuo's blog is http://home.wangjianshuo.com/.
4. The phrase 'SARS epidemic' did not occur in the sampled materials. To find this particular example I had to revisit Google Groups. There were 1600 'hits' for this phrase during the three and a half months which are examined here, though many of these will be repetitions within the same thread. The quantity of hits however shows that its absence from the sample is just by chance.
5. CDC could also be listed under 'science/medicine/health' in view of its content, with the appropriate adjustments within the table. This would make the role of 'governmental' websites much less prominent than it is in Table 5.3, and would inflate the presence of the 'science' area even more.

6. MMR and autism

1. The URL for Whale is http://www.whale.to.
2. This is quite apart from questions of pornography on the net, where the issue of what is and is not public and on what terms has a different character.

7. Constructions of risk: change, conflict and trust

1. The results indicated here are consistent with other types of research into trust for online information. Briggs and Burford (2002) for example, report that source credibility is one of the most important predictors for whether an online source is found to be trustworthy or not.
2. Interestingly, in the UK the possibility of a mobile phone/cancer link was exploited for the purposes of TV drama in a prime-time BBC courtroom series *Judge Deed,* starring Martin Shaw. The moral dynamic of the story favoured the link, and the case against the deceitful manufacturers was proven within the storyline. The victim, a single mother, dies, leaving her orphaned son to be adopted by her barrister and the judge. Unlike *Hear the Silence,* a drama about the MMR/autism link, the use of this theme for dramatic purposes and its dramatization of corporate deceit as well as technological hazard provoked no public controversy.
3. On the low status of epidemiology compared with *in vitro* and *in vivo* laboratory studies in the rhetoric of EMF debates, see Mercer (2002).

8. The internet and the public interest

1. 'Troll', like 'blog' is a new internet-related lexical addition to English. As a verb, it refers to the practice of sending a deliberately provocative message to a forum. As the examples in this chapter show, it can also be used as a noun referring to the person sending the message. This usage may be influenced by the older meaning of the form 'troll' where it refers to a kind of mythical being along with elf, dwarf, fairy and the like.

Appendix: List of Sampled Newsgroups, by Topic

Mobile phones

1. Alt.cell-phone.tech
2. Alt.cellular
3. alt.cellular.fido
4. Alt.cellular.gsm
5. alt.cellular.motorola
6. Alt.cellular.nokia
7. alt.cellular.verizon
8. Alt.cellular-phone-tech
9. Alt.folklore.science
10. Alt.folklore.urban
11. alt.health
12. alt.support.cancer
13. Alt.support.mult-sclerosis
14. Alt.support.tinnitus
15. alt.uk.virgin-net
16. Aus.comms
17. Aus.comms.mobile
18. aus.radio.scanner
19. bit.listserv.skeptic
20. Comp.dcom.telecom
21. Misc.consumers
22. misc.consumers.frugal-living
23. rec.radio.amateur.antenna
24. rec.radio.amateur.policy
25. Sci.electronics.repair
26. sci.engr.electrical.compliance
27. sci.environment
28. sci.life-extension
29. sci.med
30. Sci.med.diseases.cancer
31. sci.med.physics
32. Sci.physics
33. Sci.physics.electromag
34. Sci.skeptic
35. seattle.politics
36. Soc.culture.singapore
37. Uk.telecom
38. Uk.telecom.mobile

MMR

1. alt.disability.blind.social
2. alt.fan.cecil-adams
3. alt.parenting.solutions
4. alt.politics.british
5. alt.support.attn-deficit
6. alt.support.autism
7. alt.tv.er
8. bit.listserv.autism
9. misc.health.alternative
10. misc.kids
11. misc.kids.breastfeeding
12. misc.kids.health
13. misc.kids.moderated
14. misc.kids.pregnancy
15. nz.general
16. sci.med
17. soc.culture.malaysia
18. uk.comp.sys.mac
19. uk.local.thames-valley
20. uk.local.warwickshire
21. uk.media.radio.archers
22. uk.people.health
23. uk.people.parents
24. uk.rec.competitions

SARS

1. alt.consumers.experiences
2. alt.design.graphics
3. alt.elvis.king
4. alt.fan.pratchett
5. alt.personals.toronto
6. alt.politics.bush
7. alt.politics.org.cia
8. alt.punk

9. alt.sports.football.pro.sea-seahawks
10. alt.support.childfree
11. alt.support.lupus
12. alt.support.mult-sclerosis
13. aus.politics
14. balt.general
15. can.politics
16. misc.emerg-services
17. misc.health.aids
18. misc.health.alternative
19. misc.immigration.australia+nz
20. misc.invest.stocks
21. misc.kids.breastfeeding
22. misc.kids.moderated
23. misc.news.internet.discuss
24. misc.survivalism
25. nz.general
26. or.general
27. rec.arts.sf.fandom
28. rec.arts.sf.written
29. rec.crafts.jewelry
30. rec.gambling.poker
31. rec.pets.cats.health+behav
32. rec.sport.golf
33. rec.sport.skating.ice.figure
34. rec.travel.air
35. rec.travel.asia
36. rec.travel.europe
37. rec.travel.misc
38. sci.med
39. sci.med.immunology
40. soc.culture.cambodia
41. soc.culture.malaysia
42. soc.culture.singapore
43. soc.culture.taiwan
44. soc.retirement
45. soc.singles.moderated
46. talk.politics.medicine
47. uk.local.isle-of-wight
48. uk.local.London

References

Allan, S. (2002). *Media, Risk and Society.* Buckingham, Open University Press.

Alonzo, M. and M. Aiken (2004). 'Flaming in Electronic Communication'. *Decision Support Systems* 36: 205–13.

Andersen, B. (1991). *Imagined Communities.* London, Verso.

Anderson, J.Y. (1996). 'Not for the Faint of Heart: Contemplations on Usenet', in *Wired Women: Gender and New Realities in Cyberspace,* ed. L. Cherny and R. Weise. Seattle, Seal Press: 126–38.

AoIR (Association of Internet Researchers) (2002). 'Ethical Decision-Making and Internet Research: Recommendations from the AoIR Ethics Working Committee',. http://www.drury.edu/ess/aoir/ethics.html.

Arterton, F.C. (1987). *Teledemocracy: Can Technology Protect Democracy?* Newbury Park, Sage.

BAAL (1994). 'Recommendations on Good Practice in Applied Linguistics', http://www.baal.org.uk/goodprac.htm.

Bakardjieva, M. (2003). 'Virtual Togetherness: an Everyday-Life Perspective'. *Media, Culture and Society* 25: 291–313.

Bakhtin, M. (1981). *The Dialogic Imagination.* Austin, University of Texas Press.

Bar-Ilan, J. (1997). 'The "Mad Cow Disease", Usenet Newsgroups and Bibliometric Laws'. *Scientometrics* 39(1): 29–55.

Baron, D. (2000). 'From Pencils to Pixels: the Stages of Literacy Technology', in *Passions, Pedagogies, and 21st Century Technologies,* ed. G. Hawisher and C. Selfe. Logan, UT, Utah State University Press: 220–41.

Baron, N.S. (1998). 'Letters by Phone or Speech or by other Means: the Linguistics of Email'. *Language and Communication* 18(2): 133–70.

Baron, N.S. (2000). *From Alphabet to Email: How Written English Evolved and Where it's Heading.* London, Routledge.

Baron, N.S. (2003). 'Why Email Looks Like Speech: Proofreading, Pedagogy and Public Face', in *New Media Language,* ed. J. Aitchison and D.M. Lewis. London, Routledge: 85–94.

Barthes, R. (1977). *Image, Music, Text: Essays Selected and Translated by Stephen Heath.* New York, Hill and Wang.

Barton, D. (1994). *Literacy: an Introduction to the Ecology of Written Language.* London, Blackwell.

Basso, K.H. (1974). *Explorations in the Ethnography of Speaking,* in *Explorations in the Ethnography of Speaking,* ed. R. Bauman and J. Sherzer. Cambridge, Cambridge University Press: 425–32.

Bauman, Z. (1995). *Life in Fragments.* Oxford, Blackwell.

Baym, N. (1993). 'Interpreting Soap Operas and Creating Community: Inside a Computer-Mediated Fan Culture'. *Journal of Folklore Research* 30: 143–76.

Baym, N. (1995a). 'The Performance of Humor in Computer Mediated Communication'. *Journal of Computer Mediated Communication,* http://www.ascusc.org/jcmc/vol1/issue2/baym.html.

Baym, N. (1995b). 'From Practice to Culture on Usenet', in *The Cultures of Computing*, ed. S.L. Star. Oxford, Blackwell: 29–52.

Baym, N. (1995c). 'The Emergence of Community in Computer-Mediated Communication', in *Cybersociety: Computer-Mediated Communication and Community*, ed. S.G. Jones. London, Sage: 138–63.

Baym, N. (1996). 'Agreements and Disagreements in Computer Mediated Discussion'. *Research on Language and Social Interaction* 29: 315–25.

Baym, N. (1997). 'Interpreting Soap Operas and Creating Community: Inside a Computer-Mediated Fan Club', in *Culture of the Internet*, ed. S. Kiesler. Mahwah, NJ, Lawrence Erlbaum Associates: 103–20.

Baym, N. (1998). 'The Emergence of On-Line Community', in *Cybersociety 2.0: Revisiting Computer-Mediated Communication and Community*, ed. S.G. Jones. London, Sage: 35–68.

Baym, N. (2000). *Tune in, Log on: Soaps, Fandom, and Online Community.* Thousand Oaks, CA, Sage.

Beacco, J., C. Claudel et al. (2002). 'Science in Media and Social Discourse: New Channels of Communication, New Linguistic Forms'. *Discourse Studies* 4: 277–300.

Bechar-Israeli, H. (1995). 'From ⟨Bonehead⟩ to ⟨cLoNehEAd⟩: Nicknames, Play, and Identity on Internet Relay Chat'. *Journal of Computer-Mediated Communication* 1(2), http://www.ascusc.org/jcmc/vol1/issue2/bechar.html.

Beck, U. (1992). *Risk Society: Towards a New Modernity.* London, Sage.

Bell, A. (1996). 'Text, Time and Technology in News English', in *Redesigning English*, ed. S. Goodman and D. Graddol. London, Open University Press/Routledge.

Bennett, P. and K. Calman (1999). *Risk Communication and Public Health.* Oxford, Oxford University Press.

Benoit, W.L. and P.J. Benoit (2000). 'The Virtual Campaign: Presidential Primary Websites in Campaign 2000', http://www.acjournal.org/holdings/vol3/Iss3/curtain.html.

Berners-Lee, T. (1999). *Weaving the Web: Origins and Future of the World Wide Web.* London, Texere Publishing.

Bit-Babik, G., D.K. Chou et al. (2003). 'Estimates of the SAR in the Human Head and Body due to Radiofrequency Radiation Exposure from Handheld Mobile Phones with Hands-Free Accessories'. *Radiation Research* 159: 550–7.

Bolter, J.D. (1991). *Writing Space: the Computer, Hypertext, and the History of Writing.* Hillsdale, NJ, Lawrence Erlbaum.

Briggs, P. (2003). 'Bodies Online: Information and Advice Seeking in the Health and Fitness Domain', http://www.london.edu/e-society/Projects/Bodies/bodies.html.

Briggs, P. and B. Burford (2002). 'Trust in Online Advice'. *Social Science Computer Review* 20(3): 321–32.

Brown, P. and S. Levinson (1987). *Politeness: Some Universals in Language Usage.* Cambridge, Cambridge University Press.

Bruckman, A.S. (1996). 'Gender Swapping on the Internet', in *High Noon on the Electronic Frontier*, ed. P. Ludlow. Cambridge, MA, MIT Press: 315–25.

Burnett, G. and L. Bonnici (2003). 'Beyond the FAQ: Explicit and Implicit Norms in Usenet Newsgroups'. *Library and Information Science Research* 25: 333–51.

Bush, V. (1945). 'As We May Think'. *Atlantic Monthly*, July 1945.
Camp, L.J. (1996). 'We are Geeks, and We are not Guys: the Systers Mailing List', in *Wired Women: Gender and the new Realities in Cyberspace*, ed. L. Cherny and E.R. Weise. Seattle, WA, Seal Press: 114–25.
Carlo, G. and M. Schram (2002). *Cell Phones: Invisible Hazards in the Wireless Age*. New York, Carroll & Graf.
Castells, M. (1996). *The Rise of the Network Society*. Malden, MA, Blackwell.
CBC On Air (no date). 'History of Thalidomide', http://www.tv.cbc.ca/witness/thalidomide/extrahis.htm.
Chandler, D. (1998). 'Personal Home Pages and the Construction of Identities on the Web', http://www.aber.ac.uk/media/Documents/short/webident.html.
Cherny, L. and E.R. Weise, eds (1996). *Wired Women: Gender and the New Realities in Cyberspace*. Seattle, Seal Press.
Cheung, C. (2000). 'A Home on the Web: Presentations of Self on Personal Home Pages', in *Web.Studies: Rewiring Media Studies for the Digital Age*, ed. D. Gauntlett. London, Arnold: 43–51.
Choice Healthcare Services (2004). 'MMR and Single Vaccines: Alternative Frequently Asked Questions', http://www.choicehealthcare.co.uk/mmr_faqs.html.
Collot, M. and N. Belmore (1996). 'Electronic Language: a New Variety of English', in *Computer-Mediated Communication*, ed. S.C. Herring. Amsterdam, John Benjamins: 12–28.
Consumers Association (2000). 'Assessment of Hands Free Kits for Mobile Telephones: Technical Summary'. *Which?* Special Report: 11–17.
Corner, J. (1995). *Television Form and Public Address*. London, Edward Arnold.
Corner, J. (1996). *The Art of Record*. Manchester, Manchester University Press.
Corner, J., K. Richardson et al. (1990). *Nuclear Reactions: Form and Response to Public Issue Television*. Luton, John Libbey.
Cottle, S. (1998). 'Ulrich Beck, "Risk Society", and the Media: a Catastrophic View'. *European Journal of Communication* 13(1): 5–32.
Crawford, A. (2002). 'The Myth of the Unmarked Net Speaker', in *Critical Perspectives on the Internet*, ed. G. Elmer. Oxford, Rowman & Littlefield: 89–104.
Crowston, K. and M. Williams (1996). 'Reproduced and Emergent Genres of Communication on the World-Wide Web', hyperion.math.upatras.gr/commorg/webgenres.html.
Crystal, D. (2001). *Language and the Internet*. Cambridge, Cambridge University Press.
Dahlberg, L. (2001). 'Computer-Mediated Communication and the Public Sphere: a Critical Analysis'. *Journal of Computer-Mediated Communication* 7(1), http://www.ascusc.org/jcmc/vol7/issue1/dahlberg.html.
Dahlberg, L. (2004). 'Internet Research Tracings: Towards Non-Reductionist Methodology'. *Journal of Computer-Mediated Communication* 9(3), http://www.ascusc.org/jcmc/vol9/issue3/dahlberg.html.
Dahlgren, P. (1995). *Television and the Public Sphere: Citizenship, Democracy and the Media*. London, Sage.
Danet, B. (2001). *Cyberpl@y: Communicating Online*. Oxford, Berg.
Danet, B. (2002). 'Studies of cyberpl@y: ethical and methodological aspects', http://unixware.mscc.huji.ac.il/~msdanet/papers/ethics2.pdf.

Danet, B. and S. Herring (2003). 'Introduction: the Multilingual Internet'. *Journal of Computer-Mediated Communication* 9(1), http://www.ascusc.org/jcmc/vol9/issue1/intro.html.

Davis, B.H. and J.P. Brewer (1997). *Electronic Discourse: Lingustic Individuals in Virtual Space.* Albany, NY, State University of New York Press.

Dearing, J. (1995). 'Newspaper Coverage of Maverick Science: Creating Controversy through Balancing'. *Public Understanding of Science* 4: 341–62.

Dibbell, J. (1993). 'A Rape in Cyberspace; or How an Evil Clown, a Haitian Trickster Spirit, Two Wizards and a Cast of Dozens Turned a Database into a Society', in *High Noon on the Electronic Frontier*, ed. P. Ludlow. Cambridge, MA, MIT Press: 375–96.

Directremedies.com (2004). 'Single MMR Vaccines', http://www.directremedies.com/vaccines.htm#autism.

Dolan, G., R. Iredale et al. (2004). 'Consumer Use of the Internet for Health Information: a Survey of Primary Care Patients'. *International Journal of Consumer Studies* 28(2): 147–53.

Durant, J. (1993). 'What is Scientific Literacy?' in *Science and Culture in Europe*, ed. D. John and J. Gregory. London, Science Museum: 129–38.

Dyer-Witheford, N. (2002). 'E-Capital and the Many-Headed Hydra', in *Critical Perspectives on the Internet*, ed. G. Elmer. Oxford, Rowman & Littlefield: 129–63.

Eagleton, J. (2004). 'SARS: "It's as bad as we feared but dared not say". Naming, Managing and Dramatizing the SARS Crisis in Hong Kong'. *English Today 78* 20(1): 34–45.

Eastin, M.S. (2001). 'Credibility Assessments of Online Health Information: the Effects of Source Expertise and Knowledge of Content'. *Journal of Computermediated Communication* 6(4), http://www.ascusc.org/jcmc/vol6/issue4/eastin.html.

Engebretsen, M. (2000). 'Hypernews and Coherence'. *Journal of Digital Information* 1(7): 12–19.

Fairclough, N. (1992). *Discourse and Social Change.* Cambridge, Polity Press.

Fairclough, N. (1995). *Media Discourse.* London, Edward Arnold.

Ferrara, K. (1991). 'Interactive Written Discourse as an Emergent Register'. *Written Communication* 8(1): 8–34.

Fish, S. (1980). *Is There a Text in this Class?* Boston, Harvard University Press.

Fist, S. (2000a). Electric Words, http://www.electric-words.com/.

Fist, S. (2000b). 'The Cellphone-Health Debate: Where I Stand', http://www.electric-words.com/.

Flanders, V. and M. Willis (1998). *Web Pages that Suck.* San Francisco, Sybex.

Foot, K.A., S.M. Schneider et al. (2003). 'Analyzing Linking Practices: Candidate Sites in the 2002 US Electoral Web Sphere'. *Journal of Computer-mediated Communication* 8(4), http://www.ascusc.org/jcmc/vol8/issue4/foot.html.

Foucault, M. (1972). *The Archaeology of Knowledge.* London, Tavistock.

Foucault, M. (1977). *Discipline and Punish.* London, Allen Lane.

Fowler, R. (1991). 'A Press Scare: the Salmonella in Eggs Affair', in *Language in the News: Discourse and Ideology in the Press*, ed. R. Fowler. London, Routledge.

Gaines, B.R. (1997). 'Modelling the Human Factors of Scholarly Communities Suported through the Internet and World Wide Web'. *Journal of the American Society for Information Science* 48(11): 987–1003.

Garrett, L. (1994). *The Coming Plague: Newly Emerging Diseases in a World out of Balance.* Harmondsworth, Penguin.
Garrett, L. (1997). 'Covering Infectious Diseases', in *A Field Guide for Science Writers*, ed. D. Blum and M. Knudson. Oxford, Oxford University Press.
Gauntlett, D. (2000). 'Web Studies: a User's Guide', in *Web.Studies: Rewiring Media Studies for the Digital Age*, ed. D. Gauntlett. London, Arnold.
Giddens, A. (1990). *The Consequences of Modernity.* Cambridge, Polity Press.
Giddens, A. (1991). *Modernity and Self-Identity: Self and Society in the Late Modern Age.* Cambridge, Polity Press.
Giddens, A. (1999). *Runaway World: how Globalisation is Reshaping our Lives.* London, Profile Books.
Gillies, J. and R. Cailliau (2000). *How the Web was Born: the Story of the World Wide Web.* Oxford, Oxford University Press.
Globalreach (2004). 'Global Internet Statistics (by language)', http://globalreach.biz/globstats/index.php3.
Goffman, E. (1979). *Gender Advertisements.* Boston, Harvard University Press.
Goffman, E. (1981). *Forms of Talk.* Philadelphia, University of Pennsylvania Press.
Goggin, G. (2000). 'Pay Per Browse? The Web's Commercial Futures', in *Web.Studies: Rewiring Media Studies for the Digital Age*, ed. D. Gauntlett. London, Arnold: 103–12.
Golding, P. (1998). 'Worldwide Wedge: Division and Contradiction in the Global Information Infrastructure', in *Electronic Empires: Global Media and Local Resistance*, ed. D.K. Thussu. London, Arnold: 135–48.
Goodman, S. (1996). 'Visual English', in *Redesigning English: New Texts, New Identities*, ed. S. Goodman and D. Graddol. London, Routledge: 35–105.
Granic, I. (2000). 'The Self-Organisation of the Internet and Changing Modes of Thought'. *New Ideas in Psychology* 18(1): 93–107.
Gregory, J. and S. Miller (1998). *Science in Public: Communication, Culture and Credibility.* Cambridge, MA, Basic Books.
Gruber, H. (2000). 'Scholarly Email Discussion List Postings: a Single New Genre of Academic Communication?', in *Words on the Web: Computer-Mediated Communication*, ed. L. Pemberton and S. Shurville. Exeter, Intellect.
Gwyn, R. (2002). *Communicating Health and Illness.* London, Sage.
Habermas, J. (1989/1962). *Structural Transformation of the Public Sphere.* Cambridge, Polity Press.
Hargreaves, I. and G. Ferguson (2000). *Who's Misunderstanding Whom?* London, ESRC.
Hargreaves, I., J. Lewis et al. (2003). *Towards a Better Map: Science, the Public and the Media.* London, ESRC.
Harrington, C.L. (1998). 'Is Anyone Else Out There Sick of the News?! TV Viewers' Responses to Non-Routine News Coverage'. *Media Culture and Society* 20(3): 471–96.
Harris, L., ed. (1995). *Health and the New Media: Technologies Transforming Personal and Public Health.* Mahwah, NJ, Lawrence Erlbaum.
Harris, R. (1995). *Signs of Writing.* London, Routledge.
Harris, R. (2000). *Rethinking Writing.* London, Athlone.
Harrison, S. (2000). 'Maintaining the Virtual Community; Use of Politeness Strategies in an Email Discussion Group', in *Words on the Web: Computer Mediated Communication*, ed. L. Pemberton and S. Shurville. Exeter, Intellect.

Hauben, M. and R. Hauben (1997). *Netizens: on the History and Impact of Usenet and the Internet.* Los Alamitos, CA, IEEE Computer Society Press.

Hawisher, G.E. (1993). 'Electronic Mail and the Writing Instructor'. *College English* 55: 627–43.

Hawisher, G.E. and C.L. Selfe, eds (2000). *Global Literacies and the World-Wide Web.* London, Routledge.

Hearit, K.M. (1999). 'Newsgroups, Activist Publics and Corporate Apologia: the Case of Intel and its Pentium Chip'. *Public Relations Review* 25(3): 291–308.

Hellsten, I. (2003). 'Focus on Metaphors: the Case of "Frankenfood" on the Web'. *Journal of Computer-Mediated Communication* 8(4), http://www.ascusc.org/jcmc/vol8/issue4/hellsten.html.

Heritage, J. (1985). 'Analyzing News Interviews: Aspects of the Production of Talk for an "Overhearing" Audience', in *Handbook of Discourse Analysis 3: Discourse and Dialogue,* ed. T.V. Dijk. London, Academic Press: 95–119.

Herring, S. (1994). 'Politeness in Computer Culture: Why Women Thank and Men Flame', in *Cultural Performances: Proceedings of the Third Berkeley Women and Language Conference,* ed. M. Bucholtz, A.C. Liang, L. Sutton and C. Harris. Berkeley, CA, Women and Language Group: 278–93.

Herring, S. (1996/1999). 'Bringing Familiar Baggage to the New Frontier: Gender Differences in Computer-Mediated Communication', in *Cyberreader,* 2nd edition, ed. V. Vitanza. Needham Heights, MA, Allyn and Bacon: 190–201.

Herring, S. (1996a). 'Two Variants of an Electronic Message Schema', in *Computer-Mediated Communication: Linguistic, Social and Cross-Cultural Perspectives,* ed. S. Herring. Amsterdam, John Benjamins: 81–106.

Herring, S. (1996b). 'Posting in a Different Voice', in *Philosophical Perspectives on Computer-Mediated Communication,* ed. C. Ess. Albany, State University of NY Press: 115–45.

Herring, S. (1999). 'Interactional Coherence in CMC'. *Journal of Computer-Mediated Communication* 4(4), http://www.ascusc.org/jcmc/vol4/issue4/herring.html.

Herring, S. (2000). 'Gender Differences in CMC: Findings and Implications'. *CPSR Newsletter* 18(1), Computer Professionals for Social Responsibillty, http://www.cpsr.org/publications/newsletters/issues/2000/Winter2000/index.html.

Herring, S. (2001). 'Gender and Power in Online Communication', http://www.slis.indiana.edu/CSI/WP/WP01-05B.html.

Herring, S. (2004). 'Slouching towards the Ordinary: Current Trends in Computer-Mediated Communication'. *New Media and Society* 6(1): 26–36.

Hilgartner, S. (1990). 'The Dominant View of Popularization: Conceptual Problems, Political Uses'. *Social Studies of Science* 20: 519–39.

Hiltz, S.R. and M. Turoff (1978). *The Network Nation: Human Communication via Computer.* Cambridge, MA, Addison-Wesley Publishing Company, Inc.

Honeywill, P. (1999). *Visual Language for the World Wide Web.* Exeter, Intellect.

Horlick-Jones, T. (2003). 'Managing Risk and Contingency: Interaction and Accounting Behaviour'. *Health, Risk and Society* 5(2): 221–8.

Hymes, D. (1972). 'Models of the Interaction of Language and Social Life', in *Directions in Sociolinguistics: the Ethnography of Communication,* ed. J. Gumperz and D. Hymes. New York, Holt, Rinehart and Winston: 35–71.

IEGMP (2000). 'Mobile Phones and Health'. Report of an Independent Expert Group on Mobile Phones. Chilton, NRPB.

Illingworth, N. (2001). 'The Internet Matters: Exploring the Use of the Internet as a Research Tool'. *Sociological Research On Line* 6(2): 96–112.

Joinson, A. (2002). 'Psychological Aspects of Information Seeking on the Internet'. *Aslib Proceedings* 54(2): 95–102.

Joinson, A.N. (2001). 'Self-Disclosure in Computer-Mediated Communication: the Role of Self-Awareness and Visual Anonymity'. *European Journal of Social Psychology* 31(2): 177–92.

Jones, S.G. (1995). 'Understanding Community in the Information Age', in *Cybersociety: Computer-Mediated Communication and Community*, ed. S.G. Jones. London, Sage: 10–35.

Jones, S.G., ed. (1999a). *Doing Internet Research: Critical Issues and Methods for Examining the Net.* London, Sage.

Jones, S.G. (1999b). 'Studying the Net: Intricacies and Issues', in *Doing Internet Research*, ed. S.G. Jones. London, Sage: 1–27.

Kahn, R. and D. Kellner (2004). 'New Media and Internet Activism: from the "Battle of Seattle" to Blogging'. *New Media and Society* 6(1): 87–95.

Kaplan, N. (1995). 'E-literacies: Politexts, Hypertexts, and other Cultural Formations in the Late Age of Print'. *Computer-Mediated Communication Magazine* 2(3), http://www.ibiblio.org/cmc/mag/1995/mar/kaplan.html.

Karpf, A. (1988). *Doctoring the Media.* London, Routledge.

Kayany, J.M. (1998). 'Contexts of Uninhibited Online Behavior: Flaming in Social Newsgroups on Usenet'. *Journal of the American Society for Information Science* 49: 1135–41.

Kemshall, H. (2002). *Risk, Social Policy and Welfare.* Buckingham, Open University Press.

Kemshall, H. (2003). *Understanding Risk in Criminal Justice.* Buckingham, Open University Press.

Kiesler, S., ed. (1997). *Culture of the Internet.* Mahwah, NJ, Lawrence Erlbaum.

Kiesler, S., J. Siegel et al. (1984). 'Social Psychological Aspects of Computer Mediated Communication'. *American Psychologist* 39(10): 1123–34.

Kitzinger, J. (1993). 'Understanding AIDS – Media Messages and What People Know about Acquired Immune Deficiency Syndrome', in *Getting the Message*, ed. J. Eldridge. London, Routledge: 271–304.

Kitzinger, J. (1998a). 'Media Impact on Public Beliefs about AIDS', in *The Circuit of Mass Communication*, ed. Jenny Kitzinger, David Miller, Kevin Williams and Peter Beharrell. London, Sage: 167–91.

Kitzinger, J. (1998b). 'Resisting the Message: the Extent and Limits of Media Influence', in *The Circuit of Mass Communication*, ed. D. Miller, J. Kitzinger, K. Williams and P. Beharrell. London, Sage: 192–212.

Kitzinger, J. (2000). 'Media Templates: Patterns of Association and the (Re)Construction of Meaning over Time'. *Media, Culture and Society* 22(1): 61–84.

Kollock, P. and M. Smith (1996). 'Managing the Virtual Commons: Cooperation and Conflict in Computer Communities', in *Computer-Mediated Communication: Lingistic, Social and Cross-Cultural Perspectives*, ed. S. Herring. Amsterdam, John Benjamins: 109–28.

Kot, M. (2003). 'Zipf's Law and the Diversity of Biology Newsgroups'. *Scientometrics* 56(2): 247–57.

Kress, G. (1989). *Linguistic Processes in Sociocultural Practice.* Oxford, Oxford University Press.

Kress, G. (1997). 'Visual and Verbal Modes of Representation in Electronically Mediated Communication: the Potentials of New Forms of Text', in *Page to Screen: Taking Literacy into the Electronic Era,* ed. I. Snyder. Sydney, Allen & Unwin: 77–93.

Kress, G. and T. van Leeuwen (1996). *Reading Images: the Grammar of Visual Design.* London, Routledge.

Kress, G. and T. van Leeuwen (2001). *Multimodal Discourse: the Modes and Media of Contemporary Communication.* London, Arnold.

Lakoff, G. and M. Johnson (1980). *Metaphors We Live By.* Chicago, University of Chicago Press.

Landow, G. (1997). *Hypertext: the Convergence of Contemporary Critical Theory and Technology.* Baltimore, Johns Hopkins University Press.

Langford, I.H., C. Marris et al. (1999). 'Public Reactions to Risk: Social Structures, Images of Science, and the Role of Trust', in *Risk Communication and Public Health,* ed. P. Bennet and K. Calman. Oxford, Oxford University Press: 33–50.

Launspach, S. (2000). 'Literal or Loose Talk: the Negotiation of Meaning on an Internet Discussion List', in *Words on the Web: Computer Mediated Communication,* ed. L. Pemberton and S. Shurville. Exeter, Intellect: 87–95.

Leach, J. (1999). 'Cloning, Controversy and Communication', in *Communicating Science: Professional Contexts,* Reader 1, ed. E. Scanlon, R. Hill and K. Junker. London, Routledge/Open University: 218–30.

Lee, J.Y. (1996). 'Charting the Codes of Cyberspace: a Rhetoric of Electronic Mail', in *Communication and Cyberspace: Social Interaction in an Electronic Environment,* ed. Lance Strate, Ronald Jacobson and Stephanie B. Gibson. Cresskill, NJ, Hampton Press: 275–96.

Lewenstein, B.V. (1995a). 'From Fax to Facts: Communication in the Cold Fusion Saga'. *Social Studies of Science* 25: 403–36.

Lewenstein, B.V. (1995b). 'Do Public Electronic Bulletin Boards Help Create Scientific Knowledge – the Cold-Fusion Case'. *Science, Technology and Human Values* 20(2): 123–49.

Lewenstein, B.V. (1999). 'Cold Fusion and Hot History', in *Communicating Science: Professional Contexts,* Reader 1, ed. E. Scanlon, R. Hill and K. Junker. London, Routledge/Open University: 185–217.

Lewis, D.M. (2003). 'Online News: a New Genre', in *New Media Language,* ed. J. Aitchison and D.M. Lewis. London, Routledge: 95–104.

Lewis, J. and T. Spears (2003). 'Misleading Media Reporting? The MMR Story'. *Science and Society* 3: 913–18.

Liewvrouw, L.A. (2004). 'What's Changed about New Media? Introduction to the Fifth Anniversary Issue of New Media and Society'. *New Media and Society* 6(1): 9–15.

Livingstone, S. (2002). *Young People and New Media.* London, Sage.

Livingstone, S. (2004). 'The Challenge of Changing Audiences: or, What is the Audience Researcher to do in the Age of the Internet?' *European Journal of Communication* 19(1): 75–86.

Livingstone, S. and P. Lunt (1994). *Talk on Television: Audience Participation and Public Debate.* London, Routledge.

Lords Select Committee on Science and Technology (2000). *Science and Society,* the United Kingdom Parliament.

Ludlow, P., ed. (1993). *High Noon on the Electronic Frontier.* Cambridge, MA, MIT Press.

Lull, J. (1990). *Inside Family Viewing.* London, Routledge.

Lupton, D. (1994). *Medicine as Culture.* London, Sage.

Lupton, D. (1990). *Risk.* London, Routledge.

Lyman, P. and B. Kahle (1998). 'Archiving Digital Cultural Artifacts', *D-lib Magazine*, July/August 1998, www.dlib.org/dlib/july98/07lyman.html.

Lynch, P. and S. Horton (1999). *Web Style Guide: Basic Design Principles for Creating Web Sites.* New Haven, Yale University Press.

MacKinnnon, R. (1997). 'Searching for the Leviathan in Usenet', in *Cybersociety: Computer-Mediated Communication and Community*, ed. S.G. Jones. London, Sage: 112–37.

Mann, C., ed. (2000). *Internet Communication and Qualitative Research: a Handbook for Researching Online.* London, Sage.

Marcoccia, M. (2004). 'On-Line Polylogues: Conversation Structure and Participation Framework in Internet Newsgroups'. *Journal of Pragmatics* 36: 115–45.

Mclaughlin, M.L., K.K. Osborne et al. (1995). 'Standards of Conduct on Usenet', in *Cybersociety: Computer-Mediated Communication and Community*, ed. S.G. Jones. London, Sage: 90–111.

Meinhof, U. and J. Smith (2000). *Intertextuality and the Media: from Genre to Everyday Life.* Manchester, Manchester University Press.

Mercer, D. (2002). 'Scientific Method Discourses in the Construction of EMF Science: Interests, Resources and Rhetoric in Submissions to a Public Inquiry'. *Social Studies of Science* 32(2): 205–33.

Miller, D. and S. Macintyre (1999). 'The Relationships between the Media, Public Beliefs and Policy-Making', in *Risk Communication and Public Health*, ed. P. Bennet and K. Calman. Oxford, Oxford University Press: 229–40.

Mitra, A. (1997). 'Virtual Commonality: Looking for India on the Internet', in *Virtual Culture: Identity and Communication in Cybersociety*, ed. S.G. Jones. London, Sage: 55–79.

Mitra, A. and E. Cohen (1999). 'Analyzing the Web: Directions and Challenges', in *Doing Internet Research: Critical Issues and Methods for Examining the Net*, ed. S.G. Jones. London, Sage: 179–202.

Mobile Phone Health Registry 2002. http://www.health-concerns.org/health_concerns/registry.asp.

Morley, D. (1992). *Television, Audiences and Cultural Studies.* London, Routledge.

Morris, M. and C. Ogan (1996). 'The Internet as a Mass Medium'. *Journal of Communication* 46(1): 39–50.

Moulder, J., L.S. Erdreich et al. (1999). 'Cell Phones and Cancer: What is the Evidence for a Connection?' *Radiation Research* 151: 513–31.

Murphy, B.M. (2002). 'A Critical History of the Internet', in *Critical Perspectives on the Internet*, ed. G. Elmer. Oxford, Rowman & Littlefield: 27–48.

Myers, G. (2004 Forthcoming). *Matters of Opinion: Dynamics of Talk about Public Issues.* Cambridge, Cambridge University Press.

Naylor, R., S. Driver and J. Cornford (2000). 'The BBC Goes Online: Public Service Broadcasting in the New Media Age', in *Web.Studies: Rewiring Media Studies for the Digital Age*, ed. D. Gauntlett. London, Arnold: 137–48.

Negroponte, N. (1995). *Being Digital.* New York, Alfred A. Knopf.

New London Group (1996). 'A Pedagogy of Multiliteracies: Designing Social Futures'. *Harvard Educational Review* 66: 60–92.

Ngini, C.U., S.M. Furnell et al. (2002). 'Assessing the Global Accessibility of the Internet'. *Internet Research: Electronic Networking Applications and Policy* 12(4): 329–38.

NRPB (2003). 'Health Effects from Radiofrequency Electromagnetic Fields: Report of an Independent Advisory Group on Non-Ionising Radiation'. Documents of the NRPB.

Oblak, T. (2003). 'Boundaries of Interactive Public Engagement: Political Institutions and Citizens in New Political Platforms'. *Journal of Computer-Mediated Communication* 8(3), http://www.ascusc.org/jcmc/vol8/issue3/oblak.html.

Office of National Statistics (2003). 'Internet Access 11.9 Million Households Online', http://www.statistics.gov.uk/cci/nugget_print.asp?ID=8.

Office of Science and Technology and the Wellcome Trust (2000). *Science and the Public: a Review of Science Communication and Public Attitudes to Science in Britain.* London, OST/Wellcome Trust.

Orr, M. (2003). *Intertextuality: Debates and Contexts.* London, Polity.

Osborne, L.N. (1998). 'Topic Development in Usenet Newsgroups'. *Journal of the American Society for Information Science* 49(11): 1010–16.

O'Sullivan, P.B. and A.J. Flanagan (2003). 'Reconceptualizing "Flaming" and other Problematic Messages'. *New Media and Society* 5(1): 69–94.

Pagetutor (no Date). Pagetutor.com: HTML Tutorials for the rest of us, http://www.pagetutor.com/pagetutor/makapage/index.html.

Paolillo, J. (2001). 'Language Variation on Internet Relay Chat: a Social Network Approach'. *Journal of Sociolinguistics* 5(2): 180–213.

Pew (2003a). 'Internet Health Resources', http://www.pewinternet.org/pdfs/PIP_Health_Report_July_2003.pdf.

Pew (2003b). 'America's Online Pursuits', http://www.pewinternet.org/pdfs/PIP_Online_Pursuits_Final.PDF.

Phillips, D. (1996). 'Defending the Boundaries: Identifying and Countering Threats in a Usenet Newsgroup'. *The Information Society* 12(1): 39–62.

Philo, G. (1999). 'Media and Mental Illness', in *Message Received,* ed. G. Philo. New York, Addison Wesley Longman: 54–61.

Postman, N. (1993). *Technopoly: the Surrender of Culture to Technology.* New York, Vintage Books.

PublicTechnology.net (2003). 'Latest UK Web Access and Usage Patterns from National Statistics: Dec 2003', http://www.publictechnology.net/.

Rafaeli, S. and F. Sudweeks (1997). 'Networked Interactivity'. *Journal of Computer-Mediated Communication* 2(4), http://www.ascusc.org/jcmc/vol2/issue4/rafaeli.sudweeks.html.

Rainie, L. and P. Bell (2004). 'The Numbers that Count', *New Media and Society* 6(1): 44–54.

Rampton, S. and J. Stauber (2002). *Trust Us, We're Experts: How Industry Manipulates Science and Gambles with Your Future.* New York, Tarcher and Putnam.

Reilly, J. (1999). 'Just Another Food Scare? Public Understanding and the BSE Crisis', in *Message Received,* ed. G. Philo. New York, Addison Wesley Longman.

Rheingold, H. (1993). *The Virtual Community: Homesteading on the Electronic Frontier.* Reading, MA, Addison-Wesley.

Rheingold, H. (2002). 'Foreword: the Virtual Community in the Real World', in *The Internet in Everyday Life,* ed. B. Wellman and C. Haythornthwaite. Oxford, Blackwell: xvii–xviii.

Richardson, K. (2001). 'Risk News in the World of Internet Newsgroups'. *Journal of Sociolinguistics* 5: 50–72.

Richardson, K. (2003). 'Health Risks on the Internet: Establishing Credibility on Line'. *Health, Risk and Society* 5: 171–84.

Roberts, M. (2002). 'Agenda Setting and Issue Salience Online'. *Communication Research* 29(4): 452–65.

Robinson, K.M. (2001). 'Unsolicited Narratives from the Internet: a Rich Source of Qualitative Data'. *Qualitative Health Research* 11(5): 706–14.

Rogers, A. and N. Mead (2004). 'More Than Technology and Access: Primary Care Patients' Views on the Use and Non-Use of Health Information in the Internet Age'. *Health and Social Care in the Community* 12(2): 102–10.

Rogers, C.L. (1999). 'The Importance of Understanding Audiences', in *Communicating Uncertainty: Media Coverage of New and Controversial Science,* ed. S.M. Friedman, S. Dunwoody and C.L. Rogers. Mahwah, NJ, Lawrence Erlbaum.

Rogers, R., ed. (2000). *Preferred Placement.* Maastricht, Jan van Eyck Academie/ Debalie.

Roscoe, T. (1999). 'The Construction of the World Wide Web Audience'. *Media, Culture and Society* 21: 673–94.

Runciman, D. (2004). 'The Precautionary Principle'. *London Review of Books* 26(7): 16–18.

Sallis, P.J. (1998). 'Usenet Newsgroups' Profile Analysis, Utilising Standard and Non-Standard Statistical Methods'. *Journal of Information Science* 24(2): 97–104.

Sallis, P.J. (2000). 'Computer-Mediated Communication: Experiments with Email Readability'. *Information Sciences* 123: 43–53.

Savolainen, R. (1999). 'The Role of the Internet in Information Seeking. Putting the Networked Services in Context'. *Information Processing and Management* 35(6): 765–82.

Savolainen, R. (2001). '"Living Encyclopaedia" or Idle Talk? Seeking and Providing Consumer Information in an Internet Newsgroup'. *Library and Information Science Research* 23(1): 67–90.

Scannell, P. (1996). *Radio, Television and Modern Life.* Oxford, Blackwell.

Scharf, B.F. (1999). 'Beyond Netiquette: the Ethics of Doing Naturalistic Discourse Research on the Internet', in *Doing Internet Research; Critical Issues and Methods for Examining the Net,* ed. S.G. Jones. London, Sage: 243–56.

Schneider, S.M. (1996). 'Creating a Democratic Public Sphere through Political Discussion: a Case Study of Abortion Conversation on the Internet'. *Social Science Computer Review* 14(4): 373–93.

Schneider, S.M. and K.A. Foot (2004). 'The Web as an Object of Study'. *New Media and Society* 6(1): 114–22.

Silver, D. (2000). 'Looking Backwards, Looking Forwards: Cyberculture Studies 1990–2000', in *Web.Studies: Rewiring Media Studies for the Digital Age,* ed. D. Gauntlett. London, Arnold: 19–30.

Silverstone, R. (1992). *Consuming Technologies: Media and Information in Domestic Spaces.* Routledge, London.

Sinclair, J. and M. Coulthard (1975). *Towards an Analysis of Discourse: the English used by Teachers and Pupils.* Oxford, Oxford University Press.

Slevin, J. (2000). *The Internet and Society.* Cambridge, Polity.

Snyder, H. (1996). 'Chaotic Behavior in Computer Mediated Network Communication'. *Information Processing and Management* 32(5): 555–62.

Snyder, I., ed. (1997). *Page to Screen: Taking Literacy into the Electronic Era.* London, Allen and Unwin/Routledge.

Snyder, I., ed. (2002). *Silicon Literacies: Communication, Innovation and Education in the Electronic Age.* London, Routledge.

Sontag, S. (1988). *Illness as Metaphor and Aids and its Metaphors.* New York, Picador.

Spears, R. and M. Lea (1994). 'Panacea or Panopticon? The Hidden Power in Computer-Mediated Communication'. *Communication Research* 21(4): 427–59.

Sproull, L. and S. Kiesler (1986). 'Reducing Social Context Cues: Electronic Mail in Organizational Communication'. *Management Science* 32: 1492–512.

Starr, P. (2000). 'The Electronic Commons'. *The American Prospect* 11(10), http://www.prospect.org/web/page.ww?section=root&name=ViewPrint&articleId=4367.

Steele, G., D. Woods et al. (1983). *The Hackers Dictionary.* New York, Harper and Row.

Street, B. (1984). *Literacy in Theory and Practice.* Cambridge, Cambridge University Press.

Street, B. (1995). *Social Literacies: Critical Approaches to Literacy in Development, Ethnography and Education.* London, Longman.

Taylor, B., E. Miller et al. (1999). 'Autism and Measles Mumps Rubella Vaccine: No Evidence for a Causal Association'. *Lancet* 353: 2026–9.

Terence Higgins Trust (2004). 'HIV Facts', www.tht.org.uk/hiv_info/facts.htm.

Thomas, J. (1996). 'Introduction: a Debate about the Ethics of Fair Practices for Collecting Social Science Data in Cyberspace'. *The Information Society* 12: 107–17.

Thompsen, P.A. (1996). 'What's Fuelling the Flames in Cyberspace? A Social Influence Model', in *Communication and Cyberspace: Social Interaction in an Electronic Environment*, ed. L. Strate, R. Jacobson and S.B. Gibson. Cresskill, New Jersey, Hampton Press.

Tosca, S.P. (2000). 'A Pragmatics of Links, Article no. 22'. *Journal of Digital Information* 1(6).

Trumbo, C.W. (2001). 'Use of E-mail and the Web by Science Writers'. *Science Communication* 22(4): 347–78.

Turkle, S. (1995). *Life on the Screen: Identity in the Age of the Internet.* New York, Simon and Schuster.

Vincent, D. (2000). *The Rise of Mass Literacy: Reading and Writing in Modern Europe.* London, Polity.

Wakefield, A. (1998). 'Ileal-Lymphoid-Nodular Hyperplasia, Nonspecific Colitis, and Pervasive Developmental Disorder in Children'. *Lancet* 351: 637–41.

Wakeford, N. (2000). 'New Media, New Methodologies: Studying the Web', in *Web.Studies: Rewiring Media Studies for the Digital Age*, ed. D. Gauntlett. London, Arnold: 31–41.

Warschauer, M. (2000). 'Language, Identity, and the Internet', in *Race in Cyberspace*, ed. B.E. Kolko, L. Nakamura and G.B. Rodman. New York, Routledge: 151–70.

Warschauer, M., G.R. El Said et al. (2002). 'Language Choice Online: Globalization and Identity in Egypt'. *Journal of Computer-Mediated Communication* 7(4), http://www.ascusc.org/jcmc/vol7/issue4/warschauer.html.

Wellings, K. (1988). 'Perceptions of Risk: Media Treatment of AIDS', in *Social Aspects of AIDS*, ed. P. Aggleton and H. Homans. London, Falmer.

Wellman, B. (1997). 'An Electronic Group is Virtually a Social Network', in *Culture of the Internet*, ed. S. Kiesler. Mahwah, NJ, Lawrence Erlbaum Associates: 53–67.

Wellman, B. and C. Haythornthwaite, eds (2002). *The Internet in Everyday Life*. Oxford, Blackwell.

Wilhelm, A.G. (1998). 'Virtual Sounding Boards: How Deliberative is Online Political Discussion?' *Information, Communication and Society* 1: 313–38.

Williams, F., ed. (1988). *Research Methods and the New Media*. New York, The Free Press.

World Health Organization (1999). *Report on Infectious Diseases: Removing Obstacles to Healthy Development*. Geneva: World Health Organization, http://www.who.int/infectious-disease-report/.

World Health Organization (2003a). *Severe Acute Respiratory Syndrome (SARS): Status of the Outbreak and Lessons for the Immediate Future*. Geneva, World Health Organization, http://www.who.int/csr/media/sars_wha.pdf.

World Health Organization (2003b). 'Initiative for Vaccine Research p. 10 – Measles', http://www.who.int/vaccine_research/documents/new_vaccines/en/index9.html.

Wouters, P. and D. Gerbec (2003). 'Interactive Internet? Studying Mediated Interaction with Publicly Available Search Engines'. *Journal of Computer Mediated Communication* 8(4), http://www.ascusc.org/jcmc/vol8/issue4/wouters.html.

Yates, S. (1996). 'English in Cyberspace', in *Redesigning English: New Texts, New Identities*, ed. S. Goodman and D. Graddol. Buckingham, Open University/Routledge: 106–40.

Yazbak, F.E. (2002). 'The MMR-Autism Debate: How Relevant is the Latest Study From Denmark?', http://www.casiquest.org/autism_debate.html.

Index